April 1982

To Jane Hoffman:
Good luck in your new
home!
From the 8th Floor Gang

HEARTLAND BEAT

HEARTLAND BEAT By Nina Rubel

The Kerning Arts Press · 719 South Elm Boulevard · Champaign, Illinois 61820

Acknowledgments

The articles and the accompanying photos dated from May 1974 through March 1979 all appeared previously in *The Courier*, later called *The Morning Courier*, and are reprinted with permission by Donald M. Lindsay, Champaign. The articles and the accompanying photos dated from August 1979 through March 1981 all appeared previously in *The News-Gazette* and are reprinted by permission by *The News-Gazette*, Champaign. Almost all the articles appear here in slightly revised form.

Designed by **Charles T. Flora**.

Photographs by

Curt Beamer Jacket and pages 12-14, 44, 46, 65, 74, 76-78, 87-88, 90-92, 95-96, 98-104, 149, 210, 218-221 and 238-241.
John C. Dixon Pages 31-34, 170-171 and 184-188.
Phil Greer Pages 56-58, 61, 119, 158, 198-199 and 227.
Jerry Lower Pages 110, 117 and 132.
Lou McClellan Pages 16-17, 53, 215-216, 223-225 and 236.
Robert K. O'Daniell Pages 20-27 and 126.
Joe Wilske Pages 80-84 and 230-233.

First Printing, November 1981
Second Printing, January 1982

Production Notes:

Sonnie Schrock • *Typesetting* (Crouse Printing)
Joe Livingston • *Printing* (Andromeda)
Shanebrook Graphics • *Color Separations*

Heartland Beat. © 1981 by Nina Rubel.

ISBN 0-9606956-0-5
Library of Congress Catalogue Card Number: 81-90390.

To Lee, Mark and Sasha — the mainstays of my life —

and to the readers of *The Courier* and *The News-Gazette*
who make the beat of a feature writer truly a Heartland Beat.

For men and women are not only themselves; they are also the region in which they were born, the city apartment or the farm in which they learnt to walk, the games they played as children, the old wives' tales they overheard, the food they ate, the schools they attended, the sports they followed, the poets they read, and the God they believed in.

W. Somerset Maugham, *The Razor's Edge*.

Contents

Introduction

For us who live in Champaign-Urbana, Nina Rubel is homefolks. For several years now, her vivid feature stories (really intensely personal essays) in the local newspapers have been showing us, in loving detail, what it is like to be at home in Champaign-Urbana.

It is hard to do justice to Nina's vision of her hometown, even after rereading the best of these essays, all together in this volume. But surely the core of it is the sort of shock of wonder many of the early Illinois settlers felt when they rode out of the timberlands to the east and the south and saw the great prairies of Illinois rolling out before them. The first man to call Champaign-Urbana home was apparently one Runnel Fielder, who in 1822 pulled up his horse and put down his stakes in Big Grove, a piece of woodland in the middle of "a wilderness of wild grass—nothing but grass from Decatur to Danville." What Runnel Fielder felt about making a home on a tiny islet in a sea of grass is lost to history. But if he was like innumerable other Illinois immigrants of the period, he must have caught his breath when he first looked out on the magnificent emptiness of the Great Prairie. Those voices, faint but clear from old letters and diaries, tell us over and over of the complex mingling of exhilaration and terror in the first glimpse of the Illinois prairies, exhilaration at the seemingly boundless freedom, the infinite possibilities, terror at the potential dangers of such formlessness, such loss of limits and boundaries.

Nina Rubel's essays catch the quality of that shock and that wonder even now, when the prairie has seemingly been tamed and bounded by the human grids of roads, fences, and property lines. Maybe part of her sense of wonder comes from having grown up in Denmark and coming to Champaign-Urbana as an adult. But then the economics of the region and the presence of the University of Illinois make Champaign-Urbana a town full of immigrants, true heirs of Runnel Fielder in that respect at least. (I met one person who, on being asked if he was a native, replied, "Not me! I'm from Bondville"—five miles away. But he was just less of an immigrant than most of us.) And immigrants or not, we like the way Nina articulates for us, precisely and with delight, the delicate interplay of the native and the exotic in Champaign-Urbana—a beautiful Greek Orthodox baptismal service in the middle of the corn and soybean country, a mother who maintains a meticulously organized Germanic household in the Champaign suburbs, a Russian and a Scotsman attending a Fighting Illini football game.

The wonder and the delight come, too, from Nina's keen sense of people and the ingenious ways they find of expressing who they are. Nina seems to like successful people, not necessarily those who have acquired fame and wealth, but those who have been successful in discovering who they are and finding a rewarding way of life. The little boys, now grown, who constructed an elaborate model of an imaginary kingdom in the crawlspace under the family house, the woman who bucked her mother's notion of being a "lady" to become an automobile mechanic, the woman who brings dignity and professionalism to the job of cleaning houses, the man who describes his thirty years of farming with a wry, self-deprecating kind of country pride — all emerge from these pages with a vividness in which we sense not only their pleasure in achievement but Nina's joy in the infinite possibilities of living.

She finds delight in language, too, the rich, nut-like flavor of ordinary speech. The man who built the University's music building as a memorial tribute to his wife writes of their first meeting, "Since that time I have loved her with all my heart until now, when my heart is broken on account of her death, and I am writing these lines with blinding tears." A man in the general store in Hugo, Illinois, tells Nina, "We doctor in Urbana anymore, not in Tuscolie." She catches the rhythms of a 96-year-old woman remembering how she first came to Champaign: "I had to do something to support the children, so I came to Champaign, where my first cousin, Carl Hansen, lived, and opened a boarding house. Carl sent all his unmarried fellows at his creamery to me for room and board, and that's how I got started."

Nina has the rare gift of really listening to people and catching not only their turns of speech but their ways of looking at the world, not only in moments of pride and contentment but at darker moments, too. Four women recall their husbands' deaths; "Most people seem to feel that if they have you for dinner once as a widow, that is it." "I appreciate my body more than I did before," says an 18-year-old girl whose leg has been amputated. "I realize my body is vulnerable and is not going to last, and that is why I am putting my trust in something that will last. Putting my trust in something eternal, in God, I know I won't be disappointed."

Exhilaration and terror — these are still, for Nina Rubel, the human reactions to the prairie: exhilaration at the infinite possibilities of making a life for oneself, terror at the dangers hidden in that existential emptiness. This is, Nina seems to be saying, life in prairie land.

In one of her essays, Nina gives us eighteen ways of telling if you're really at home in Champaign-Urbana, including being able to discern the subtle change in topography that gives "Yankee Ridge" its name. There is a nineteenth: reading Nina Rubel. When we read these essays, we know, down deep in our bones, that we're home.

James Hurt, *Professor of English, University of Illinois*

ARCHITECTURAL PLEASURES

Crawlspace Castles

Once upon a time, more than a score of years ago, when dogs still roamed the twain cities unrestrained by leashes, two small boys liked to play in a dark, gloomy dungeon below their parents' homestead.

While the wind howled like a banshee and the stinging rains swept in from the great expanses south of their house, the two little boys created a wondrous landscape of castles and villages perched near a winding river above which craggy mountains hover and the spirit of knights in shining armor reigns.

Today the two little boys, Richard and Robert McClintock, are grown men and their widowed father, E.C. McClintock, Jr., has placed on the market the pseudo-Tudor house in whose 10-foot by 12-foot by four-foot crawlspace the castle landscape is contained.

But the golden imagination and fabulous ingenuity that created the magic landscape still glows in all its enduring and unique beauty.

The Urbana house above the crawlspace is itself like a small castle with its vine-covered walls of red brick and massive chimney framed by towering evergreens.

When the McClintocks moved into the house 25 years ago, Richard and Robert, then ages 12 and 9, quickly staked out the crawlspace below the dining room, next to the regular basement, as a place to play on rainy days.

"We were inspired by our interest in fairy tales, castles, history and architectural history," Robert McClintock said. "Combined with our hobby of making models the landscape, which we called Canyonland, just evolved from that."

The landscape includes at least five major castles, none of them taller than a foot, roads, bridges, a river that the boys used to fill with water, several villages including a grouping with a windmill and a house with a cantilevered second story, and many mountains.

Railroad tracks with miniature trains wend through part of the landscape. Several of the bridges are shaped with graceful Roman arches while others are fortified with ramparts.

The landscape also includes many small lookout towers and small huts and is embellished with countless details such as a two-inch-high religious figure forming a roadside shrine.

Twigs of dried evergreens are used as trees and small groves throughout.

Several of the castles—crenelated battlements, towers, turrets and all—are built of inch-long bricks molded by hand and put up wet without the use of mortar with only an occasional nail inserted to keep them in place, Robert McClintock said.

The material used for the buildings, mountains and tiny sculptures was the clay-like soil of the crawlspace floor.

The brothers worked on their creation throughout their teens with Richard retaining his interest in the project through his early college years.

The possessor of a doctorate in Latin, he is now 37 and is the assistant to the president of Hampden-Sydney College in Hampden-Sydney, Va.

He has retained his interest in model making and recently built a complete museum display of the original college buildings for the school. He also rebuilds ornate antique clocks. He and his wife, Deborah, have four children, Andrew, 8, Victoria, 6, Anne, 4, and Rebecca, 2.

Robert McClintock is now 34 and lives in Urbana with his wife, Leslie, and their son, Matthew, 3, and 2-week-old daughter, Elizabeth Aura.

He has earned two undergraduate degrees, in history and classics, as well as a master's degree in medieval history and a master's degree in vocational education, which he will probably extend into a Ph.D. He holds a part-time research assistantship at the University of Illinois.

He also is a certified foreign car mechanic and has maintained his interest in model making.

Richard and Robert McClintock's mother, Elizabeth McClintock, who died in February, was a private school administrator who founded one school and headed several others in Virginia, where the McClintocks lived before moving to Urbana.

The men's father, E.C. McClintock, Jr., retired in 1976 as professor of general engineering at the University of Illinois, where he also served for several years as director of publications and technical information for the College of Engineering.

A dragon lives forever
But not so little boys
Painted wings and giant strings
Make way for other toys.

From 'Puff The Magic Dragon'
By Peter, Paul And Mary

He continued to teach and do research at the university several years following his retirement.

He said he and his wife always encouraged their sons in the creation of Canyonland, which he describes as "frozen poetry or architectural poetry."

A few years after the boys had started their venture the poet Robert Frost visited the McClintock home for breakfast during a visit to the University of Illinois campus to give a poetry reading.

"The boys showed him Canyonland and he was delighted with it and very enthusiastic about their creativity," Mr. McClintock said.

Now that the house, which was built in 1928, is up for sale, the priceless creation of many rainy afternoons' labor will pass out of the family's possession.

"I hope that whoever buys the house will not keep their kids out of Canyonland," Robert McClintock said.

"My brother may feel differently but, as far as I am concerned, the children who may move into the house can go ahead, play in here, modify it or knock it down and start over again if they want to."

September 1980

2nd Place, Illinois UPI 1980 feature contest (with "Becki Conway" and "The Abandoned Farm")

14

The House That Jack Built

Jack Sherman Baker lives in a self-created environment of protected court-yards and rooms where 14-foot-high walls meet exposed ceiling beams and large glass windows contrast with thriving plants.

Professor Baker is an architect and teaches architecture at the University of Illinois. He bought his 19th Century building in 1957 for $20,000.

Formerly a wagon shop with a forge for shoeing horses on the main floor, the building is located in a once run-down commercial area near the Illinois Central station in Champaign.

With the exception of a shop on the street side and a studio apartment in the back of the shop, the entire two-story building is occupied by Professor Baker.

The street-side entrance opens on a stairway to the second floor which houses Professor Baker's office, a 22-foot by 60-foot living room, a study, a bedroom, two bathrooms and a multilevel theater.

From a small balcony outside the theater, a wooden stairway leads to one of the two large enclosed courtyards.

The living room opens onto a large deck, from which stairs lead to the second courtyard. Professor Baker's main-floor rooms, a drafting room and a conference room, are reached from this courtyard, which also serves the apartment.

The house embodies the professor's belief that a house should reflect its user's lifestyle and philosophy.

His philosophy, he said, is that in an increasingly crowded and violence-ridden society, people need to retreat to an "introverted environment of courtyard schemes and surrounding walls."

Professor Baker's lifestyle permeates the house with its white-painted brick walls and original wide-boarded pine floors sanded and finished with a tough bowling alley surface.

The living room is flooded by light from a skylight and a wall of glass facing the courtyard with its many trees, planted by Professor Baker.

In front of the fireplace a sunken seating area, once an elevator shaft, is bordered on three sides by pillow-filled sofas.

The kitchen is a rectangular bar holding the stove top, double sink and counterspace. The stove top and sink can be converted into serving areas by flipping a hinged cover over them.

The living room also contains a dining area, a wide couch covered with a fur throw, a small pump organ and a stereo.

For all its vastness—it has housed performances by dance and theater groups and the Walden string quartet—it has small secluded areas. One is located behind an arrangement of floor-to-ceiling plants below the skylight, where a Charles Eames leather chair and hassock invite reading.

The theater, which is almost ready to be used for dance and drama performances, has a double-deck stage that also was originally an elevator shaft through which wagons were brought to the second floor.

Professor Baker has retained the hand mechanism used to operate the elevator as a design element.

The theater has a gas-powered fireplace and its own kitchen area, above which a padded platform serves both as extra sleeping space and a place from which to view the performance. The platform is reached by climbing metal rungs embedded in the wall.

In addition to three drafting tables lined up next to the northern exposure windows, the office features a wall of bookshelves with a movable library ladder. The second-lowest shelf is extra wide to serve as desk space and for display of memorabilia.

The office also has a fireplace, surrounded by a coffee table and four safari chairs. Displayed in the room are photographs and models of houses and a theater boat designed by Baker.

Downstairs, the doors separating the conference room from the drafting room are made of two stained glass windows from an old church.

The apartment is next to these two rooms and occupies a 25-foot by 25-foot area two stories high. Baker removed a section of the upper floor to create a sleeping loft and to allow the original skylight to provide natural illumination for both levels.

A circular metal staircase connects the two levels. The glass wall to the courtyard allows for a visual connection between the gravel of the courtyard floor and a rectangular gravel area inside the windows.

Professor Baker did most of the remodeling himself.

"It took several months to clear the junk out of the living room area alone, and the courtyard area was full of old cars and batteries," he said.

"The building was in a bad state of disrepair. The window frames were falling out. The rear stairs and deck were decayed and a fire hazard. The brick walls, parapet and chimneys were in bad need of repair and repainting, and most of the plumbing had failed many years earlier."

Professor Baker's first efforts were to improve the exterior. He planted ivy along all outside walls and fought for years before obtaining a permission from the city to plant trees in the sidewalk.

These trees became the first planted on streets in the downtown areas of Champaign-Urbana, Professor Baker said, and later became an inspiration to the tree-planting efforts of Champaign Community Development Council.

The building has received two awards of excellence from the American Institute of Architects and has been visited by many major architects from all over the United States and Europe.

Baker said the house often is used for seminars by students in architecture, landscape design, planning, music and dance. He said he has held many receptions for visiting architects.

"In cities like New York, old buildings have been restored and recycled, but you seldom see this done in small towns. I think it is important to bring people back to the city to live over the stores to make the inner city areas viable at all times," he said.

"I am encouraged by the fact that many of my former students have gone on to rehabilitate old buildings in cities where they now live."

September 1975

Hidden Treasures

The University of Illinois abounds in architectural glories easily visible to anyone who works on or visits the campus.

The striking Georgian facade of the Illini Union with four pairs of white columns lends itself to viewing. The handsome proportions of the English Building, the only University of Illinois structure designed by McKim, Mead and White — the most celebrated American architectural firm in the early years of this century — and the castle-like exterior of Altgeld Hall with its turreted Romanesque tower can be enjoyed on a casual stroll.

But the campus also contains hidden treasures of architectural or ornamental design of which few people, regardless of the length of their association with campus, are aware.

Among these visual delights are the former music library in Smith Music Hall, the mathematics library in Altgeld Hall, the memorial entrance hall and staircases in Lincoln Hall, a bust by sculptor Jo Davidson in Gregory Hall, the copy of the doors of the San Giovanni baptistry in the architecture building and several fragments of Louis Sullivan design north of the architecture building.

One of the most glorious rooms on the entire campus is the little-known and rarely seen Memorial Room in Smith Music Hall.

The room is the crowning glory of a building which in its conception is an American version of the Taj Mahal, built by a grieving husband to commemorate his wife and their love story.

Located on the second floor of the building directly behind the four columns that stand in the center of the harmonious eastern facade, the Memorial Room is a large rectangular room of stunning exuberance and beauty.

Designed in the style of Italian renaissance, the room is a riot of yellow and white marble and richly detailed designs of cream, pink and apple-green stucco.

Two marble fireplaces at the center of the short walls face each other across rows of flattened marble pillars along the long walls.

Three huge windows on the eastern wall are hung with cream-colored draperies with swirls of fabric in an intricate design. The ceiling and part of the walls are crammed with rosettes and scroll designs in the three pastel colors.

The floor is covered with a huge Oriental rug, a gift to the university from President and Mrs. John Corbally. The rug was stored in the attic of the president's official residence and was found to be too large for use in the home.

Smith Music Hall Memorial Room

The only defect in the jewel-like interior of the room is a pair of hideous fluorescent light fixtures. The music department has been unsuccessful in its search for someone to donate chandeliers to replace the fluorescent lights.

Built as a memorial room to house memorabilia of the building's donor, Capt. Thomas J. Smith and his wife, Tina Weedon Smith, the room became the music library in the 1940s and was used as such until 1972 when the music department moved into the new music building.

The room is used for occasional chamber recitals and student recitals and for performance classes such as William Warfield's class in oratorio roles. When not in use it is kept locked to guard the Oriental rug which is valued at between $15,000 and $20,000. The room also holds a grand piano.

With its richness of decoration and intimate feeling, the room — whose modern-day nomenclature is simply 220 Smith Music Hall — is a perfect setting for chamber concerts, giving the concert-goer a feeling of being present at a concert in Haydn's time at the home of the Esterhazy family.

Two full-length portraits of Capt. and Mrs. Smith that originally hung in the room are located at either end of the corridor surrounding the room.

According to correspondence between Capt. Smith and Edmund J. James, president of the University of Illinois from 1904 to 1920, which is stored in the university archives, similar portraits were planned of President James and James M. White, the contemporary university architect and architect of the building.

Originally called the Tina Weedon Smith Memorial Music Building, the building was completed in 1920.

It was the first university building constructed from funds which were not state-appropriated. Capt. Smith donated 770 acres of farmland in Champaign County to the University of Illinois trustees in 1914 with the proceeds from sale of the land earmarked for a music building.

At the time, the building was the greatest gift by a private citizen to the university and was termed by President James "an epochal gift."

In 1916 the trustees approved the sum of $250,000 for the complete building including $7,500 for the memorial room.

While the building was under construction, President James wrote to 5,000 prominent people in the musical world to ask for recommendations for names of great musicians to be inscribed on exterior panels of the building.

Surrounded by carved laurel wreaths, the four names chosen, Palestrina, Bach, Haydn and Beethoven, are carved around the north, east and south entrances.

The 1916-18 correspondence between Capt. Smith and President James is earmarked by many urgent requests by Capt. Smith for rapid completion of the building.

The file contains a "Statement of Captain Thomas J. Smith of Feb. 15, 1918, made at Battle Creek, Mich., where he is seeking the recovery of health so that he might prolong his life long enough to see (the building) completed and dedicated."

Writing with a nobility of sentiment and beauty of expression which is rarely found today, the 82-year-old Capt. Smith wrote:

"From the commencement of business in Champaign, Illinois, I have lived a life that is free from harm or evil as well as was in my power and now at this stage of my career, I want to say before my departure from this life that I bear no evil thoughts nor harbor no evil mind against any human being and feel at this time that if I had my life to repeat, I doubt whether I could have improved it or not."

Capt. Smith died the following April, two years before the completion of the building.

Mrs. Smith, who is described in the 1917 cornerstone laying program as "a light-hearted and high-spirited woman" who was "particularly fond of music," died in 1903 at the age of 56.

Capt. Smith was an attorney and a member of the University of Illinois Board of Trustees from 1897 to 1903.

In a memorial tribute to his wife, which appeared in an undated issue of The Champaign Daily News, Capt. Smith recalled the circumstances of his first meeting with his future wife, which evoke the plot of George Bernard Shaw's "Arms and the Man."

As an officer in the federal army in the Civil War, Capt. Smith and the company he commanded halted on a march in pouring rain outside the house in Woodbury, Tenn., where Tina Weedon lived with her widowed mother.

The company was in search of Morgan's Raiders, the famous Confederate group, March 6, 1863.

Capt. Smith's men entered the Weedon house and carried off everything they could find to eat. Informed about this by Mrs. Weedon, Capt. Smith ordered the men out and then, he wrote, "I saw Tina Weedon sitting on the table with both feet hanging down to the floor."

He wrote, "Some lively talk (followed) which soon developed the fact that she liked the rebels and hated the Yankees."

Capt. Smith gave Miss Weedon and her mother all the coffee he had as a peace offering and, at the end of the conversation, was "politely asked to call if I ever chanced that way again."

That same night the young Yankee officer wrote a letter to the Yankee-hating young woman and sent it to her by a messenger.

The following year Capt. Smith made his way through enemy lines to marry Miss Weedon. The couple was separated until the war ended the following year when the two were reunited and settled in Champaign.

At the end of his description of that momentous first meeting Capt. Smith wrote in his memorial tribute:

"Since that time I have loved her with all my heart until now, when my heart is broken on account of her death, and I am writing these lines with blinding tears."

Among eight bronze busts of famous editors in the Editors Hall of Fame in Gregory Hall is a particularly striking work by the American sculptor Jo Davidson.

The subject is Edward Wyllis Scripps, founder of the United Press and Scripps Howard Enterprises, who lived from 1854 to 1926.

The Editors Hall of Fame, a project of the Illinois Press Association from 1927 to 1943, was established to recognize the spirit and achievement of notable men and women of the press.

By 1943, when the project seemingly had faded away, 89 persons had been elected to the hall.

The eight busts were dedicated and unveiled Nov. 30, 1930, in the University of Illinois Auditorium with more than 2,000 people attending.

The busts were placed in the custody of the University of Illinois and are housed in the corridors of Gregory Hall, where the College of Communications is located.

Lincoln Hall entrance stairway

A freshly restored plaster copy of one of the greatest masterpieces of the early Italian renaissance is displayed in the Temple Buell Architecture Gallery in the University of Illinois architecture building.

The original work is considered the supreme masterpiece of Lorenzo Ghiberti (1378-1455), Florentine sculptor, goldsmith and writer.

Ghiberti spent 27 years making the bronze doors—the second pair of doors he made for the Baptistery of San Giovanni. The 11th Century Baptistery is an octagonal building next to the cathedral of Florence, Santa Maria del Fiore, whose dome by Brunelleschi is the most striking feature of the Florence skyline.

Machiavelli and Galileo are buried in the cathedral.

The Temple Buell doors are located on the west wall of the gallery and have been completely restored by Robert Youngman, professor of art at the University of Illinois, and a group of students.

The restoration work took one year, beginning two-and-a-half years ago, and included moving the doors from the south wall of the gallery and removing many layers of paint and grime.

The doors came to the university in the 1940s as part of sculptor Lorado Taft's estate.

They consist of 10 panels of Old Testament scenes framed by rich ornament with statuettes and heads in niches. Ghiberti created the biblical scenes himself and his son made the part around the door frame that shows fruits, flowers, vines, animals and birds.

The University of Illinois copy came apart in 21 pieces, Professor Youngman discovered. After reassembling the plaster pieces he found about 40 minor pieces—some as small as a few inches square—missing.

To replace the missing pieces Professor Youngman took Italian lessons and traveled to Florence last December. He unearthed the original molds, which are made of ground-up rabbit bones and skin, in the stables of the Pitti Palace on his second day in Florence.

A Florentine craftsman is casting the missing sections in plaster so the University of Illinois copies can be complete.

Copies of the doors—named "The Gates of Paradise" by Michelangelo—also can be found in San Francisco and at the Carnegie Mellon Institute in Pittsburgh.

Dedicated on Abraham Lincoln's birthday, Feb. 12, 1913, Lincoln Hall is a fitting homage to the president who lived in Illinois most of his life and was the signer of the land-grant act creating the University of Illinois.

The brick, stone and terra-cotta building is described in a 1912 booklet as "one of the noblest monuments thus far erected in this country to our martyred president."

The Illinois Legislature appropriated $250,000 for the construction of the building in 1909, the 100th anniversary of Lincoln's birth. The building was designed by W. Carbys Zimmerman, the state architect. A large addition on the west side which includes the theater was built in 1930. The addition cost $500,000 and was designed by James M. White. An earlier addition was constructed in 1927.

The building's exterior includes 10 terra-cotta panels on the eastern facade which depict scenes from Lincoln's life; tablets, medallions and inscriptions relating to Lincoln; and stucco portraits of Lincoln's contemporaries. All are seen easily by passers-by. The memorial entrance hall on the east side, however, is a hidden treasure.

Made almost entirely of white marble, the entrance hall features massive pillars topped by stucco della Robbia medallions, marble benches and a marble floor.

Lincoln Hall entrance hall

Two graceful marble stairways lead to the entrance to the theater and to a balcony overlooking the entrance hall.

A bronze bust of Lincoln is set in a niche between the start of the stairways.

In the original plans a copy of the Gettysburg Address in brass letters was designed to be sunk in the marble floor of the entrance hall. A plaque with the address is now hung on the southern wall.

Behind the walls of the staircases a small, modern enclosure of concrete blocks for seating, arranged Stonehenge-fashion in front of a curved concrete windscreen, provides a place to sit and ponder the life and times of the president commemorated by the building.

Fragments of work by Louis Sullivan, a towering figure in American architecture, serve as benches for campus strollers north of the University of Illinois architecture building.

The fragments are the two impost blocks—the blocks placed at the beginning of the curve of an arched doorway—from the Walker Warehouse which was located on South Market Street in Chicago and demolished around 1953.

The warehouse was completed in 1889 at a cost of $325,942, according to Alan K. Laing, professor emeritus of architecture at the University of Illinois. It was designed by Sullivan and built by Martin A. Ryerson, Jr.

The fragments came to the university through a former architecture student, G.L. Calhamer, who noticed the building being torn down and alerted architecture department members they might obtain the impost blocks. The rest of the building was used to build a breakwater in Lake Michigan.

The library of Altgeld Hall, the mathematics building, is a room of beauty that hits the first-time visitor with great impact.

The impact comes from perfect proportions, pillared arches, a plethora of pillars along the walls, rich mural decorations everywhere and, above all, four mural paintings of classic motifs.

In the words of Muriel Scheinman of Urbana, who wrote her master's thesis on Altgeld Hall:

"A fortuitous blend of Romanesque, Gothic, Classical and Byzantine motifs, Altgeld Hall is an imposing stone monument dominated by a square carillon tower, its aura of weighty tradition reinforced by isolation from surrounding buildings."

The building was completed in 1897 and was built and used as the university library for almost 30 years. The building next housed the College of Law for almost 30 years and became the mathematics building in 1955.

Its architect was Nathan C. Ricker, a University of Illinois graduate who founded the department of architecture and served as dean of the College of Engineering for many years.

Mathematics Library in Altgeld Hall

In 1940 the building was named for John Peter Altgeld during whose term as governor of Illinois (1893-97) the university received significant appropriations and whose personal enthusiasm for medieval architecture led to the rejection of two earlier designs, according to Allen S. Weller's book, "100 Years of Campus Architecture at the University of Illinois," published in 1968.

The building's original name was Library Hall.

Mrs. Scheinman writes in her thesis:

"To its planners, Library Hall was an especially significant structure, tangible evidence that the 'cow college' of 1868 had been transformed into an institution of higher education worthy of a place in the ranks of the select.

"Of the elements of the design, none more than the murals furnish an insight into the sensitivities of those closely associated with the project: the allegorical paintings were more than artistic embellishment for they suggest by their very existence — as well as by their lofty themes — the University's commitment to scholarship and culture."

The murals are contained in four spaces below a large dome. Each space is bounded by a crescent-shaped curve on top and five smaller arches below.

The subject of the murals are "The Sacred Wood of the Muses," "Arcadia," "The Laboratory of Minerva" and "The Forge of Vulcan."

They are executed in rich colors. The remaining wall decorations are mainly painted in pallid green, dark red and muted blue for the architectural details and, in addition to these colors, dulled pink and more intense greens and blues for the floral decorations.

Although the room is stunning by any standards today, it must have been far more beautiful at its original creation.

Mrs. Scheinman writes:

"As originally built, the University rotunda conveyed a sense of openness and space because of the double stories extending upwards to the elliptical ceiling, and the reading rooms which stretched out from either side; a skylight suspended over the opalescent domed stained glass ceiling reinforced the airy effect by allowing natural and artificial light into the delivery room below."

Today the glass ceiling is covered with paint and the rooms are partitioned to allow room for book shelves and study space.

November 1979

28

Joyce's Georgian Door

Shari and Bernard Benstock searched all over Dublin for the perfect Georgian door only to find it literally on their own doorstep in Champaign.

The Benstocks, who are both James Joyce scholars, wanted a photograph of a beautiful Georgian door for the cover of their book, "Who's He When He's at Home," which was published this month by the University of Illinois Press.

Subtitled "A James Joyce Directory," the book is a guide to all fictional, mythological, legendary and real-life characters mentioned in Joyce's writings with the exception of "Finnegans Wake" for which a directory already exists.

The search, conducted on many visits to Dublin fair city, came to an end when the couple returned to their house in Champaign from the latest of these trips and realized that their own front door is a fine example of Georgian architecture.

It seems fitting that the house, which the Benstocks bought at their arrival to Champaign 5½ years ago, enters into their book—the result of five years of joint work—because the house constitutes, along with their 12-year-old son, Eric, and their absorption in literature and each other, the major loves of their lives.

Shari Benstock said, "We absolutely adore the house, in spite of the day-to-day trials of coping with a place this size."

Built in 1895, the white frame house contains 8,000 square feet of floor space on three floors in addition to a large basement.

The house has had only five owners in its 85 years of existence. It was built by Wolf Lewis, founder of one of Champaign's first department stores, W. Lewis and Co., which closed a few years ago, and his wife, Rachel.

The Lewises lived in the house for 26 years. The second owners, Isaac and Rose Kuhn, kept the house for 22 years. Mr. Kuhn was owner of Jos. Kuhn & Co., a clothing store on Main Street in Champaign, and the son of the store's founder, Joseph Kuhn.

The Kuhns sold the house in 1953 to John and Barbara Nixon, who owned it until 1961. Mr. Nixon was employed by U.S. Industrial Chemical Co. in Tuscola. Mrs. Nixon was a member of the McIlhenny family of New Iberia, La., of Tabasco fame.

The next owners were Shirley and Richard Newman, who lived in the house for 13 years until they sold it to the Benstocks in August 1974.

Newman is president and Mrs. Newman is vice president and copy chief of Richard Newman Associates, Inc., an advertising and public relations firm in Champaign.

The abstract for the house, which is generally considered one of Champaign's great old houses, indicates that the land it stands on was sold by the

U.S. government to Richard Logan in 1849. An 1851 entry in the abstract shows the land involved in that transaction was 160 acres.

Champaign was then known as West Urbana.

The white frame house looks out on Central High School. For all its massiveness, the house — unlike the great houses on University Avenue between the school and Prospect Avenue — is set on a small lot cheek-by-jowl with the neighboring houses.

The facade of the house features a porch with six white-painted terra cotta Ionic pillars, a second-floor balcony and two towers on the third floor — one square and one with a peaked, five-sided roof.

"We took on the house knowing it would be an adventure but not knowing if we could survive the challenge of caring for it," Mrs. Benstock said. "Well, it has been an adventure and we have survived."

The survival efforts have included replacing the furnace during the Benstocks' first Christmas in the house, a ghastly bout last winter when water pipes froze and cracked, sending water down onto the walls of newly painted rooms, and the on-going addition of a new roof and gutters at a cost of about $12,000.

But the Benstocks still love the house.

"It serves as a retreat when the world is too much with us," Mrs. Benstock said.

"We discovered during a year spent in England in 1977-78 that we can't live without the house. We were desperately homesick for it."

A native New Yorker, Professor Benstock teaches English and comparative literature and is director of the program in comparative literature at the University of Illinois.

In addition to the new book, he is the author of four books on Joyce and two on Sean O'Casey as well as many scholarly articles.

The new book is Mrs. Benstock's first book. She has written many scholarly articles on, among others, Joyce, T.S. Eliot, Virginia Woolf, Harold Pinter and Henri Matisse.

She grew up in an Iowa farm town and has a Ph.D. in English but has not been able to obtain a university job in her field locally. She works as staff associate in student affairs in the schools of basic medical sciences and clinical medicine at the University of Illinois.

Although the house is a magnificent structure throughout, its greatest glories are a splendid dining room with hand-painted murals depicting the four seasons, an exquisitely proportioned main stairway with a semicircular balcony jutting out at the half landing, the huge amounts of leaded, beveled glass in many windows and doors and the oval, convex stained-glass windows of rare beauty ornamenting several rooms.

Other lovely aspects of the house are renovated oak floors and 12-foot ceilings throughout and a plethora of bay windows.

The baronial dining room features a dark-stained, beamed oak ceiling and wainscoting. The southern wall holds a large built-in oak buffet with glass-fronted china cabinets at the sides and leaded-glass doors on the cabinet above the center.

Two oval stained-glass windows above the china cabinets filter the light.

The murals, which cover the upper parts of the four walls, were painted on canvas in the early years of the house's existence by an artist commissioned through Mandel Brothers department store in Chicago, according to Leonard Lewis, Champaign, the son of Wolf and Rachel Lewis.

Mr. Lewis, who is 96 years old, moved into the house at the age of 11 and lived there about 20 years.

Richard Newman repainted the murals during a three-year period of his ownership of the house. He left two narrow panels between the panes of the bay window in their original state. These panels now have the muted appearance of Chinese scrolls while the remaining paintings glow in strong colors.

Mrs. Benstock built the glass-topped dining table set on a frame and legs of dark wood. The family handyperson, she also has done much of the painting and plastering in the house. Her husband, a master chef, prepares many of the tempting delicacies served on the table.

The dining room is entered from a center hall that is larger than many modern living rooms and was used in the youth of Ruth Youngerman of Champaign, a daughter of the Isaac Kuhns, for dances for as many as 12 couples, Mrs. Youngerman said.

The hall is dominated by the graceful main stairway and by the entrance door and its surrounding panels, all of which are decorated throughout with leaded glass.

A small vestibule separates the entrance to the hall from the front door.

In addition to the dining room the main floor contains a living room with a fireplace worthy of a palace, a connected parlor with a wall-long window seat below a bay window, a library which serves as Professor Benstock's study and an enclosed porch off the library.

It also holds a large kitchen, a butler's pantry with floor-to-ceiling built-in storage space, the former summer kitchen which the Benstocks have remodeled into a summer dining room, a guest lavatory and a side entrance hall which leads out to a porte-cochere.

The kitchen holds a built-in wall refrigerator and a dishwasher — each of which belongs to the first line of appliances made by their respective manufacturers and which still functions.

The Benstocks have decorated the house with striking, modern pieces of furniture. A large abstract painting dominates the parlor and living room area.

The main stairs and the large landing on the second floor are utilized as a gallery for posters and prints.

The second floor holds a sitting room with a fireplace that connects through a large portal with the master bedroom. Mrs. Benstock uses the sitting room as her study.

The floor also holds Eric's room (the former solarium), two guest bedrooms, a maid's room used for storage and two bathrooms.

The master bathroom has a shower stall of solid marble, an old pedestal sink and an equally old dentist's sink at chest height, all possessing the original faucet handles.

The master bathroom and Eric's bathroom as well as the half-landing are ornamented with oval stained-glass windows.

The third floor contains two efficiency apartments and two one-bedroom apartments. The apartments were created by the Newmans.

A wide second stairway serves the apartment dwellers. An additional narrow stairway, which is now boarded up, in earlier times provided access to the kitchen for the maids.

The house also has a full basement containing a mural painted by Mrs. Youngerman's sister, Helen — now Mrs. B. B. Wiese of Champaign — and her friends, Mrs. Youngerman said.

The two sisters are among a number of local residents who still have glowing memories of the house.

Leonard Lewis recalls that in his boyhood the house's stable sheltered two horses. The living room was called the Gold Room because it was fur-

nished with delicate, small-sized pieces of furniture covered with gold leaf, he said.

Among Mrs. Youngerman's memories are three weddings held in the house, those of herself and two of her sisters.

Her parents considered buying Wilber Mansion, the present Champaign County Historical Museum, which was for sale in 1921 when they acquired the house, but preferred what is now the Benstocks' house.

The library, Professor Benstock's study, had walls covered with satin and a ceiling painted with angels when her family moved into the house, she said.

A coach house with an apartment on the second floor—which burned beyond repair during the Benstocks' year in England—held a small electric car which her mother drove, she said.

The house had a speaking system made of copper tubing for communication between floors in her childhood, she said.

"Mother planted lilies-of-the-valley next to the entrance to the coal bin like everyone else did in those days," she said.

"It was a wonderful house—a marvelous place to grow up," she said.

Mrs. Newman said, "That house is my favorite place in the whole town. It is the place I will always think of as home."

The Newmans brought up their three children in the house and Mrs. Newman recalls occasions when the house held 150 youngsters for an Edison Junior High School cast party or 25 to 30 girls for overnight stays for state youth conventions.

"It was a house that adapted itself to the kind of good time young people enjoy while allowing the parents to be comfortable at the same time," she said.

The Newmans renovated the house when they bought it.

"The Nixons had moved away and the house had stood empty for two years. It truly looked like a Charles Addams cartoon," Mrs. Newman said.

"The water pipes had burst and the canvas had pulled off the walls in many rooms. Every room but the dining room was damaged."

The remodeling was designed by James Edsall, a member of the University of Illinois architecture department.

"The renovation work was done by the university's finest, from freshmen to Ph.D. candidates," Mrs. Newman said.

"My husband used to joke that I cooked from the army field cookbook during those years. The deal was $1.50 an hour and all you could eat, and did they ever eat!"

She said she had expected the house to take many months to sell when she and her husband put it on the market in 1974. Instead it sold in 10 days.

"The real estate salesperson showed it to us just because she wanted us to see this glorious house," Mrs. Benstock recalled.

"We saw it, loved it, went out for lunch at a restaurant and plotted economics on a paper napkin, returned and made the offer, and in 18 hours the whole thing was done," she said.

"It took all the money we had. We didn't have a dime left for anything, including furniture."

The following Christmas Eve the Benstocks had gathered a large group of family and friends when the furnace cracked down the middle and was pronounced irrepairable.

"On Christmas Day I called the president of the savings and loan association where we had a savings account with next to no money in it," Mrs. Benstock said.

"I told him we needed a commercial furnace but had no money. He said, 'Let this be my Christmas present to you. We'll give you a loan so you can order the furnace immediately.'

"It made me realize we had come to a town full of wonderful people and that the house truly was meant to be ours."

February 1980

A GARLAND OF WOMEN

Sharp Under the Hood

When Elizabeth Sharp was a little girl living on an Air Force base, she watched over her father's shoulder as he repaired household appliances and broken toys.

Her mother, who grew up in the South and had definite ideas about what a girl should be interested in, discouraged Liz's interest.

"So whenever a household item broke, I would take it apart in my mother's absence, fix it, then undo it back to the broken stage and, in the evening, watch with satisfaction when my father would fix it and affirm my diagnosis," Ms. Sharp said.

"Today Dad is proud of me, but my mother still thinks it's off-color that I am a mechanic."

A mechanic and attendant at Bruce Taylor's Shell station in Champaign, Ms. Sharp has behind her two years as a service writer for L and L Imports Inc. in addition to previous work for Taylor. She is a full-time student at the University of Illinois, now in her last year of study for a bachelor's degree in physical education.

"Right now I only work 11 hours a week, on Saturdays, because of the so-called gas shortage. The men with families need the work more than I do. Before the shortage I put in 35 hours a week plus going to school, earning 4.5 averages and 5.0 in summer school. But it has taken me a long time to get it all together like this."

Ms. Sharp, 26, moved around a great deal in her childhood. Her father's job in the Air Force brought the family to Hawaii, where Liz was born, and to Germany, Alaska and most of the mainland states. She graduated from high school in Virginia after never having spent more than two years in one place.

"It was hard at the time," she said, "But I learned to adapt in a way that really helps me now. I would never have given up the opportunity to see so much of the world as a child."

After high school graduation she came to Champaign-Urbana.

"I went to the University of Illinois majoring in P.E. and flunked out," she said. "Then I flunked out of Parkland twice, was allowed to register for a third time, finally made good grades and was graduated in 1970.

"About this time I was hired by Bruce Taylor to pump gas. Meanwhile Lyman Larson, who owns L and L, had been observing the women's liberation movement and decided it was time he had a woman working for him, so he approached me to work as a service writer."

The service writer makes appointments for service on cars, writes the orders, assigns the cars to mechanics and follows through on how much work was done and how much to charge.

"There was an understanding that the mechanics did their jobs and I did mine, but when a job needing small hands would come up—such as working behind the dashboard—they would often ask me to help.

"The really important thing I learned at L and L was to diagnose what was wrong with a car. It got so I often could tell what the trouble was from looking at and listening to the engine.

"The first few months at L and L I had a tough time establishing myself with some of the male customers, and it was often so frustrating. Some of them gave me no credit whatsoever for knowing anything about cars, and they took a lot of convincing before they'd allow me near their cars.

"Women were much better. Many of them seemed happy at dealing with a woman, feeling she would take them more seriously. I would explain the trouble with their cars in terms of things around the house; for instance, that a valve is like a stopper in a sink, and a piston like a plunger.

"I am grateful to my two employers. Bruce Taylor, for instance, has two sons and has never had a woman work for him before. Yet he has never treated me any differently, never expected more or less from me than from the guys, and taught me as much as he teaches them.

"When I first worked for L and L, I'd work there 7:30 a.m. to 4:30 p.m. and then go on to Bruce Taylor's and pump gas from 5 p.m. until midnight. I didn't mind—I was making pretty good money and learning a lot," Ms. Sharp said.

"When winter came, though, I began getting sick a lot from working outside so much, and finally I got very ill and had to quit the gas-pumping job. I had a lot of emotional problems at the time, but since I became a Christian two years ago there has been a terrific change in my life. I take no credit at all for getting good grades now after flunking out three times. It only came about when I became a Christian."

Ms. Sharp went back to work at Taylor's nearly a year ago.

Ms. Sharp has overhauled her own Volkswagen and worked on friends' cars and small appliances. When she tore down her VW last year and found she needed some expensive parts, she contacted the owners of an independent garage to see if she could order the parts through them. She ended up reorganizing their office, including building floor-to-ceiling shelves on two walls by herself. In return she got the needed parts free and the use of special tools.

"As a mechanic I work on whatever comes in—some people ask for me by now—but I specialize in VWs. I prefer working on small-engine cars because the trend in modern culture to look at cars as luxury items and not as necessities just destroys me."

With all her love for mechanics, Ms. Sharp plans to make her lifetime career in physical education. She wants to coach women's sports at the college level because she feels strongly that girls' sports should receive support equal to that for boys' sports. Now a member of the University of Illinois women's track team, Ms. Sharp plans to do her graduate work at Michigan State University.

"I love being a mechanic and will never give up being involved with cars. When I was at L and L, I had several professors of mechanical engineering as customers, and they would sometimes try to talk me into switching to their field. But I feel very committed to working in physical education for women. I think it is an area where I can make a real contribution."

May 1974

Miss Betsy Ross at 75

The advertising slogan, "You are not getting older, you are getting better," could have been written with Betsy Ross in mind.

At an age when many women stick close to their firesides Miss Ross, who for 12 years acted as hostess in the University of Illinois President's House, lights up countless social occasions with her beautiful presence.

In the last month, her youthful face, framed with tendrils of white hair, the back of her head ornamented with the black velvet bow that is her trademark, has been seen at the Krannert Center at the performances of "Joan of Arc at the Stake" and "Hippolytus" and at the Symphony Guild benefit at Market Place.

Between these and other social occasions she found time to entertain 40 members of Mu Phi Epsilon, an honorary music society of which she is patron, at her Urbana home; attended work sessions as a member of the Krannert Art Museum Associates; and followed a series of lectures on prints, lithographs and etchings at the museum.

Perhaps the best measure of her youthfulness is the fact that her 75th birthday party last fall was arranged by a 13-year-old neighbor ("He and I are chums," she said) who enlisted his mother's help to put on a Bicentennial Year Betsy Ross party with red, white and blue balloons and streamers as decorations and a large number of guests who brought depictions of the first flag-maker as gifts to her namesake.

Miss Ross enjoyed every minute of her party although, she said with a sigh, there are times when she gets tired of the remarks her name brings forth from strangers meeting her for the first time.

"I often simply give my name as B. Ross in shops and offices," she said.

Miss Ross did celebrate the Bicentennial year by making a 13-star flag but only because a cousin in Washington, D.C., presented her with a flag-making kit at Christmas 1975.

"It was a terrible job. I don't think my cousin realized what she let me in for," she said. After completing the flag she mailed it to the cousin who arranged, through U.S. Rep. Edward Madigan of Lincoln, to have the flag flown over the Capitol building before returning it to Miss Ross.

Miss Ross is not a descendant of the first flag-maker. "My ancestors helped settle the State of Illinois. Several generations later one of them went to Washington as secretary to a congressman and both my parents were born in Washington," she said.

Miss Ross's father, Col. Tenney Ross, who died in 1960, was commanding officer during his army career of various army outposts, and Miss Ross often helped her parents represent the United States through their home.

"In San Juan, Puerto Rico, for instance, we lived in an old castle overlooking the harbor and held open house once a month, so I gained quite a lot of experience in running a big house," she said.

This experience became valuable when Arthur Cutts Willard became president of the University of Illinois in 1934. Miss Ross was the niece of Mrs. Willard and was asked by the Willards to live with them as their salaried social secretary.

"Mrs. Willard was not very rugged, and so I was asked to be the hostess in my dual capacity of social secretary and member of the family," Miss Ross said.

The President's House on Florida Avenue had only been in use for a few years when Mr. Willard became president. Miss Ross lived and worked in the house until President Willard's retirement 12 years later and continued to live with the Willards until President Willard died in 1960.

She first came to the University of Illinois from Washington as a voice student in the music department and also lived with the Willards during her college days in Champaign-Urbana.

She said about her years in the President's House, "Mr. Willard felt the house should be the center of everything on campus. You must remember that the Illini Union had not been built then, and so the President's House had to fulfill many functions.

"We had a $1,000 fund a year for official entertainment. The university had about 10,000 students when Mr. Willard became president and reached from 12,000 to 14,000 students at its highest point during his presidency. Money was very tight because of the Depression. My uncle decided against having an inauguration, for instance, to save money. He just took his hat and hung it up on a peg in his office, and that was that."

An internationally noted engineer, President Willard joined the University of Illinois faculty in 1913 and was head of the mechanical engineering department for many years and later served as its dean before becoming president of the university.

While a faculty member at the University of Illinois, he designed the ventilation system for the Holland Tunnel between New York City and New Jersey, the first vehicular tunnel in the world.

In spite of the tight money situation the Willards did indeed succeed in making the President's House the campus center the president wanted it to be, Miss Ross said.

"We held an open house the first Sunday afternoon of every month when the university was in session. Everyone on the faculty was invited, and through notices in the newspapers all the townspeople were invited as well," she said.

"We had hundreds of guests attend the open house each month. We served tea, coffee, sandwiches, cakes and mints. It was part of my job to arrange for faculty wives to pour the tea, for young faculty women and wives to act as assistant hostesses to make sure everyone had someone to talk to, and for inviting students who were the daughters or nieces of faculty to serve in the dining room."

Mrs. Willard and Miss Ross were in charge of the housekeeping. Miss Ross also handled the accounts and the lists of invitations. Before the war the staff included a houseman-butler, a cook, two maids and a woman to do the laundry, as well as a night watchman provided by the university. For the large teas and receptions extra staff was hired including serving women, a sandwich-maker and two dishwashers, Miss Ross said.

With Miss Ross handling the arrangements, the Willards also gave football luncheons for as many as 50 guests before every home football game of the season, held luncheons at commencement time, gave frequent dinner parties for 16 guests and held evening musicales in the drawing room.

"We also ran a regular hotel. People would call from the various university departments and ask us to have a visiting VIP stay overnight, and we were always able to do it," Miss Ross said.

Among the many illustrious names in Miss Ross's guest book are those of the singer Marian Anderson; the then Prime Minister of Norway, Carl Hambro; Life magazine photographer Margaret Bourke-White; Eve Curie, the author and daughter of Pierre and Marie Curie; and many Illinois legislators and University of Illinois trustees.

Miss Ross recalled having the pianist Arthur Schnabel as a houseguest with particular tenderness.

"Mrs. Willard was ill and could not attend his concert. The morning after the concert she came down to the drawing room in her dressing gown and Mr. Schnabel played for her," she said.

February 1977

44

Twin Duality

Maureen Pletcher and Colleen Howley Gosselin believe that their being identical twins has had far-reaching effects on their lives.

On the positive side they say the closeness they shared prepared them to be better marriage partners and more able to respond with warmth and empathy to others.

Being twins also provided the spur for their going to college and in general rising above the blue-collar background of their family.

On the negative side they count considerable pain when they first were separated and the struggles each has gone through to establish an individual sense of identity and self-worth.

Born in Princeton, N.J., the 29-year-old sisters spent their first 22 years together. After six years' separation they have lived for the last year in Champaign-Urbana.

Maureen, who has chosen Sam as her nickname in order to separate herself from the twin names of Maureen-Colleen, has lived here for six years. She has been a teacher at Edison Middle School for one year and before that taught at Central High School for three years.

She is the wife of W. Randall Pletcher, a graduate student in sociology at the University of Illinois.

Colleen lived in the East for six years after the twins' graduation from college. She has taught at Washington School in Urbana since her arrival in Champaign-Urbana last August, and will be a graduate student in administration at the University of Illinois this fall.

Her husband, Laurent Gosselin, is program director at the University of Illinois Child Development Laboratory.

The sisters are united in Champaign through a fluke, Colleen said.

"My husband applied for jobs all over the country after getting his doctorate and it was by chance that he got one in the town where Sam lived," she said.

The twins grew up in Princeton as the youngest of seven children, sharing the same room and sleeping in the same bed until they graduated from Princeton High School.

They were roommates throughout their college careers at New Jersey's Glassboro State College, where they both majored in education.

Only one of their siblings has a college degree.

"In a poor family it was a very proud thing for parents to have twins. Somehow the expectations for us were different than for the older children," Colleen said.

Being twins also helped them in their social relationships in Princeton, a town of great affluence and high educational level with a sharp demarcation between town and gown people.

Colleen Howley Gosselin, at left, and Maureen Pletcher

"We were accepted in an upper-class group in high school because we were twins," Sam said. "And we would do a lot of baby-sitting together for wealthy families who took an interest in us and encouraged us to go to college."

She said she felt the combination of being poor and being twins helped them obtain scholarships in college.

"The most unusual part about being a twin is being so close to another person. You always have someone on hand with whom you can share your innermost feelings. We were almost inseparable while we were growing up," Sam said.

She and Colleen developed a private language when they were small. They still often start conversations with each other in mid-sentence and found during their six-year separation they would somehow realize if the other one was upset and needed a comforting phone call.

Their siblings often would feel threatened and excluded by this closeness when the twins lived at home, Colleen said.

"It was particularly hard on the sister closest to us in age, who is three years older, also because we got so much more attention from our parents because of being twins," Sam said.

The twins were dressed alike until they were in the eighth grade and always received identical presents. They said they found it hard to establish their own taste in clothes as they became older.

"Everyone wants to be unique. Sometimes it is upsetting always to be with someone so alike," Sam said.

The sisters were placed in the same class throughout their schooling and had the same friends until they left college. They spent all vacations together and developed the same hobbies such as swimming and tennis.

Sam said she would stress the individuality of each child if she became the parent of twins, giving the children dissimilar names, dressing them in non-alike clothes, and insisting they be placed in separate classrooms whenever possible.

The most difficult part about separating after 22 years together was learning to be alone, Colleen said.

"Leaving home for me was associated with leaving Sam," she said. "I had to learn to deal with loneliness. It has taken me a long time to deal with being separate in the world."

She pointed out that by having each other's constant companionship she and Sam missed out on needed time to be alone and had, for instance, little opportunity to fantasize.

On the other hand the sisters believe they make good marriage partners because of their experience in communicating intensely.

"Both of us are real sensitive to other people's moods and can read people well. Both our husbands and friends value this," Sam said.

The "psyching up" each provided for the other helped them meet challenges in school work and sports, she said.

When they were first apart, they frequently felt they were becoming selfish, they said. "Just the experience of eating a whole candy bar by myself seemed a very selfish thing," Colleen said.

The twins, who were impossible to tell apart as children, today have developed somewhat different looks.

Their inner development also has moved along different lines.

"I am very active in the women's movement. I want to obtain power through administrative work. I am much more liberal and have extended my value systems to a lot larger framework than Sam has. I am into social change and a great believer in support systems of any kind," Colleen said.

Sam said, "I am more conservative, partly because of my religious commitment. I follow the teachings of my Guru, Sant Kirpai Singh Maharaj, which require meditation and introspection and forbid drinking and smoking. The code covers all aspects of my life and has changed me significantly. I intend to follow these teachings for the rest of my life."

"We have become so different that if it wasn't for our strong relationship it would be hard for us to work things out," Colleen said.

"But because of our backlog of shared experiences, even though the relationship can be painful at times, I feel that in years to come it can be a tremendous comfort to us."

July 1978

Elizabeth Klein, Writer

Since Elizabeth Klein decided to become a professional writer nine years ago, she has spent 5,760 hours (give or take a few) on her writing and earned about $1,350.

These figures leave her with an hourly income of 23½ cents from her writing, but Ms. Klein is not discouraged.

"The real motivation of my writing is not the money — although I certainly would be ecstatic if I sold the novel I'm working on and it made a lot of money," she said.

"But I realize there are perhaps no more than a hundred fiction writers and poets in this country who are able to support themselves solely on their income from writing.

"I write because it is the most exquisite experience in the world. When I'm writing it's a 'high.' It's like nothing else on earth and worth all the aggravation it costs me."

The mother of three children aged 7 to 11 and the wife of Michael Shapiro, associate professor of English at the University of Illinois, Ms. Klein made the decision to become a professional writer after she and her husband arrived in Champaign-Urbana in 1966.

Shortly after her arrival she suffered a skull fracture in an automobile accident. In the period of reassessment which followed the brush with death she decided "to commit my life to being a poet in the broad sense of the word," she said.

Before coming to Champaign-Urbana Ms. Klein had received her bachelor's degree from Elmira College in Elmira, N.Y., and a master's degree in 16th Century literature from Columbia University in New York. She also had worked for two years as an editorial researcher for Newsweek magazine and taught English as a second language for 2½ years at New York University.

The total of 5,760 hours spent writing since she made her commitment nine years ago has been chalked up by working 10 hours a week during the first 7½ years and six hours a day five days a week during the last 1½ years since her youngest child started the first grade.

During the years when she spent 10 hours a week on her writing she also taught 10 hours weekly in the Writing Laboratory at the University of Illinois. A babysitter hired for 20 hours a week freed her to pursue both careers.

The $1,350 income came from an article about the problem of being a full-time mother and a part-time professional which appeared in McCall's magazine in 1973 and earned $1,000, from giving poetry readings and from payments for several poems.

"I have published somewhere between 25 and 30 poems but most poems are paid for in copies of the magazine," she said.

She was accepted for listing in "A Directory of American Poets" this year, an honor which pleases her.

Ms. Klein is searching for a publisher for a book of her poems. A number of her poems has been chosen for inclusion in anthologies. She also has written several unpublished short stories.

The novel she is writing has the working title of "Reconciliations." She described it as being about an extended Jewish family which undergoes a traumatic event.

"I write about things I love, that concern me, that interest me, even that appall me occasionally," she said.

She currently is reading books for background for the novel.

"One of the characters is a high school teacher whose literary tastes were developed by the novels of the 1920s and 1930s, so I am reading those. Another character is a grandmother who admires Emma Goldman, and therefore I am reading about her," she said.

Ms. Klein writes her first draft in longhand and then revises her writing while typing.

An active participant in the creation of the writers' community in this area, she is president and one of the founders of Illinois Writers Inc., a founder and member of an informal workshop for writers that meets every two weeks, and a member of the Red Herring Poetry Workshop. She is editor of Illinois Writers' newsletter and one of the arrangers of the conference for writers held this spring in Champaign-Urbana.

In the non-writing part of her life she teaches Sunday School at Sinai Temple, is den mother for one of her sons' Cub Scout troop, and "carts the kids to guitar lessons, Hebrew school and orchestra."

Her husband enables her to keep her regular 9 a.m. to 3 p.m. writing schedule by coming home to give the children lunch on the two days a week when they do not eat at school.

"I have a very supportive husband. It would have been very difficult for me to pursue my writing without his encouragement and help," she said.

The next few years will be crucial to her career.

"I give myself 2½ years until the need to support three children through college draws near," she said.

"If I don't feel I have the chance of earning more money through my writing by then, I will have to limit my writing drastically and teach or do editorial work full time."

March 1977

Note: Elizabeth Klein's novel, "Reconciliations," was bought by Simon and Schuster, New York, in the spring of 1981 for 1982 publication.

Charlene Buoy's Signs of the Times

When Charlene Buoy shops on the square in Monticello, she looks around her with a feeling of pride.

"All the new signs on the square are mine," she said.

As the blonde, slender grandmother puts the finishing paint strokes on a large outdoor mural for radio station WVLJ on the outskirts of Monticello, she waves her free hand towards the highway and says, "Almost every truck that goes by here is one of mine, too."

A self-taught sign painter, Mrs. Buoy (pronounced Booie) has been working at her trade five years. She originally did sign painting for a while after she married 20 years ago, but stopped to concentrate on rearing her four children.

The children are Becky, 14, Jan, 15, Philip, 17, and a married daughter, Gail Gaddis, who presented Mrs. Buoy with her first grandchild, Ben, seven weeks ago.

Mrs. Buoy's father, who died when she was 11, was a sign painter, and she ascribes her unusual career choice to having become interested in sign painting while going out with him on assignments when she was a child.

She received no training from anyone but learned the technique through trial-and-error.

"My first signs were pretty bad. I guess they were my practice efforts," she said.

Originally from Atwood, Mrs. Buoy and her husband, Arnie, lived in Monticello until six years ago, when they moved first to Daytona, Fla., and then to Nashville, Tenn. They returned to Monticello 2½ years ago.

Mr. Buoy travels through the state of Illinois to sell, install and service air conditioners, ice machines, refrigeration units and soda-dispensing machines.

While living in Nashville, Mrs. Buoy designed billboards for Minnesota Mining and Manufacturing Co. Some of her designs—including a billboard for Scottish Inns—were displayed on billboards from coast to coast.

Working an average of 30 to 40 hours a week during the outdoor painting season and 15 to 20 hours in winter, Mrs. Buoy has painted a great variety of signs. Much of her work involves doing lettering on trucks and the doors of business establishments.

Among the unusual signs she has painted are a farm sign in the shape of a steer and a one-foot tall, 20-feet long sign for a restaurant listing every item on its menu.

She usually starts her day at 5:30 a.m. To execute the mural for the radio station, she worked from 10 a.m. to around 3 p.m. in the broiling sun with the temperature reaching the mid-90s.

In true country style, no money changed hands for the job. Instead Mrs.

Buoy traded air time for commercials for her labor. She said the cash cost of the job would have been between $60 and $75.

She first makes a scale drawing that she presents to the client for approval and modification. She then draws the layout with charcoal on the wall or door and paints the design and lettering with brushes.

She is left-handed and paints with her left hand. As she works, four diamond rings on her left ring-finger sparkle in the sun.

Most of the jobs require one coat of paint, although some truck lettering occasionally calls for two coats. The charcoal lines wash off when it rains.

She uses a ladder for the radio station mural and at times has worked on scaffolding on large designs.

She does not have a workshop in her Monticello home although she paints many smaller signs there.

"I work wherever I can find space to put a sign," she said. "Sometimes the better part of the living and dining rooms will be taken up for two weeks by a big sign."

Mrs. Buoy painted many pastel portraits on commission when her children were young. She now does pen and ink, pencil or charcoal drawings for clients, but prefers to work on needlepoint and make applehead dolls.

"Mom does everything. She cooks, fixes radios, TVs and toasters, does carpentry, makes dolls and does needlepoint. Today she fixed the dog's chain with a bobbypin," said Jan, who kept her mother company on the WVLJ job together with Becky and several friends.

While the three younger children have no plans to follow in their mother's footsteps, Gail wants to learn the trade from her when Ben is a little older.

Mrs. Buoy tries to fit in as much time as possible to be with her grandchild, but her sign-painting keeps her pretty busy.

"I finished a sign for my own business two months ago, but I haven't had time to put it up yet," she said.

June 1976

On the Road with Chantilly Lace

Every truckin' day during the school year Chantilly Lace rolls down the superslab between ol' Champaign-town and that Bloomington-town, modulating with Mama Boo-Boo, Topless Turtle and One-Eyed Jack.

Or, in plain English, every workday during the academic year Sheila Goldberg commutes on Interstate 74 between Champaign and Bloomington, talking with some of her Citizens Band Radio friends.

In private life, Mrs. Goldberg of Champaign is the wife of a University of Illinois professor and the mother of three children, Julye, 23, Barry, 21, and Jay, 15.

A high-school drop-out, she began college when her youngest child was 7, and finished her undergraduate work and doctorate in three years.

She is an assistant professor of child development at Illinois State University at Bloomington-Normal.

About a year ago, Mrs. Goldberg found herself getting bored with the 63-mile, one-and-a-half hour drive twice a day, and a little frightened at being alone on the highway.

Then Barry gave her a CB-radio for her birthday.

Now the time seems to fly on the trips as she visits with truckers and other new friends over the radio and checks in with housebound radio chums along the route.

And she has learned to feel a lot safer.

"I used to be terribly tense driving on the highway, but not anymore. It's really like in the song, 'Me and old CB'," she said.

"Once this winter I panicked, feeling that my little 95-pounder (Fiat station-wagon) was too light to handle on the icy road. After I said so on the radio, two fellows escorted me all the way from Bloomington to Champaign, one guarding my front door, the other the back door."

The brother- and sisterhood of CBers is always ready to help a fellow driver, as she found out again a few weeks ago when she had trouble with the electrical system of her car and pulled off on the shoulder.

"Many truck drivers stopped to help me. After one of the fellows fixed it, and I drove off the Interstate, I could hear the truckers asking each other, 'Did anyone see Chantilly Lace? Did she make it all right?'," she said.

Mrs. Goldberg has learned from experience not to tell her airwave friends what she does for a living.

"It puts them under pressure and turns them off, even if I say it in a roundabout way like 'I teach teachers'," she said. "Usually I just parry questions about what I do."

She loves the camaraderie of the highway and enjoys picking up the CB-lingo. On a drive with this reporter she spoke frequently into her microphone, talking easily with a driver named Lone Wolf who told her, "The Bears look hungry today."

"We have a lot of names for the police, like Bears, Tijuana Taxis, Smokies, Mounties and Plain Wrappers (unmarked police cars)," she said.

"I often modulate with a Mahomet-based policeman whose handle is Gentle Ben."

She stressed that, contrary to widespread beliefs, CBers have many concerns other than locating the position of police cars.

"I belong to REACT (Radio Emergency Associated Citizens Team) which assists the police in all forms of local emergencies by furnishing information," she said.

"During the manhunt for an escaped convict last year all we CBers maintained radio silence about the whereabouts of the Bears so as not to aid the convict.

"REACT members also monitored the recent Boneyard Walk and will help monitor the 4th of July parade."

As we drive along, Mrs. Goldberg translates the CB-parlance. When a male voice describes the position of "two beavers in distress," she explains this means two female motorists with car trouble. Sure enough, a few minutes later, we see the women's car on the shoulder with an "18-wheeler" (big truck) stopped ahead of it and the truck driver working under the car's hood.

A little later, a man on the radio tells another, "You've got two attractive seatcovers coming up," meaning a car with two women.

Other CB-terminology heard during the drive is Circle City (Indianapolis), Windy City (Chicago), Negatory (no), "Do you have your ears on?" (Are you out there?), "Come back" (What), and "Blowing your door off" (passing the car).

"Watch for me on the flipper" means "Let's talk again on the return journey." "I've got this rubberband stretched as far as it will go" is "I'm going top speed." "Green stamps" is a speeding ticket, and "takin' your picture" means "radar in operation."

Mrs. Goldberg followed a lot of byroads to become a college professor. Born in England, she went to Canada with her parents to live during World War II and later moved to the United States.

She dropped out of high school in order to spend four years on a kibbutz in Israel. During this time she was a member of Operation Magic Carpet which helped bring the Yemenite Jews to Israel.

"It was very moving," she said. "They were primitive people who had never seen an airplane in their lives. But they had been told that the Messiah would arrive out of the air on big wings someday, and when the huge planes came swooping down to pick them up, they kissed the ground and walked aboard trustingly."

After many years of concentration on raising her family, she decided to further her education and entered the University of Illinois in 1968.

In the course of three years she obtained her bachelor's, master's and doctor's degrees.

Except for the truckers who stopped to help her when her car was disabled, Mrs. Goldberg has never met any of her CB friends, although invitations to have a cup of coffee at a truckstop are frequent.

She did break her rule about describing her job when she discovered that one of her regular contacts, whose CB-name is Candy Cane, is a woman who also lives in Champaign and teaches child development at Normal.

On their first CB-exchange, the two women explored the possibilities of doing a research project together.

Asked if they have considered forming a car pool, she answered, "Yes, we have.

"But having a passenger would mean I'd have to quit talking on the CB, and I enjoy that far too much to give it up."

May 1976

Relief in Bronze

Moving with great caution, Isabella Pera lifts a bucket filled with 150 pounds of bubbling, bright yellow bronze from a furnace heated to 2,000 degrees Fahrenheit.

Attached to the hook of an overhead crane hoist, the bucket is moved inch by inch up from the fiery furnace, while Ms. Pera grips it with a pair of home-made, long-handled tongs.

When the bucket handle is free of the hoist, she lifts the bucket with tongs into a metal ring in the center of a long rod.

A helper, Flora Mace, grasps one end of the rod as Ms. Pera holds the other. Together they lift the rod, and, with Ms. Pera controlling the action with her hand, carry it several feet and pour the molten bronze into six plaster molds.

"This is a unique moment," whispers Frank Gallo, the sculptor. "It is extremely rare anywhere in the world to see a woman sculptor do her own casting.

"It is the first time on this campus the entire process has been done by a woman by herself."

Last spring Ms. Pera and Jane Needle became the first women at the University of Illinois to cast their works together, but they received some aid from male sculptors.

Mr. Gallo directs the University of Illinois Graduate Sculptors Workshop that is housed in a metal shed on Griffith Drive west of the Herman M. Adler Zone Center in South Champaign.

He and Roger Blakley, who teaches bronze casting, are watching the casting together with a group of graduate sculptors who have gathered in the workshop to help or provide moral support. Everyone seems to hold his or her breath throughout the pouring process and breaks spontaneously into applause when the last drops of bronze bubbles in the molds.

Ms. Pera pushes her welder's helmet back and throws her arms up in triumph. Then a round of hugs and handshakes begins.

"She's been a nervous wreck all week," says Ann Cowperthwaite.

Jane Needle says, "So many steps throughout the five-day process can go wrong. She had to nurse the kiln like a mother. And she is an Italian, a real emotional person!"

Before the week of the casting, Ms. Pera had shaped six sculptures in clay. After the casting, four pieces were to be fitted together to form a wall relief, and two pieces would be combined to make an abstract torso.

As part of the preparations, she covered each piece with three or four coats of plaster and then broke the plaster molds open to remove the clay. She covered the inside of the empty plaster molds with four coats of wax and fitted them back together.

Then she removed the plaster mold and threw it away and covered the wax with an investment, a mixture of sand and plaster, to form a cylinder.

Ms. Pera's vigil began on a recent Tuesday morning and ended with the casting on the following Saturday morning.

She placed the six cylinders, each approximately two feet high, in the kiln to start the burning-out process, during which the wax and excess moisture are eliminated.

She watched over the kiln from 8 a.m. to midnight every day for four days, with time out for cat naps on an old couch.

"It took 12 hours on Tuesday to bring the kiln up to 1,000 degrees F. and another 12 hours at the end to bring the temperature down slowly," she said.

"On Wednesday the pilot light went out at least 15 times. Something was wrong with the mechanism, and I couldn't figure out what it was. I kept changing all the controls, trying to shut out the air draft. Finally I must have touched the right ones."

All the costs of the supplies, including the bronze at one dollar a pound, were borne by Ms. Pera.

The five chambers that made up the foundry (the kiln, sand pit and melting furnace interspersed with two chambers for access) are underground for safety, with their tops at floor level.

On the morning of the casting, Ms. Pera started the melting furnace and brought it up to the 2,000-degrees F. Using the crane, she lifted the six molds from the kiln one by one into the sandpit and covered their tops with heavy white paper and fastened it with metal wire.

57

Then she shoveled sand around the molds to the level of the tops. The sand holds the molds and keeps them from breaking open.

She was aided in the shoveling by six other graduate students and by 5-year-old Amy Baur (daughter of sculptor student Michael Baur, and the lab mascot) who ran back and forth throwing in handfuls of sand.

The helpers vacuumed sand off the tops of the molds.

As the feeling of tension rose, Ms. Pera, dressed in a full-length industrial apron, a suede jerkin and workman's gloves and with heavy rubber covers over her boots, placed the bronze ingots in the furnace with long tongs.

"It's dangerous stuff," said Miss Needle in a low voice. "Two guys were pouring bronze here a few years ago, when rain came through the roof and made a drop of bronze splatter up. It shot behind the protective leg covering on one guy and burnt him clear to the bone."

As the bronze heated, it was evident that Ms. Pera's friends were trying to ease her tension. One bought her a soft drink, and another asked facetiously, "Wanna sit down and put your feet up?"

Ms. Pera tested the heat of the bronze with a pyrometer, a long L-shaped rod, several times. After the last test, she motioned to Miss Mace, by now also dressed in protective clothing, and together they lifted the glowing bucket, and the pouring began.

After the pouring ended, a case of beer was brought out, and the students cooked hot dogs on the after-heat of the furnace.

Beaming with relief, Ms. Pera munched a mustard-laden hot dog and said her two finished sculptures will be shown in the Graduate Art and Design Exhibition at the Krannert Art Museum.

Mr. Gallo patted her on the shoulder and said, "We used to have all men in the Sculpture Lab. This year nine out of the 11 students are women. It just turned out that the female applicants were better than the male this year."

"We women are taking over the world," Ms. Pera said.

January 1976

Room Rappers

Their jobs might drive some women up a wall but Sunny Lovell and Linda Noddle find their work enchanting.

"Sure, it's a hard job, physically difficult and quite tiring, but we really get off on changing a room and making it pretty," Mrs. Noddle said.

"We work three days a week and we make a tremendous amount of money," Mrs. Lovell added.

The two young women started a wallpapering business with the catchy name of "Room Rappers" a little over a year ago and have been booked solid at least a month in advance since the first day.

Since most of their bookings are arranged over the telephone, many clients do a double-take when Mrs. Lovell and Mrs. Noddle arrive for the first time in their blue jeans and workman's aprons with the words Room Rappers appliqued in calico print.

Neither fits most people's preconceptions of a blue-collar worker. A tall willowy brunette, Mrs. Lovell worked as a model for three years before her marriage and is now doing some television commercials. Her petite colleague is equally glamorous with her wedge haircut and flashing grin.

Their background also is an unexpected one for two laborers who take pride in hanging 22 rolls of wallpaper a day and whose commitment to their work is so great that last spring Mrs. Noddle worked for two months with her broken leg in a cast.

Mrs. Lovell, who moved to Champaign one-and-half years ago, is married to Merle Lovell, a commodities broker at Stotler & Company. She and her husband have two daughters, Tiffany, 8, and Jessica, 3.

She grew up in Pittsburg, Kan., and attended Pittsburg State College. In her modeling career with the Kim Dawson Agency in Dallas, she was featured in national television and print ads and did fashion modeling. After their marriage in 1968, the Lovells lived in Kansas City until moving to Champaign.

Mrs. Noddle, who has just joined the Junior League of Champaign-Urbana as a provisional member, is the wife of Jeffrey Noddle, vice president of merchandising at J. M. Jones. She and her husband have two daughters, Julie, 5½, and Stacey, 2.

She grew up in Highland Park, has a bachelor's degree in education and has worked as a teacher. She and her husband moved to Champaign two years ago after having lived in Iowa, Louisiana and California.

"We both had been housewives for a number of years and wanted to work. We wanted big money and to be able to choose our own work hours," Mrs. Lovell said.

"Linda and I both had hung a lot of wallpaper for many years and ran out of friends and relatives to work for. We decided it was the only thing we were good enough at to do for money."

"We were two spoiled brats who decided to go into business," Mrs. Noddle added with a smile.

Getting started was simplicity itself. Each husband staked the company with $50. Cards were printed and distributed, a ladder, old door, sawhorses, brushes and pans were acquired, baby sitters were contacted, and Room Rappers were off and rolling.

"It just took off and snowballed from the beginning. We have been booked a solid month ahead from the day we started, and now we are getting come-backs, jobs for people we have worked for earlier," Mrs. Lovell said.

In a charming gesture typifying their unique blend of society background and hardnosed working-man's philosophy, they send a rose to each customer who refers new trade to them.

The women say they have never run into any prejudice either from clients or from other workers because of their sex.

"If anything it seems to be an advantage to be female wallpaper hangers. People seem more comfortable having two women come into their homes. Maybe they feel we project our own nest-making concerns to their house," Mrs. Noddle said.

The women charge from $10 to $13 per roll, depending on whether it is regular wallpaper or a specialty covering such as grass cloth or foil. Trimmed wallpaper is $1 extra, and extra charges are made for bathrooms and kitchens and for the use of scaffolding.

"You can spend a day hanging three-and-a-half rolls in a bathroom and hang 22 rolls in a large room in the same time," Mrs. Lovell said.

Estimates usually are made over the phone with the customers ordering their own wallpaper from a store.

"We are strictly blue collar. We don't measure for paper or order it," Mrs. Noddle said.

The women's blue-collar philosophy stops when it comes to spending their earnings. Each keeps control of her Room Rappers income with the full encouragement of her husband.

"I'll never stop spending my husband's money — to do so was instilled in me early," Mrs. Lovell said.

She recently acquired a white 1961 Jaguar.

"It will be restored and painted so that it's really beautiful. It will be my toy — one of those cars you polish on Saturday and drive on Sunday," she said.

Mrs. Noddle confided with a grin that "No one will ever see my Room Rapper earnings except the department stores and my charge accounts."

"I don't know how many women could take our kind of schedule. But I'm a bundle of energy; I have to be moving all the time. For Linda and me the tiredness of the evening, the hurting feet and the calluses on our hands are worth it," Mrs. Lovell said as Mrs. Noddle nodded in agreement.

October 1978

A Professional in the House

"I feel I'm a real professional. If there was a degree handed out for excellence in housework, I feel I'd get it."

Roberta Aikens has spent a lifetime cleaning other people's houses, first in her native South Carolina and for the last 21 years in Champaign-Urbana.

"When I started I didn't have any choice. I have had chances to get out of it since, but I like it. As a matter of fact I love it," the soft-spoken woman said.

"Many people think it's dirty work but it isn't. I like the freedom of it. I like being my own boss. I like making a house look beautiful and I enjoy the different people I work for."

The child and grandchild of South Carolina sharecroppers, Mrs. Aikens was orphaned at the age of 2 and was brought up by her grandfather, who died when she was 12.

At this age she was taken into the household of her aunt and uncle. The couple was already raising three small children of their own and soon after her arrival extended their family with four small boys left motherless with the death of the aunt's youngest sister.

"My aunt and uncle were the most beautiful people. They are now in their 70s, and I love them dearly," she said.

"I had about six years of school, off and on, and left school at 12½ to work fulltime cleaning houses," she said.

"I worked from early morning to well into the evening. The pay was 50 cents a day, sometimes 75 cents, and then you'd get a lot of magazines you couldn't read and clothes and shoes that didn't fit you."

In the span of her long career Mrs. Aikens feels she has seen housework change from despised underpaid work in which "you were regarded as little more than a slave" to a remunerative and well-regarded profession.

Today she works nine four-hour days for eight families—"I finally cleared one morning for myself and I'm going to hold on to that, no matter how many people call me"—at fees ranging from $16 to $20 for four hours.

As a comparison it may be noted that the bulletin board at Job Service (the former Illinois State Employment Service) this week featured two openings for cleaner-housekeepers in a motel and a nursing home, both at the pay scale of $2.65 an hour.

In addition to paying both her and their share of the Social Security tax, all Mrs. Aikens' employers pay her two weeks vacation at her regular weekly rate and pay for sick-days and holidays when they happen on their regular day.

"I had a time working that in when I first began to ask for vacation, holiday and sick pay some five to 10 years ago," she said. "I had to let some people go over that issue."

When she began working in Champaign-Urbana 21 years ago, the hourly rate for housework was $1. As recently as 14 years ago her pay was $1.50 an hour.

Mrs. Aikens has worked for most of her employers for many years. The longest relationship with a family goes back 20 years.

"The oldest son in that family got married recently and I thought to myself, 'My! I used to pin diapers on him,' " she said with a laugh.

Since many of her employers know each other, in many cases having originally obtained her services through word-of-mouth recommendations from a family already on her list, she is careful never to discuss them with each other.

"It's a professional job just like a doctor's. He doesn't discuss his patients with other people, and I don't talk about my people," she said.

Mrs. Aikens and her employers have developed close personal relationships, sharing many joys and sorrows, she said. She has stayed in touch by letter and Christmas card exchanges for many years with employers who have moved away.

Over the years she has filled openings in her schedule from a waiting list of people composed of friends and acquaintances of her various employers.

"I have had letters from out-of-state and from as far away as Australia from people who are moving to town and have gotten my name from people here," she said, shaking her head in disbelief.

In her job she performs all basic housecleaning duties but refuses to shampoo rugs—"That's a $200 to $300 job for a professional rug cleaning service in some cases"—and to undertake major window-washing jobs.

She said she much prefers being allowed to make decisions about what supplies to use and the order of the cleaning jobs.

"I've been in most of the homes so long, I know much more about caring for them than the people themselves do," she said.

To obtain the high school education she never had she spends two evenings a week on top of her heavy work schedule attending classes at Urbana High School for her General Equivalency Diploma (GED) and many evening and weekend hours studying for her classes.

She enrolled in the GED program last January.

Her three daughters, Emily, Janet and Sonia, all graduated from high school and attended Illinois Commercial College in Champaign. "They were among the first blacks to attend the college," she said.

All three are now working in white-collar jobs. Emily is an employment counsellor at a medical center in Denver. Janet works in the price control department at Lowry Air Force Base in Denver and is married to a sales adviser for Ford Motor Co. who is a college graduate. Sonia is a data processor working for the county in Los Angeles and is the wife of an actor.

The three young women have provided their mother with five grandchildren—four boys and one girl.

Mrs. Aikens is the wife of William Aikens, who is employed at Kraft, Inc. in Champaign.

Working both through her church, Salem Baptist Church, and on her own, she has in her own quiet way for many years helped many members of the black community through tough spots.

She has done this not only through advice and her own example but also by channeling to them the large quantities of linens, clothes and household goods given to her by employers.

"Some of the youngsters I helped are grown now and have beautiful educations and some of the women, who needed help so desperately, are steppin' high now," she said with quiet pride.

"One woman said to me, 'Honest to God, you kept my children going'."

Her only quarrel with her job is with its nomenclature.

"I don't like terms like 'cleaning woman' and 'maid,' and I hate the word 'domestic'. I am a 'professional in housecleaning'."

November 1978

Dorthea Means God's Gift

"My mother's name, Dorthea, means gift from God. I can't think of anyone having a more appropriate name."

Elma Hendrix of Champaign is talking about her 96-year-old mother, "Dora" Twenstrup, who makes her home with Mrs. Hendrix and her husband, Richard.

Although Mrs. Twenstrup has suffered five minor strokes in recent years, she is an active participant in the life of the family.

She frequently bakes rye bread and prepares the family's favorite recipes from her native Denmark such as klejner (a deep-fried cookie), frikadeller (fried meatballs) and a hearty soup with dumplings and tiny meatballs.

Mrs. Twenstrup's favorite pastime is needlepoint which she executes from her own design. She has made two needlepoint pictures of houses and has almost finished a third. She also crochets, knits and does embroidery.

She often can be found washing dishes and always makes her own bed.

For 18 years she has sent birthday cards to all the residents of the Champaign County Nursing Home as a work contribution to her church, Grace Evangelical Lutheran. For January this meant addressing and signing 18 cards; the youngest recipient of a card was born in 1915, 36 years after Mrs. Twenstrup's birth.

Her hearing seems perfect. She speaks in a clear, small voice with only a hint of a Danish accent. Her eyes are strong enough, with the help of glasses, for her beloved needlepoint and much reading.

She walks with the help of a "walker" and rarely leaves her daughter's house.

Her quickness of mind is constantly evident. When asked what her brother, Norman Twenstrup of Champaign, does for a living, Mrs. Hendrix's thoughts were elsewhere for the moment. Her mother quickly answered for her, "He is an assistant to the manager of an apartment complex of condominiums."

She seems to inspire a strong affection in those who know her, not just in the immediate family, which includes her daughter, Julie Isley, of Milwaukee, but reaching out as far as Alaska.

Last summer descendants of her husband, who died more than 50 years ago, came to Champaign to visit her, and the previous year a nephew and his wife traveled from Denmark to see her.

She also receives frequent visits from the descendants of the family she worked for on her arrival in the United States in 1903, and from her three granddaughters who call her "Nana."

Yet her life has not been an easy one. In a 10-year period she lost her husband, mother and three sons—one who died at birth and twins who died at age 4 and 6.

Her brother was killed by a German soldier in 1945 during the German occupation of Denmark.

"Yes, I have had a hard life, but I guess I am just a stubborn Dane. By the grace of God I have managed," she said.

Mrs. Twenstrup's father died when she was very young. Later her mother and stepfather kept an inn, and she worked for them. She also at one point kept house for her grandfather, who had a small farm.

As was customary at the time, she left school at 14, and served an apprenticeship learning how to do laundry and ironing. She still hand-irons the collars of the choir robes for her church.

She later spent three months at a special Danish school specializing in adult education and still remembers a woman whose inspired teaching and respect for learning, she said, influenced her life.

In 1903 she crossed the Atlantic Ocean on a steamer and came to Kempton, near Kankakee, where she found work as a housekeeper on a cattle farm.

After three years in Kempton she returned to Denmark at the urging of her mother. She arrived in Copenhagen in time to watch the funeral cortege of King Christian IX which was attended by the greatest number of crowned heads ever seen in one place.

Back in Denmark, she married "the boy next door," Julius, and after the birth of their first child, Elma, returned with him to the United States in 1913 for good.

They settled in North Dakota, where Julius entered the meat business with his brother.

"My husband was the best meat cutter I have ever seen," Mrs. Twenstrup said. "His father was a meat cutter before him, and my husband learned the trade from him and as an apprentice in Germany."

She learned meat cutting from her husband and would cut meat and wait on customers while her husband went around the countryside buying cattle.

"Then he got diabetes and died at 46 years of age, two years before the discovery of insulin. It was terrible. We were left without a penny. Everything went for doctors' bills and funeral expenses.

"I had to do something to support the children, so I came to Champaign, where my first cousin, Carl Hansen, lived, and opened a boarding house. Carl sent all his unmarried fellows at his creamery to me for room and board, and that's how I got started.

"Imagine feeding a working man for $7 a week, and that often included the room. One thing, the fellows could always have all the butter they wanted, because my cousin provided that."

A widower, Carl Hansen, 80, now retired as vice president of Beatrice Foods Co., visits Mrs. Twenstrup and the Hendrixes every Saturday night for dinner, and the two older people spend many hours together reminiscing. They are the only two members of their family left in their generation.

"He always greets me with 'Goddag og Guds fred' (How do you do and God's Peace)," Mrs. Twenstrup said.

"Even at the prices of that time, I couldn't feed the fellows at a dollar a day," she continued, "and I got tired of running the boarding house and went to work taking care of apartments for students. They were not very neat in their housekeeping, so I had a lot to do when I came in once a week.

"Oh, well, with the children helping out we got along somehow."

Mrs. Twenstrup has through her life had a strong religious faith. Mrs. Hendrix said the first sign that the power of speech had returned to her mother after her stroke early in January came when Mrs. Hendrix heard her pray in Danish, 24 hours after the stroke. Her English speech returned later.

On last Christmas Eve, the pastor of Mrs. Twenstrup's church, the Rev. William A. Petrillo, for the first time did not preach a sermon of his own composing but read instead a translation made by Mrs. Twenstrup of a Danish Christmas sermon.

Since Mrs. Twenstrup was unable to attend the service, a friend taped the reading and brought her the recording, enabling her to listen to the words that have sustained her through her long and arduous life.

February 1975

FARM FOLK

Earl's for Coffee

"This is one of the few stores of its kind left in Illinois. The day Earl gets too old to run it, we will see the end of it."

The speaker is one of the early morning coffee drinkers at the Hugo General Store. Located at a crossroads in the tiny community of Hugo with the Embarras river behind it, the store is also known as "Earl's Place."

Together with the Hugo Community Church across the road, the crossroads provides a focal point for the people living within a five-mile radius.

The owner, Earl Entler, opens the store around 6 every morning including Sunday, rain or shine. One of his first tasks is to put on the big coffee pot.

"I don't make much (from the store) but I like seeing the neighbors," Mr. Entler said. "As long as they don't take my old-age pension away, I am going to keep it going."

He does see the neighbors. The coffee crowd often numbers as many as 10 farmers at a time. They drive up in pickup trucks, wearing work clothes and John Deere or DeKalb visored caps, and help themselves to coffee, leaving a dime on the top of the refrigerated case.

The largest number arrives between 8 and 9 a.m.

Most of the space in the small store is given over to an area furnished with a row of five wooden seats from an old church, and wooden armchairs grouped around a gas stove.

Here the talk goes on about crops and drainage, cattle and the weather. Information may be exchanged about the health of a neighbor. The talk is flavored with the good-natured joshing of people who see each other every day and still has a regional identity. "We doctor in Urbana anymore, not in Tuscolie," one fellow said.

All the coffee drinkers are men. Women in print dresses or pant suits stop by for staples, meat and dairy products, but do not sit down. They exchange greetings with the men and sometimes leave a message for someone with Mr. Entler.

Children and teenagers frequently arrive on mini-bikes or motorcycles and buy pop from Mr. Entler's three soft drink cases. They fill their tanks from one of the gasoline pumps outside and walk to the counter with change for their purchase.

Small children brought by their mother run to Mr. Entler for a hug and at times cuddle in his lap for a few minutes before heading for the candy case.

Mr. Entler closes between noon and 4 p.m. when, he said, "not a soul comes by." He opens again from 4 to 7 p.m.

Besides grocery staples, the merchandise includes spools and silk thread,

flashlights, drill heads, hog rings and other necessities for a farming community. Chewing tobacco sells well along with cigars and cigarettes.

Tuesdays are busier days than normal for Mr. Entler. Women come in for supplies for a noon potluck dinner in the church basement. The women gather in the church for Bible study in the morning and a quilting bee in the afternoon and are joined by the men for dinner.

A faded color reproduction of President Eisenhower hangs over one doorway.

"The other day a blacksnake crawled up and draped itself over the doorsill below that picture," Mr. Entler said. "I poked it down with a yardstick and chased it outside."

Mr. Entler's 14-year-old dog, Pat, follows him around, when it is not napping near the stove.

"That dog is all I've got left outside of the neighbors," Mr. Entler said.

Mr. Entler's wife through 45 years, Flossie, died last December. "Flossie was just precious," Lillian Brothers, a next-door neighbor, said, her eyes misty.

Mr. Entler has spent most of his life in Hugo. His father, Fred Entler, founded the store in 1931 and operated it with his son's help until the elder Mr. Entler's health failed. He died in 1965, and Earl Entler has managed the store since.

In addition to the store, Mr. Entler has a sawmill in back, powered by an old tractor. He also produces and sells honey from beehives behind the store.

The store's back room is a workshop and tool room stocked with thousands of nails, bolts, cotter pins, washers and tractor belts.

"If you need a replacement piece for, say, a tractor and Earl doesn't have it, he will make it for you," one of the coffee drinkers said.

When Mr. Entler turned 67 last May 10, more than 200 people attended a surprise birthday party held at the church. A seven-piece band played Country and Western music, and Mr. Entler was presented with a television set.

The people in Hugo are proud of the general store with its bare concrete floor and fading painted walls.

"In New England a store like this would be all fancied up with checked curtains and a quaint pickle barrel," a young farmer said. "Earl's store looks the way it has always looked, and we like it that way."

September 1974

75

From Mighty Oak to Farm Lumber

Winter is the time when people who farm catch up on jobs they put aside during the busy seasons of the farm year.

It is the time of year when 68-year-old Earl Entler, proprietor of the Hugo General Store, finds time to operate his ancient sawmill on the banks of the Embarras River.

On a recent warm December day, Mr. Entler got together with two friends, farmers Martin and Glenn Prosser, to cut up a 15-foot-long oak trunk belonging to Martin.

The Prossers (father and son) worked smoothly as a team together with Mr. Entler to operate the sawmill, which is powered by a derelict Case tractor.

With grappling hooks attached to three long poles, they pulled the almost three-foot diameter trunk onto a wheeled carriage in line with the sawblade. The wheels of the carriage run on strips of iron on top of wooden beams. The blade assembly is under a shed.

Standing on top of the log, Martin Prosser trimmed an uneven part from the log with an ax before the three men pulled two vertical levers on the carriage, called head blocks, toward the whirring five foot-wide circular sawblade.

Pulling the carriage forward by hand, Mr. Entler sliced off the first piece, which consisted mainly of bark. That piece was thrown on a slab pile. Then the real cutting began.

The oak grain began to appear as several inch-wide lengths were cut. They looked remarkably like pieces of salami coming off the butcher's slicer at a delicatessen.

The log was pulled over with the grappling hooks so that it lay on the cut side. The men wedged in pieces of wood to steady the log and again sliced off a bark-covered piece to be thrown on the slab pile and several long boards. This process was repeated twice until the end of the log was perfectly square.

After taking time out to regulate the tractor motor that powers the saw by means of a heavy rubber belt attached to the tractor wheel at one end and the saw mechanism at the other, the men made a cut almost through the length of the log. Then they turned the log 180 degrees and proceeded to cut it into planks.

The planks were stacked on Martin Prosser's flatbed truck.

The slab pile would be "buzzed up" later on a saw attached to another old tractor into firewood lengths for the use of Mr. Entler and "some neighbors with not much money," a kibitzing farmer, Harold Rhoades, said.

The oak planks, whose beautiful grain led to thoughts of coffee tables and chests, would be used to build hog houses during the winter, Martin Prosser said.

December 1975

Portrait of a Farmer

He has the calm, serene gaze of a man whose eyes have looked on the wind-swept plains of Central Illinois farmland all his life, lifting often to scan the skies for tomorrow's weather.

The blue eyes of Harold Rhoades—who is called Shorty by everyone except his immediate family—reflect the steadfastness, patience and durability of a race of men whose unceasing labors help feed the nation.

Self-deprecating to a fault, he is sure to squirm at seeing himself described in such epic terms. In his book he is simply a man doing a job he knows well and having a good time doing it.

The love he has for the land he has farmed for almost 30 years and for his work is as evident to an observer accompanying him on his morning chores as is his reluctance to put his feelings into words.

"I like farming fine," he says, adding that he has never really considered any other kind of work since boyhood.

Certainly farming shows itself from its finest aspect as Mr. Rhoades's wiry, denim-clad figure—the name of Shorty must have been bestowed on him by a breed of giants because he appears to be about five feet nine inches tall—moves among his Hereford cattle throwing out bales of hay from his pickup truck in the stockfield.

The hay supplements the leftover ears of corn, leaves and husks which serve as food for some 30 cows and 30 calves wandering about the harvested corn fields that make up the stockfield.

Steam rises from the cows' muzzles as they lumber bellowing toward the bales of hay in the sunny, cloudless November morning. The hoarfrost glittering on the grass of the nearby pasture disappears in tiny patches under the hooves of a few calves who approach skittishly.

The bone-chilling treks from the farmhouse to the nearby feedlot in sub-zero temperatures on early winter mornings and the agony of seeing an early killer frost ruin the corn and beans and cut profits almost to the bone, as it may in some years, seem very far away although their reality is as valid a part of a farmer's life as this idyllic morning.

"Livestock farmers are always shutting gates," Mr. Rhoades says with a grin as he climbs back into the pickup truck after closing the gate to the lovely pasture—"the prettiest part of my farm"—through which a small river winds its meandering course.

Like the tall trees in the pasture forming the northern part of the farm near Hugo, six miles east of Tuscola, Shorty Rhoades has deep roots in the area.

The son of Ross and Julia Rhoades, he grew up on their farm half a mile south of his own, attended Hindsboro High School and, aside from two years of working for the International Harvester dealer in Hindsboro right after high school graduation, has farmed all his life.

He and his wife, Clara Mae, moved to the 103-acre farm in 1950. The farm has 33 acres in pasture and 70 in farm ground.

His parents have sold the farm on which they reared Mr. Rhoades and his four sisters and a brother — now a nematologist and professor of horticulture at the University of Florida in Sanford — and now live on a 60-acre farmstead immediately south of the Rhoades farm and just across the blacktop road from their earlier home.

Mr. Rhoades farms his parents' acreage on a cash-rent basis and farms about 270 acres for two other farm owners on a 50-50 arrangement, bringing the total he farms to more than 400 acres. In a 50-50 farming arrangement the farmer provides labor, machinery and operating expenses and the owner provides the land. All farming expenses involved in the year's harvest and the harvest itself are shared equally.

Mr. Rhoades has about 90 head of cattle on his farm, 30 in the feedlot and about 60 in the stockfield. He soon will take the feedlot animals to the Indianapolis stockyards in his big truck, 10 at a time, to sell. At selling time the steers weigh about 1,050 pounds, the heifers about 950.

He considers cattle-raising the most enjoyable part of farming, he said, although he clearly takes much pleasure in the growing of corn and soybeans on the 400 acres.

The buildings on his farmstead include the farmhouse with an attached garage, a 60-foot by 81-foot machine shed (a pole barn he and his son, Robert, and a few neighbors put up one-and-a-half years ago), a gabled barn, four silver-colored corn and bean bins, a harvest storage bin to hold high-moisture corn, and several smaller sheds and buildings.

A small pond to the north of the buildings provided a favorite swimming hole for the four Rhoades children when they were younger.

The equipment includes a venerable Allis-Chalmers tractor, the pickup truck and the large truck, a combine, planter and field cultivator and several wagons.

The cycle of a farmer's year is marked by periods of intense activity when work in the fields goes on from 6 a.m. to midnight, followed by calmer months with time for fencerow cutting, machinery repair and painting and upkeep of buildings.

The busiest months for Mr. Rhoades are April, May, June and October.

In April he plows and chisels the fields, cultivates and spreads chemical fertilizer. If the weather cooperates, he starts planting during the last part of the month.

May is planting season, earmarked by constant, backbreaking work. June is the time for cutting and putting up hay for the cattle and cultivating.

The bean harvest starts late in September. October is another peak month with harvesting of beans and corn, and the early part of November also is busy with the winding up of the harvest as well as fall plowing.

Year-round chores for Mr. Rhoades involve the feeding of the cattle which are moved into the barn in February with the added chore of cleaning the barn, and the mending of fences.

"Them old cows have a way of knowing when a place is getting weak so they can bust through," Mr. Rhoades said.

Among the ongoing duties is the mountain of paperwork and record-keeping which he does on a weekly basis—"It's OK if you sit down every week and do the posting," he said—and runs to one of the nearby towns or to Champaign-Urbana for supplies.

A challenging job through the fall and winter months is following the changing prices for corn and beans in order to try to sell at the most advantageous prices.

In his outline of the year's cycle for a farmer's work Rhoades in his off-hand, self-minimizing way—he typically refers to himself not as I but as "a fellow"—makes many of the months' workloads sound light.

His description of January, for instance, goes, "Well, a fellow feeds the brood calves and fat cattle at night and works on machinery. The rest of the time is spent drinking coffee, messing around and out tromping in the fields."

But a closer investigation of the major strands that make up the fabric of Mr. Rhoades's life in addition to farming — his family, the Hugo Community church, the fellowship with the neighbors, his deep concern for conservation, his love for his two spare-time pursuits of hunting and arrowhead collecting — shows a man constantly on the go, often performing acts of concern and kindness for others.

"Dad is always keeping busy," said Mr. Rhoades's daughter, Wanda, who lives a few miles east of her parents' farm in an old farmhouse completely rebuilt and renovated by her father and her husband, Roy R. Bird, who owns a construction firm.

"Anyone who needs anything done knows they can just call Dad. He is always scooping snow off a driveway or hauling rocks for a widow who needs his help. He has done a lot of work for the church. For us kids he is always doing something — you just have to mention it and he is there," she said.

"He is very eventempered, a very plain person, the perfect dad. He may be small but there is none who does more for others."

The Rev. Leslie C. Wolfe, who has served the Hugo Community Church as pastor since 1954, said about Mr. Rhoades, "He is a multiple person, rich in friendship, stable, helpful — and there is something steady about everything he does. He is not temperamental. He weighs a situation with patience and clarity and possesses a richness of spirit. He is that friend of friends."

The most forceful comment came from Steve Prosser, a 20-year-old farmer and the son and grandson of Hugo area farmers, who along with Mr. Rhoades, Mrs. Bird, the Rev. Wolfe and many of the neighbors were participating in one of the weekly Tuesday noon dinners served in the church basement to the area farmers and their wives by the church women.

Mr. Prosser said with great emphasis, "I don't think there's anybody better on this earth than ol' Shorty Rhoades. He is my second father."

Among the jobs carried out by Mr. Rhoades — a self-taught crackerjack carpenter — recently during slow periods on the farm are the remodeling of the church on which he worked steadily for three weeks in August, the complete remodeling of the kitchen in his farmhouse and the erection of the machine shed.

Much time is spent with his dad who will soon be 90 and his mother, 84; his children, who in addition to Mrs. Bird and Robert, who works as a roofer in Tuscola, number Pat McCool, who lives at Ridge Farm near Paris with her husband, Steven, a UPS driver, and Dorothy, the youngest who lives at home and works at Fabrionics in Camargo; and the two sons-in-law and five grandchildren.

In all his undertakings he is backed by the constant help and support of his wife — a model farmwife who in a typical act had arisen at 5:30 a.m. on the day of the newspaper folks' visit to bake chocolate chip cookies for their morning coffee before leaving for an all-day training session for her job.

Mrs. Rhoades works from January through March on the tax books for the Farm Business and Farm Management Company in Tuscola.

Mr. Rhoades's organizational involvements include membership in the Douglas County Farm Bureau and serving as an elected committee member of the Agricultural Stabilization and Conservation Service Tuscola office.

A daily ritual in his life is dropping in for a cup of coffee along with most of his farmer neighbors every morning between 6:30 and 7 at the tiny Hugo General Store operated by Earl Entler.

In his leisure time he has given up hunting near his home — "It's all hunting and no shooting anymore," he says — but still enjoys a yearly late-fall deer hunting trip to Southern Illinois with several neighbors.

His favorite recreation is roaming around alone in nearby fields searching for arrowheads and other Indian relics to add to his already sizable collection.

"I just found a nice scraper sticking out of the ground while combining beans the other day," he said.

His handle on CB radio — a much-appreciated aid to communications for farmers — is Arrowhead, while Mrs. Rhoades's is Pocahontas and Wanda Bird's is Sugarbucket.

His concern for conservation is constantly in evidence.

"It's terrible the way they're abusing this river," he said, pointing to the oilslicks in the water during the morning feeding of cattle.

He mourns the wild animal population in the area which, he says, has declined markedly during the last 10 years. Although he owns several dogs, he refuses to own a cat because of the damage it might do to baby rabbits and birds.

He is not optimistic about the future for small farmers such as himself.

"Everything has went up with inflation. Repairs are almost unbelievable anymore. I hardly ever spend money on nitrogen in the winter but they said it was going up $40 a ton, so I may have to this year," he said.

Asked if farm profit is adequate, he said, "I'm not sure there is a profit anymore."

He added, "Farmers have to be able to make a living. With combines now costing from $50,000 anywhere up to $100,000 I don't see how young people starting out and having to buy all that expensive machinery can make a living.

"I see the trend towards bigger farms as growing all the time. A young man can only get into farming if he has relatives who'd let him take over and buy used equipment from them."

With his son working as a roofer and the sons-in-law engaged in non-farm jobs he sees no one in the family who can take over his farm after him.

"When I retire I'll just quit and sell the farm," he said.

But Wanda Bird says later over a cup of coffee in her kitchen, "There is so much love in our family but we are awfully bad at telling it to each other in words.

"We children are going to keep the farm somehow when Daddy quits.

"I would like it always to be known that Harold Rhoades lived on this land and farmed it all his life."

December 1979

How to Catch a Turtle:
Very Carefully

Standing knee-deep in water near the bank of a drainage ditch, Dave Boyd felt something under his shoe and said to his companion, "Is that your foot, Buster?"

"No."

"Then it's the turtle," said Dave, shifting his weight to his right foot.

The two young men were engaged in one of their favorite hobbies: catching snapping turtles with their bare hands.

Dave had checked his hooked lines the previous night and found that the bait, a chunk of raw beef heart, had attracted a large turtle.

Upon their return the next evening, they saw that the turtle had burrowed deeply into a hole on the ditch bank and was hiding in the root system of a dead tree.

They took turns poking a large stick into the hole hoping the turtle would grab the stick in its powerful jaws, so it could be hauled out.

In the process, the turtle managed to free itself from the hook and slither into the ditch. The young men quickly moved their tennis shoe-clad feet around on the ditch bottom trying to step on it, and the above exchange took place.

As soon as Dave realized that he was standing on the turtle, he reached down and replaced his foot with one hand on the center of the shell. With his other hand, he felt around carefully, spreading the fingers out from the center to the edges of the shell until he felt the saw-toothed edge above the tail.

Then he grabbed the turtle by the tail and pulled it out of the water, just as Buster lost his footing and fell into the drink.

The turtle was a fear-inducing apparition. Covered with mud and snapping ferociously, it looked and smelled like it came straight from a primeval swamp, as it hung under Dave's firm grip.

Its ridged shell measured about 18 inches in length. Dave estimated its total length including the head and tail was 28 to 30 inches, and that its weight was around 12 pounds.

Dave handed the turtle to Buster who clambered up the steep bank, crawled under an electric fence and jumped over a barbed-wire fence with the turtle in his hand. He then stopped to tie a length of steel wire around the turtle's tail for carrying it back to the farm.

The hunt took place on the farm of Dave's parents, near Murdock. A truck driver, Dave, 24, lives in Newman. Buster Albin, 15, lives in Camargo.

Besides catching turtles on double-hooked 50 pound-strength nylon

lines, the two young men hunt snappers by walking through creeks and ditches in rubber-soled canvas shoes until one of them feels a turtle under his foot.

"You kind of develop a feeling for it," Dave said. "When something feels like a turtle, you shove down on him real quick. As long as you keep your hand straight down on the shell, he can't reach you with his jaws, but only poke you with his head."

Dave said that while his friends often sell their catches for $2 a pound dressed weight, he eats the turtles he catches.

Along with a smaller turtle he had caught, he puts the turtle in water in a large trash can and left it there for several days before killing it by cutting its head off with an ax. He dressed it by skinning the legs and deboning the meat in the shell.

"You parboil the meat first and either barbecue or fry it or make soup with it," he said.

He said the dark meat has a strong fishy taste, while the white meat tastes milder and sweeter.

Dave has been catching snapping turtles for three years and estimates he has caught at least a dozen every summer. He introduced Buster to the sport last year.

"They can easily chomp off a guy's finger, and once they get hold, they don't let go till you cut off their head," he said.

"But so far, I've never been bit."

September 1975

Weathered Stones

Like the briers that grew around The Sleeping Beauty's castle, thickets of blackberry brambles form an almost impenetrable wall around the graves of this tiny cemetery, guarding the eternal sleep of those buried here generations ago.

In the wild bursts of fecundity of the Central Illinois spring and summer, wildflowers and hardy weeds vie with the blackberry shrubs to hide the cemetery from view, their greenery blending in against the dense forest of trees that lines the banks of the Embarras River a stone's throw to the west.

Only in the barrenness of winter might the taller gravestones — jutting out like the teeth of an abandoned rake — catch the eye of a traveler speeding along the blacktop road some hundred yards to the east.

Haunted only by fox, deer and opossum and a few stray human visitors including, perhaps, some particularly brave youngsters at Halloween, the cemetery is the size of a small city block.

In its time it was known as Shady Side Cemetery but the name, along with recollections of those buried here, has been all but forgotten by the folk in its locality of Hugo, six miles east of Tuscola.

Today Hugo is a farming community with only two buildings establishing its core, the Hugo Community Church and Earl Entler's small general store.

But during the time when Shady Side was in use, Hugo contained two churches, a post office, a grocery store, a blacksmith shop, a mill, a harness shop and a millinery shop and housed a doctor and a barber.

Judging from the about 20 surviving stones in Shady Side, the cemetery was in use at least from 1862 to 1899.

The most recent burial date to be found is that of Wiley B. Green who died March 2, 1899, at the age of 70. The oldest burial date is that of William Green, Jan. 11, 1862.

According to the 1900 edition of "Historical and Biographical Record of Douglas County," Hugo was once an Indian trading post and village.

The last Indians left the area in 1833, three years after the advent of the first white settlers. The earliest entries of land were made in June 1833 by Samuel C. Gill, October 1833 by John Davis and February 1836 by the Barnett family, the work states.

A store or trading post was kept by Godfrey Vesser, a Frenchman, and a man named either Bulbory or Hubbard, depending on which page in the book is consulted, in Hugo in 1829 and 1830.

According to listings of Illinois post offices, the settlement was first known as Bridgeford from its location on a horseshoe bend in the Embarras, near the location of Earl Entler's store.

From 1864 to 1872 it was called Cottage Grove, and from 1872 until

1903 the post office was listed as Hugo, after the French writer Victor Hugo.

Shady Side Cemetery is located less than half a mile, as the crow flies, east of the lovely, well-kept Antioch Cemetery which is still in use.

Named for one of the two churches which existed during the flourishing period of Hugo's history, the Antioch Christian Church, built in 1881, the Antioch Cemetery must have co-existed in its early days with the Shady Side Cemetery.

The earliest inscriptions of dates of death in Antioch are from the 1850s, and many of the gravestones record death dates in the period from 1860 to 1900.

Elmer Waggle, custodian for both cemeteries, remembers being told in his youth that "Daddy Gill (Shiloah Gill, an early settler) moved three or four from his family" from Shady Side to Antioch.

Waggle said he kept Shady Side Cemetery mowed until two years ago when he finally abandoned it to the brambles.

"I kept it looking decent. Year before last I broke the chopper behind the tractor while mowing it and again last year the same thing happened. It just got too hard to keep up," he said.

The bleached and weathered gravestones in the abandoned cemetery include many of the classical 19th Century shapes, among them heart-shaped marble stones, obelisks and oblong stones with reliefs of clasped hands or a depiction of a lamb.

Here, in the words of Gray's Elegy, "the rude forefathers of the hamlet sleep" side by side with the "busy housewife (who plies) her evening care."

Among the married couples who rest united in the little graveyard are Wiley B. Green (1829-1899) and Eliza Green (1839-1876) and M. W. Stump (1813-1875) and Sarah Stump (1816-1880).

A white obelisk commemorates Hannah E. McIntire, who died Feb. 10, 1877, "aged 53 y. 2 m. 6 ds.;" her husband, Robert N. McIntire who died Feb. 4, 1879, aged 60 years and four months; and their son, William D., who died Jan. 25, 1879, at age 22, predeceasing his father by a brutal 11 days and probably felled by the same contagious illness.

A well-preserved marble stone bears witness to the common 19th Century tragedy so often readable on old tombstones: that of parents burying more small children than it seems possible for blood and flesh to bear.

The stone is inscribed on one side with the name of William Anderson who died in May 1876 at the age of 42.

There is no sign of the burial of Mrs. Anderson, either in Shady Side or in Antioch Cemetery, although her name, Mary, survives as part of the inscription on one of the Anderson family stones. Perhaps her stone has disappeared; perhaps she was spared the illnesses that ravaged her family, living to the fullness of her days with a surviving child.

For them no more the blazing hearth
shall burn,
 Or busy housewife ply her evening care;
 No children run to lisp their sire's return,
 Or climb his knees the envied kiss to
share.

 Far from the madding crowd's ignoble
strife,
 Their sober wishes never learned to stray,
 Along the cool sequestered vale of life
 They kept the noiseless tenor of their
way.

 Perhaps in this neglected spot is laid
 Some heart once pregnant with celestial
fire.

But the two perpendicular sides of the Anderson stone list the deaths of five children — Johnie, who died in 1871 at the age of three years and five months; an unnamed infant daughter who died four days old in 1857; Elizabeth, whose life spanned eight months in 1872; Sarah, who lived for 20 days in 1873; and Martha, who died in 1877, three months short of her 16th birthday.

The mind boggles at such devastation. Chronologically, William and Mary Anderson faced the death of their infant daughter in 1857, their 3½-year-old son in 1871, their eight-month-old daughter in 1872 and their 20-day-old infant daughter in 1873.

Cruelest of all for Mrs. Anderson, after being buffeted by these successive blows and then losing her husband, must have been seeing Martha cut down on the threshold of young womanhood.

Coming only eight months after her father's death and at an age when it must have seemed to her mother that this child at least had managed to outlive the diphtheria, infantile paralysis, malaria and fevers that preyed on 19th Century children, Martha's death must have been a crippling wound for her mother.

The large Anderson stone is surrounded by three small stones, inscribed with poignant simplicity "Elizabeth," "Sarah" and "Martha."

Leaning against the main stone as a tired child rests its brow against a parent at the end of the day is a small slab on which the inscription reads:

Johnie
son of
William and Mary
Anderson
Died
Nov. 24, 1871
aged
3 Y. 5 M. & 11 D.
Sweet in life,
Lovely in death,
Happy in Heaven.

May 1980

A Storybook Farm

Most Illinois farms today are like efficient factories for the production of corn and beans. The livestock often consists of a sole watchdog. A lawn and small vegetable garden cover the only soil not used for crops.

The farm depicted in children's story books, with chickens and hens, horses and cows, fruit trees and pumpkin patches, has become a rarity. But it does still exist.

Randall and Opal Miller (not their real names; the couple requested anonymity for the purposes of reprinting the article in this book) own such a farm not far from Champaign. A child's dream of what a "real" farm should be like, the Miller farm abounds with living and growing things.

The farm is home for seven dogs, 25 cats, 200 chickens, three geese, 16 ducks, 24 head of cattle, two palomino mares and their two colts, 11 ewes and six lambs and one donkey.

Until recently, the Millers also had two hen turkeys and a gobbler, and kept pigs. Last winter, the gobbler and one turkey hen got sick and died, and the remaining hen took off in search of a new gobbler. The last pigs went to market four months ago, and the couple has not yet restocked.

Mr. Miller, 62, farms 200 acres used for corn, beans, hay and pasture.

Mrs. Miller cares for the poultry and cans and freezes the abundant yield from the fruit trees and vegetable garden.

Shielded by a windbreak of pine trees and protected from the afternoon sun by a huge tree whose branches right now are bent low by big red apples, the white frame house sits at the side of a circular drive.

Animals are everywhere. Two white hens perch on a table groaning with butternut squash and pumpkins beneath an ash tree festooned with bouquets of Indian corn.

The horses neigh in a field behind the garden, and a donkey gallops up to visitors to have its nose nuzzled. A rooster, still crowing in late afternoon after having started his day at 3:30 a.m., perches above a feeding trough where six head of cattle munch contentedly.

The dogs and cats alternately ignore and worry each other. A look into the machine shed reveals a truck-bed heaped with huge pumpkins and, further back in the shadows, six sheep standing silently next to an old horse-drawn farm wagon.

The produce grown on the farm and the meat and poultry they raise enable the Millers to live lives of almost 19th Century self-sufficiency.

They have their own milk, cream and eggs and grow all their own fruits and vegetables. Last summer Mr. Miller came upon "an enormous swarm of bees in the pasture" and the couple started beekeeping and now produces their own honey.

"We buy sugar, salt, flour and coffee at the store, and that's about all,"

Mrs. Miller said, giving a visitor a taste of her ketchup, made tangy with the addition of red peppers.

"Every other year is my big canning year," she said, pointing to four six-foot-long shelves in a small shed, filled with rows six deep of plum, strawberry and peach jam, canned beets, yellow and red tomatoes, wax beans and green beans, whole peppers, relishes and pickles, tomato juice, peach and pear halves and apple butter.

"We made the apple butter in a big copper kettle over a wood fire in the yard," Mrs. Miller said.

The pantry shed also holds big cans of homemade sauerkraut and bushels of sweet and white potatoes.

Mrs. Miller modestly acknowledged that she recently plucked and cleaned 79 chickens in six days and baked 30 apple pies in a two-day period.

During winters the couple works together on repairing and refinishing antique chests, sideboards, beds and tables which fill the roomy house.

The Millers' love for antiques — which they refer to as "old furniture" — is perhaps an outcropping of a strong view of themselves as links in a human chain which shows constantly in their conversation.

Their 15 grandchildren, three sons and two married daughters ("The hardest thing I ever did was give my daughters away," Mr. Miller said) are constantly in their thoughts. The children all live away from the farm, but near enough for frequent visits.

Mr. Miller quotes his father who said, "You've never paid for your raisin' until you've raised children of your own."

At the same time, evocation of their ancestors is part of their daily lives. Mrs. Miller talks lovingly about her great-grandfather who was "hook-and-eye Dutch, as they called it" and a great-great-great-grandmother who was a full-blooded Indian; and Mr. Miller reminisces about his parents who brought up 11 children on a farm near Decatur and farmed 538 acres with horses.

September 1975

The Abandoned Farm

They stand like sentinels to a vanished past when the road to the nearest neighbor was shorter.

Abandoned by all but lovers and vandals to the howling winds and pipe-cracking freezes of winter and the scorching sun of summer, they stare out over the fields with sightless eyes.

Within the walls of these abandoned farmhouses, generations of children were conceived and grew precariously, nursed through the fevers of childhood by anxious mothers. New brides struggled with their first pie crust on oilcloth-covered kitchen tables, and old men and women with hands gnarled by hard work and arthritis closed their eyes for the last time.

Now the wiring in the walls is nibbled by mice and the plaster crumbles over sheaths of rotting wood.

The window panes are broken or have disappeared. Wood shutters bang against outside walls with a desolate sound and on the nearby barn, the sagging boards lean at an angle which grows increasingly lopsided every year.

Victims of an economic development that began shortly after World War II, abandoned farmhouses, along with poignant solitary remains such as a pump which indicates where a house once stood, present a picturesque view to the passer-by.

Their bleak and weathered appearance lends a rhythm to the East Central Illinois landscape and contrasts powerfully with the sleek, well-cared-for occupied farmsteads.

They are reminders of the many small farmhouses that dotted the area and were leveled in the decades after the war, as individual farms grew larger.

"The exodus from farms started happening pretty rapidly soon after the end of World War II," said Earl C. Bantz, cooperative extension director for Champaign County.

"Commodity prices dropped so low that farmers could not make it renting 80 or 160 acres so they left the farm very rapidly.

"This development was faster here than in many other areas in Illinois because this is a cash grain area. In other counties, where there are more livestock farmers, the farmers were able to hang on longer on small farms."

The exodus continued to the present time and now appears to have slowed, he said.

"Almost all of our farmers now have a farm size that makes an economic unit they can farm with enough income to fare reasonably well," he said.

He estimates this unit to be 500 acres farmed by a landlord and tenant.

While the land around the abandoned farmhouses is farmed by other farmers, the houses are torn down or left unoccupied for several reasons, Bantz said.

"They are not rented to townspeople because in many instances when they were, the renters did not take good care of them and often would not pay the rent. It was just more bother for the owner than it was worth," he said.

Also, many of the houses are not well built, are not insulated and sit on foundations of only six rocks, making them economically unfeasible to heat at today's high energy costs, he said.

In many areas of the county, the decrease in the number of farmhouses is easily evident.

For instance, Jim Akers, who farms south of Broadlands, can point to a section of land and say, "On that square mile there were four farmhouses 10 years ago. All of them have now been torn down."

Each abandoned farmhouse has a story to tell. The tales of the Half-Way House west of Champaign, the Hilderbrant place south of Homer and Laura Tracy's farm near St. Joseph are good examples.

The Half-Way House is located immediately west of Grandview Memorial Gardens on U.S. 150, the old Bloomington Road, north of The Andersons grain elevator.

The two-story wooden house has been heavily vandalized. A dilapidated barn stands nearby.

That house stands on the site of a house which for many years was a tavern. The tavern is said to have been visited by Abraham Lincoln, according to Arthur Miner of Hensley Township.

The present house served as home for many families with one of the last families living there for more than 20 years. Last year, after the house had long been abandoned to the elements, the body of a murdered man was found at the farmsite.

Built between 1915 and 1920, the house replaced the older house that served as tavern, inn and stage coach stop.

The tavern was called the Half-Way House because the site is half way between Champaign and Mahomet and also half way between Danville and Bloomington.

According to Charles W. Webster of Rantoul, a past president of the Champaign County Historical Society, the 160-acre farm on which the house was built was acquired by John Lindsey from the U.S. government, according to a deed dated March 1, 1851.

It is believed the house was built soon after that. Lindsey lived there and operated the tavern and inn for many years. Elderly residents of the Mahomet area say the original house had a large wing with a banquet hall and other facilities on the north side, Webster said.

"There were a lot of people going west in the early years of the tavern's existence. The Bloomington Road was the main road for the pioneers heading west. It had a lot of traffic of wagons and horseback riders, and many of them probably stopped at the tavern," he said.

As an indication of the intensity of the traffic he said, "We know that in 1830, there sometimes were 200 wagons parked overnight in the timber north of Urbana."

Isabelle S. Purnell of Mahomet writes in her history of the Mahomet Methodist Church, "The resident of the 'Half-Way House' had two yoke of oxen which he used to pull the stage out of mudholes along the line."

An idea of the prices at the tavern in its early years may be garnered from a rate list for innkeepers in Champaign County from 1836, a scant 20 years before the tavern opened.

The charge for keeping a man and horse one night, including supper, bed and horsefeed was 75 cents. A single meal cost 18¾ cents, a half pint of whiskey 6¼ cents and a half pint of French brandy 18¾ cents.

Ruth T. Weinard of Urbana said that according to family legend her grandfather, Benjamin Franklin Thomas Sr., walked through this area from Ohio driving cattle and was snowed in at the Half-Way House in 1856. Mr. Thomas later settled on a farm in Mahomet.

Mrs. Weinard's maternal grandfather, George B. Todd, was a carpenter and tore down the old house and built the present one, she said.

"He used some of the walnut timber from the original house to make a rocking chair for my father," she said.

Arthur Miner's mother, whose maiden name was Mary Fieldbinder, lived in the original Half-Way House as a young girl with her parents, and her father farmed the land, Mr. Miner said.

Among the tenants of the present house were Juanita and Carl Beebe, who lived in the house from 1950 to 1970 while Mr. Beebe tenant-farmed the land for the owner, Ellen Morris of Bement, who still owns the house and land.

The Beebes also lived in the house for two years in the late 1940s and moved into it again in 1950 after being away one year. The couple is now retired and lives in Parkville.

"We raised five children — two girls and three boys — in that house," Mrs. Beebe said.

"The boys shared one of the two upstairs bedrooms and the girls shared the other. My husband and I slept in the living room. The house also had a combination kitchen and dining room."

Several sets of tenants rented the house for short periods after the Beebes moved away, she said.

The house has been heavily vandalized in recent years.

"The minute you move out the vandals start damaging it," Mrs. Beebe said. "They seem to know when a house is empty."

Joe Rayburn, who farms nearby, said, "There have been guys trying to burn it down a number of times but so far they haven't made it."

Last April 20 the body of Thomas I. M. "Tim" Bentley of St. Joseph, a Snap-On Tool Co. distributor, was found on the farmsite with a gunshot wound to the back of the head. The previous day his van had been discovered on fire two miles north of Urbana. It had been robbed of $35,000 to $40,000 worth of tools.

Michael Wade LeCrone of Rantoul later was found guilty of the murder and sentenced to 80 years in prison.

During the trial, an assistant state's attorney who prosecuted the case said Mr. LeCrone shot Mr. Bentley and then allowed him to die "for hours and hours and hours."

Mute Testimony

In the southeastern part of Champaign County, a lone pump standing in a field bears mute testimony to the presence of the farmstead it once served.

Directly east of the 80 acres of farmland on which the pump stands is the beautifully maintained and restored farmhouse of Karen and J. Robert Ulbrich. The house was built in 1863.

The Ulbrichs' 5-year-old daughter, Sara, is the fourth generation of female descendants of Levi Hilderbrant to live in the house.

Mrs. Ulbrich inherited the farm from her mother, Mary Satterfield, who died in 1972. Mrs. Satterfield had inherited the farm from her mother, Lillie Morgan, the daughter of Levi Hilderbrant.

Mrs. Satterfield and her husband, Raymond, lived in the house from 1942 until 1972. Mr. Satterfield later lived in the house for two years with his second wife, Ruth, and continued to farm the land for a total of 36 seasons until his daughter and son-in-law, the Ulbrichs, took over the farming in 1977. He also farmed the land on which the pump stands.

This land now belongs to Dorothy Bohren of Lafayette, Ind., sister of Mary Satterfield and aunt of Mrs. Ulbrich.

The farmhouse and buildings, which the pump served, were torn down between 1931 and 1942, Mrs. Bohren said.

In Mrs. Bohren's childhood, the farmstead was occupied by the hired hands of her uncle, John Hilderbrant, who lived with his family in a farmstead, directly north of the pump as his father, Levi Hilderbrant, had before him. The Hilderbrant farmstead was torn down many years ago and only a barn remains.

The 1863 farmhouse is depicted in a drawing in the book, "Portrait and Biographical Album of Champaign County, Ill.," published in 1887.

The house looks much the same as it does today with the exception of a large porch added by the Ulbrichs and the absence of a so-called "Indian lookout," a railed-in platform on the top of the roof.

At the time of the publication of the album, the house was owned by James W. Humrichhouse and the farm was known as Fair Land Farm. According to the biographical sketch of Mr. Humrichhouse, the farm consisted of 320 acres at that time and was "mainly devoted to the breeding and feeding of fine cattle, hogs and draft horses."

The farm was acquired about 1910 by Levi Hilderbrant, according to Raymond Satterfield. Levi Hilderbrant's father, John W., also is profiled in the album.

According to the album, he was born in Ohio in 1822 and came to Illinois in 1865. His property consisted of 80 acres in Homer Township.

The album article says about Mr. Hilderbrant, who must have been 65 years old at the time of the writing, "Mr. H. has pursued the even tenor of his way, extracting much enjoyment from life, having been blest with good health, and never within his remembrance being attended by a physician."

The article classes John Hilderbrant among "the honored pioneers of this county" and describes these pioneers' endurance in the face of discouragement.

"Among other discouragements Mr. H. at one time tended sixty acres of corn three times over, preparing the ground each time himself and alone. In the fall he sold $1,300 worth of corn, and felt amply repaid for his perseverance," the album article says.

Beginning in 1912, the land was farmed by Levi Hilderbrant's daughter, Lillie, and her husband, Arthur Morgan. Lillie Morgan—the mother of Mary Satterfield and Dorothy Bohren and the grandmother of Mrs. Ulbrich—died in 1920. Mr. Morgan continued to farm the land and live in the 1863 house with his second wife, Alice, until the Satterfields took over.

Raymond Satterfield recalls that the house had not been painted for 48 years when he moved in. He wired the house for electricity during his first year there but the line to the house was not put in until 1947 because of short supplies due to the war effort, he said.

Raymond and Mary Satterfield had one son who died at birth. Mrs. Ulbrich is their only surviving child.

Mr. Satterfield was able to pass on his considerable farming knowledge, however, to Don Morgan, a half-brother of Mary Satterfield who is Mr. Satterfield's junior by 21 years, when Mr. Morgan first began farming at a tender age.

Many years later, Mr. Morgan returned the favor by teaching Mr. Satterfield's son-in-law, Bob Ulbrich, about farming.

Mr. Ulbrich, who has a master's degree in vocational and technical education and a degree in advanced study in school administration, both from the University of Illinois, came to farming after spending 10 years as a school administrator in Chicago suburbs.

He grew up in Bloomington and has no farm background. But, having learned about farming through doing and through Mr. Morgan's teaching, he finds he likes the life very well, Mrs. Ulbrich said.

The Ulbrichs, who both received their undergraduate degrees in business administration and business education from Illinois State University in Normal, are teaching part time at Parkland College.

Their 8-year-old son, Tim, already plans to become a farmer when he grows up.

Dorothy Bohren, Mrs. Ulbrich's aunt who owns the land where the pump stands, lived in the 1863 house from birth until high school graduation.

Speaking from her home in Lafayette, where her husband is a professor of genetics in the Purdue University animal science department, she recalled her childhood on the farm as a time when the transportation was horses and buggies and a lovely walnut grove stood west of the house where Mrs. Ulbrich now has a large garden.

"The main crops were oats and corn. At harvest time the neighbors got together for a threshing ring and went up and down the road to thresh the oats," she said.

"People used work horses for the field work. Everyone raised a lot of hay because of all the animals to feed. Most of the farmers had cattle in addition to the horses as well as pigs and chickens.

"In the summertime the men would get up at 4 a.m., feed the animals and milk the cows, come in for breakfast and be in the fields by 6 o'clock," she said.

The farm wife would arise by 4:30 a.m. to provide a breakfast of meat, eggs, cereal, hot breads, home-made jam, coffee and milk, she said.

She also would cook large dinners and suppers every day, providing for the hired hand as well, work in the garden and can the garden produce.

Farmstead Rigors

Laura Tracy, who lived for almost 50 years with her husband, Clint Archer, on her 150-acre farm south of St. Joseph, remembers the rigors of being a farm wife with fondness.

"I loved it. I helped run everything. I plowed, disced, farmed, ran a tractor," she said.

Mr. Archer retired from farming about 1956 and died in 1966 at the age of 81. Mrs. Tracy, who will be 90 on her next birthday, married George Tracy in 1968 and lives in Urbana with him and her only child, Dolores Swearingen.

The farmhouse where she and Mr. Archer spent a lifetime was rented out for a few years after the couple retired before it was left empty.

"It had to be fixed. It needed a new roof and other repairs so we gave up on it," Mrs. Tracy said.

Today, with the remnants of white paint fading on the farmhouse, the weathered, turreted barn and two cribs starkly silhouetted against the winter sky, the farm is the quintessence of the farm motifs favored by Urbana painter Billy Morrow Jackson.

The Archers bought the farm from a man known as Grandpa Bartlow.

"Mr. Bartlow's house burned in 1907, and the house we lived in was built after that," Mrs. Tracy said.

"The old oaken bucket was in the well when we moved there. I carried water from the well to the house and the outhouse every day," she said.

"We had 20 acres of timber. My husband ran a sawmill on the farm, had a threshing run and worked as a mechanic in addition to farming.

"He could do anything. We weren't there no time until we put in water.

"I had a garden, canned fruits and vegetables, washed on a washboard, ironed with irons heated on the stove and cooked on a wooden stove," she said.

"I love my farm. If I was young I'd go right back there now."

March 1980

2nd Place, Illinois AP 1980 life style contest
2nd Place, Illinois UPI 1980 feature contest (with "Becki Conway" and "Crawlspace Castles")

A GALLERY OF MEN

Two Years = Two College Degrees

At the tender age of 18 David Bade of Villa Grove is the proud possessor of a bachelor's and master's degree in linguistics from the University of Illinois — not bad for someone who two years ago had no plans to go to college.

David enrolled in the university in August 1975, and completed the work for the two degrees in four regular semesters and one summer semester.

To do so, he set himself a grueling schedule which culminated last fall semester when he carried 34 hours plus three units, adding up to a grand total of 46 academic hour credits.

In comparison, the average full-time load for an undergraduate is from 12 to 18 hours.

During the 46-hour semester he studied six languages: Palestinian and classical Arabic, Chinese, Biblical Hebrew, Russian and Serbo-Croatian. "At times I did have some trouble keeping the vocabularies apart," he admitted.

The son of Phillip and Margaret Bade of N. Henson Road, Villa Grove, David graduated with his class from Villa Grove High School last June but was permitted by the school to stop attending high school classes in June 1975, as long as he made it through his first year of college without flunking out.

David Bade said he never planned to go to college at all and only decided to go to the University of Illinois in order not to have to spend another year in high school.

"When I learned about the extended early admissions program, I decided to go and try to carry 20 hours every semester including summer school so that I could get my bachelor's degree in two years. I had no idea of what was considered a normal load," he said.

"That way it would take me only one year above my regular high school years to get through college."

He was planning to become a Bible translator and decided to obtain a master's degree as well at the recommendation of two students involved in Bible translation whom he met during his second semester at the university.

He started his college career by getting special permission from his adviser, Josephine L. Wilcock, assistant to the head of the linguistics department, to take 21 hours.

Having completed the semester with a 4.905 average, he upped his hours the following semester to 29 and then took 16 hours in summer school.

The 46-hour semester followed, and during his last semester, the just-completed spring semester, he allowed himself to "coast" with a, for him, relatively relaxed load of 30 hours while also preparing for and taking his qualifying exams for his master's degree.

The 46-hour semester load was so high that he needed the permission not only of Ms. Wilcock but also of the department head, Professor Braj B. Kachru, and the dean, Richard B. Hinely.

Asked why he took on such a heavy load during the 1976 fall semester, David said, "Well, they were offering a lot of courses I wanted to take. Up till then I hadn't had more than I could handle. As long as I was taking worthwhile material and could handle it, I reasoned 'why not?' "

A slender, blond young man with a sunny smile, David is extremely modest about his accomplishment.

"I don't think I did anything special," he said. "I went right along with everyone else right until my last year of high school and only picked up speed during these last two years."

His picking up speed entailed a schedule that might boggle the mind of less stalwart people.

"Last fall I didn't put sleep anywhere in my schedule. I just slept a few hours when I couldn't go on any longer," he said.

During the first 12 weeks of last fall semester, he said, his schedule included arising at 6 a.m. and attending classes and working at the university from 7:30 a.m. until the library cloased at 10 p.m.

"Then I would drive home to Villa Grove, eat, and start working again either until I fell asleep or until the next morning. Usually I would fall asleep around midnight and wake up again at 2 or 3 o'clock and start to work," he said.

Saturdays also were earmarked for work, usually until 4 a.m. Sunday, he said. His only rest came on Sundays when he would attend morning and evening church services with his parents, enjoy a family dinner at noon, and practice his trumpet for an hour in the afternoon.

He did allot himself four or five hours of sleep during the last four weeks of the semester. "I just couldn't keep taking it," he said.

"My parents didn't know how to stop me," he said with a smile. "After I had shown them the first year that I could do it, they let me go ahead."

He said his parents did not allow him to do much extracurricular work during his junior and senior high school years because he suffered from asthma as a child and still occasionally suffers from the condition.

His father operates a concrete contracting firm in Villa Grove together with his father, Herman. Mrs. Bade works as a teacher's aide in the Villa Grove school's kindergarten. The couple has four sons of which David is the second-oldest.

Deeply religious, David hopes to become a Biblical translator.

"I have always loved languages and loved God and the truth as it is written in the Bible, and I feel that as a Biblical translator I can bring my strongest commitments together," he said.

David, who also has studied Spanish and an African language at the University of Illinois, will attend a summer institute in linguistics at the University of North Dakota in Grand Forks this summer. The institute concentrates on teaching Bible translation and linguistic field work.

Next fall he plans to attend the Trinity Evangelical Divinity School in Deerfield, Ill., where he hopes to obtain a master of arts degree in Biblical study in one year.

He is unsure of his plans after next year but hopes he will be able to work as a Bible translator, preferably outside the United States. China would be his first choice, he said.

He does not plan to take a vacation except for possibly a week in September and currently works at the university every day finishing up papers for two classes in which he received an excused grade.

In what little time he has had available for pursuits other than studying he likes to play the trumpet and listen to records of "Jesus rock." He has attended a weekly evening Bible study class during the last year.

He also reads the Bible every day, using an English version although he owns Hebrew, Greek, Spanish and Russian Bibles.

"I would have gone crazy during that intense semester if I hadn't read the Bible every day," he said.

June 1977

Holliday Abroad

Victor R. Holliday of Champaign has been in the middle of history-in-the-making during his eight years in heavy construction work abroad.

Mr. Holliday was in Iraq during the Yom Kippur war and worked in Libya during the 1968 revolution there.

While spending three years in East Central Africa, three years in North Africa and two years in the Middle East as a technical supervisor, he has helped build port facilities and power plants and laid miles of oil pipelines.

A native of Sadorus, Mr. Holliday, 48, served in the Marine Corps in the Far East during the Second World War. Since he began work in 1966 for the Vechtel Corporation, which has its headquarters in San Francisco, he has visited 30 countries, mostly while traveling to and from construction assignments.

On each job, half of his time is spent teaching and supervising local crews, the other half in operating heavy machinery such as cranes.

Before he began his overseas assignments, he was engaged in construction work in Illinois and Indiana.

Currently in Champaign between assignments — "Next I may go to Alaska to work on the pipeline" — Mr. Holliday is catching up on the doings of his two sons, Lance, 19, and Shawn, 16. The young men live in Urbana with Mr. Holliday's former wife.

Involving 18 Atlantic crossings, Mr. Holliday's jobs have been in many locations and of a wide variety. In the Somalia Republic, he helped build a new port on the Indian Ocean.

"It was an instance of international cooperation," he said. "We Americans built the port as a U.S. Aid project, while the Russians constructed a meat-packing plant and the West Germans built highways."

In Libya he helped build a small harbor with tanker-loading facilities, laid pipelines and worked on the construction of a L.P.G. (liquefied petroleum gas) plant.

He helped lay pipelines in the United Arab Emirates, formerly the Truscial States on the Arabian peninsula, and on his last two jobs he has worked in Iraq, also on pipelines.

"On each job we work with many local people," he said. "We need unskilled and semi-skilled labor, and it is good political relations to use the local labor force.

"You quickly pick up the essential words of a language. I have 25 to 50 words in seven or eight languages and considerably more in others.

"I talk to the native workers in slow English, and they reply in a mixture of their own language and Pidgin English. It teaches you to concentrate, and you learn to talk with your hands and body.

"Often it takes me a few seconds, while I break down a word in my mind into its components and think of what the Latin root could be. Surprisingly often this enables me to understand."

Mr. Holliday said the work has great advantages and disadvantages.

"We go to places so hot and arid and lonely that we curse ourselves for coming here. But the money is very good, and many parts are terrifically rewarding.

"I have skied down an alp, swum in the Mediterranean, fished in the Indian Ocean and hunted in the African bush. How else, but through a job like this, could an ordinary person like me do that sort of thing?

"I cannot describe the euphoria I felt when I saw the Roman Colosseum, the art works of Michelangelo and the inside of the great pyramids.

"The most important benefit everywhere has been meeting the local people. If you are friendly and outgoing, it is not hard to make contact. I have walked the streets at 3 a.m. everywhere I have lived and traveled and never been bothered."

Mr. Holliday said he never felt endangered, even when he found himself in the midst of wars and revolutions. "We are aware of the events around us, but not affected by them," he said.

He said a special comradeship develops among men in his field.

"There are not that many of us across the globe," he said. "I cross paths in my field with maybe 200 people. On every job I meet 10 to 20 men I have worked with before, and we renew our friendship.

"To an outsider our meetings must sound like geographical name-dropping, because when we ask about Bill or Joe, the answer may be that Bill is in Bangkok and Joe is in Alaska."

During his years in East Africa, Mr. Holliday hunted wild game with friends several evenings every week and went on safari every Friday (the Moslem holy day) for a year.

He never used native trackers after discovering most natives had not been more than 10 miles from their huts. He hunted every kind of East African animal except rhinoceros and eland and has many trophies to prove it.

"We never hunted merely for trophies," he said. "We dressed all our kills, including birds, and brought them to native villages for use as food."

"After a day of hunting, we would sit around the campfire and talk to the natives till midnight," he said. "They would be fascinated by simple things that seem commonplace to us — beltbuckles, hats, shoes. We always managed to communicate without knowing each other's languages. Offering water in a hot country breaks down the barriers immediately."

Among his souvenirs from Africa are a quiver with poison-tipped arrows and a bag of frankincense.

Asked if he would recommend his life-style to young men eager for adventure, Mr. Holliday said, "No, not if they are married. It is difficult to find housing with a wife along, and schooling for the children is a major problem. You almost always end up sending the children to schools outside the country.

"If you are married and go alone to avoid the housing and schooling problems, it becomes very difficult.

"If you are single, it can be a great life. You make a high income and do exciting things. But if you are married, the hardship for a North American woman to fit into the life-style of these countries, or the other choice, temporary long separations, makes it just too hard."

January 1975

Renaissance Man

A. Doyle Moore lives in a charming neo-Georgian house in Champaign surrounded by objects from the last four centuries.

But ideally he should be living in a renaissance environment because Professor Moore probably comes as close as anyone in Champaign-Urbana to being a true renaissance man.

The avocations of the professor of graphic design at the University of Illinois are so varied that they defy attempts at description within the confines of orderly paragraphs linked by smooth transitions.

Spilling over frequently into his professional work, Professor Moore's avocations might instead best be enumerated in a staccato listing such as this:

—Bookmaking and bookbinding, all by hand. He sets the type, prints, binds and sells the books. During the last year alone he has received three awards for book design and production.

—Poetry. A well-known practitioner of concrete poetry, he has published five of the seven major concrete poets in America and was the organizer of the exhibition of concrete poetry at Krannert Art Museum a few years ago, the second such exhibition held in the United States. He defines concrete poetry as a movement in typographical visual poetry in which the expression is made through the visual organization of the words rather than through the poem's lyrical content.

—Material Folk Culture (the study of folk culture through objects and processes rather than through songs, legends and other forms of oral folk culture). He has invented and taught classes at the University of Illinois in this subject during which he and his students put on demonstrations of log chopping, sheep shearing, spinning and dyeing, barn construction, forging and cooking of orally transmitted recipes.

—Folk Music. Professor Moore sings and plays the autoharp. When he discovered no one had written on the history of the autoharp since 1864, he researched and wrote a history of the instrument.

—Gardening. The garden surrounding his house ranges from a formal arrangement of large square stones in front (each stone, of course, laid by Professor Moore) to a profusion of wildflowers and trees on the side and an English annual garden and herb garden in back leading to a Japanese moon-viewing platform. Professor Moore also helps work the Champaign-Urbana Herb Society's herb garden at Meadowbrook Park.

—Quilting. He owns quilts made by his great-grandmother, grandmother and mother and has made five or six. His last effort, in triple Irish chain design, was exhibited at the University of Illinois Art Faculty Show at Krannert Art Museum in December. He said he "cut 2,000 flawless squares of fabric" for this quilt on the paper-cutting machine he uses in bookmaking.

—Embroidery. He learned how to do bargello tapestry in order to make new seat covers for his three Georgian chairs which date from 1710 to 1790.

—Cake Making. He is the outgoing president of the Urbana Creative Cake Club.

—Japanese Fine Arts. Professor Moore has received three degrees in flower arranging and three in the tea ceremony in Japan. Last summer on a research grant to Japan he spent part of the time as an apprentice to a Japanese confectioner, learning how to make the sweets served in the tea ceremony. He now makes the sweets, whose main ingredient is bean curd, used in the tea ceremony at Shozo Sato's Japan House in Urbana.

—Performing. He made his stage debut earlier this month when he created the Kabuki role of Past Prime Courtesan in Sato's Krannert Center production of "The Mikado."

—Cooking. He is an ambitious cook who equally enjoys doing the daily cooking for himself and "spectacular things for parties for my friends." He is a devotee of the Cuisinart food processor—"my constant companion these last two years"—and makes a specialty of recipes gleaned from his studies of material folk culture. He also cooks many English dishes learned during a summer spent in Yorkshire a few years ago.

Other past or present pursuits include silversmithing and pottery—"I'm a good silversmith and I can throw a pot with one hand"—sheep shearing and the processing of wool from carding to weaving, beekeeping, field taxonomy, painting, singing and tap dancing. He plans to learn to lay bricks this summer.

Among his few non-participatory interests are ballet, the history of ballet and the study of the Indians of the southwestern states.

Professor Moore received his undergraduate education at Kansas State University and his graduate education at the University of Iowa.

He interrupted his undergraduate study to serve four years in the U.S. Air Force, spending the first 18 months in the San Francisco area and the last 2½ years in Japan, where he was art director of "Stars and Stripes."

He joined the University of Illinois art department right after graduate school.

"It may appear as if I do eccentric and varied things but everything I do is interrelated," Professor Moore said.

"I am essentially a designer and in all the things I deal with my main interest is the process of how things go together. I'm interested in the process rather than in the object.

"My reason for doing things is the pursuit of excellence in the craft of doing them."

He explained the variety of his pursuits by saying, "I feel I am on a great big panorama where things keep coming by and I reach out and grab them."

He added, "I take a great stability from this variety. It's the means to the end that I am studying. I don't consider myself a jack-of-all-trades and a master of none but a designer who deals with process.

"I'm not a frustrated anything. There's nothing that I've wanted to do that I haven't tried and there's nothing I've tried that I haven't wanted to do."

He added with a big smile, "I wonder what I'll be when I grow up."

May 1978

The Music Man

Sol Cohen's life centers on music and people — as it has for all of his 84 years.

He gives private piano and violin lessons to about 30 pupils every week, plays violin sonatas weekly with a pianist, is part of a community chamber orchestra and spends his summers as "the music man" at a summer camp in the Allegheny Mountains.

He attends many local concerts, sitting in one of the front rows since his hearing has decreased. He will venture out even on bitterly cold nights to hear promising young performers.

He travels and has been to New Mexico and Europe within the last six months.

He keeps up a vast correspondence with old and new friends.

A frequent dinner guest in many local homes, he maintains an active social life.

He continues his lifelong participation in the life of the Jewish community.

His capacity for new friendships has not diminished with the years. Often his pupils become friends with whom he discusses literature and philosophy.

Until two months ago, he took the bus to Champaign daily to conduct his teaching at the House of Baldwin. He now teaches at the grand piano in his Urbana home, where he was born.

"Waiting for the bus in bad weather got to be too much for me," he said. "Anyhow, I discovered the pupils like to come to the house."

One of Urbana's older homes, the house features large bay windows, ornate woodwork and an elaborately carved stairway.

"I tell people to come in and see the antiques, including me," Mr. Cohen said with a smile.

Until the death of his brother, Julius, in 1973 at age 85, the two brothers lived together. Julius Cohen was a voice teacher who discovered and trained many well-known singers, and a poet.

Mr. Cohen said that after his brother's death, "I simply had to have something living around me," so he acquired Buffy, a friendly cocker spaniel-poodle.

He rents rooms to two university students and enjoys the activity the young men bring to the house.

Mr. Cohen enjoys traveling and spent Christmas vacation with two former Urbana residents, Marian and Stanley Fletcher, in Albuquerque, N.M. He took the train both ways and spent much of the vacation playing sonatas with Mr. Fletcher, a pianist, and playing in a chamber orchestra.

He spent last September traveling in Europe with a 35-year-old friend from Champaign, a former pupil of Julius's.

They went to Italy, Switzerland, France, England and Germany where Mr. Cohen visited a former pupil, Arthur Price of Champaign, who is the American consul in Stuttgart.

Mr. Cohen learned French and German during prolonged stays in Europe in his youth. When he was 17, he left Urbana for Prague where he studied for six months with a famous violin teacher.

He went from there to Budapest, where he studied violin for two years, and was joined by Julius, who studied singing.

"One season in Budapest we went to 56 operas and dozens and dozens of concerts. We always sat way up in the top balcony in the cheapest seats," he said.

"We heard many famous singers, now forgotten. It affected my life to that degree that I am still a romanticist and don't enjoy modern music, sorry to say."

"I have many friends who are composers at the University of Illinois. I like them very much, but I must say I don't like their music."

Mr. Cohen was a member of the violin section of the Champaign-Urbana Symphony Orchestra until last year.

He is the last member of a family which for almost 100 years has been an integral part of the musical life in Urbana and Champaign.

His father, Nathan H. Cohen, settled in Urbana as a cigarmaker after having been an actor and singer in California. His mother was a former opera singer, and the family house once was described by an acquaintance as "more like a concert hall than a place of residence."

The home was a meeting place for university music students, and house-guests included musical stars who were here to perform in the old Illinois Theatre.

While Julius Cohen stayed in Urbana almost all his life, Sol Cohen spent many years away.

He was for years an associate of Ruth St. Denis, founder of modern dance in America; he toured with her and wrote music for her.

With his brother, he spent many summers at the MacDowell Colony for Creative Artists in Peterborough, N.H. He taught music for many years in private schools, including a seven-year stint at a school in Asheville, N.C.

From 1935 to 1939 he was director of the Champaign senior and junior high school orchestras and music teacher in the two schools.

In the first World War, he was a private in the U.S. Army and fought in the Meuse-Argonne offensive.

He later returned to France, where he studied music in Paris. He prides himself on never having spent a night in Paris other than on the Left Bank.

An open-minded and enthusiastic man, his friendships continue to grow. An example of this is his relationship with one of his pupils of high school age.

"This boy is simply tremendous," he said. "We are both fond of English Victorian literature. The boy reads Austen, Dickens, Trollope and Thackeray, and we discuss the books. We also correspond in French to practice the language."

He has been approached to participate in the creation of books on teaching methods but has declined.

"I cannot adopt a doctrinal approach," he said. "I work on an individual system with each student."

Mr. Cohen rewards his school-age pupils with a candy bar at the end of each lesson. When he and his brother were honored at a communitywide celebration as B'nai B'rith Men of the Year in 1972, a mother of one of his students presented him with a candy bar at the end of her tribute.

Asked the secret of his vitality, Mr. Cohen said, "It is very strange: I don't feel any older than I did 10 or 20 years ago. I don't seem to be heir to the illnesses of the flesh, and I feel no sense of age in any way.

"To me each day is an adventure, and each person I meet is a new adventure."

February 1975

Two Enemies Now Friends

In March 1945 Hans Lobitzer, a soldier in the German Army, came to the aid of an American bombardier, Irvin D. Baer, and possibly saved his life.

Mr. Baer returned May 20 from a visit with Mr. Lobitzer, who is now a prosperous businessman in his native Austria.

"Two mortal enemies are now close friends," said Mr. Baer, who has been employed by Fairchild's Camera in Champaign for more than 15 years.

When the two men met, Mr. Baer was 26 and Mr. Lobitzer was 22.

"I was a bombardier in the American Air Force, flying out of Italy," Mr. Baer said.

"On a mission to bomb the oil refineries on the north bank of the Danube in a suburb of Vienna, we were hit by flak and one engine was knocked out. We dropped our bombs on the bombing run which slowed us down so that the formation got away from us.

"Our plane headed for the Russian lines, but we were hit again by flak over Graz (Austria), and one wing started to burn."

Mr. Baer said the plane was manned by a new, inexperienced crew, and before he bailed out, he had to kick another crew member out of the plane when that man froze in the doorway.

"Just as I went out, the wing of the plane went down in a fiery spin," he said.

Three members of the crew died, while seven reached the ground safely.

Mr. Baer said that his parachute brought him down in eastern Hungary, near Lake Balaton, in the midst of a battle between the Russians and the Germans.

"Both sides were shooting at me with machine guns," he said.

When he reached the ground, he ran to hide in a shellhole where the Germans took him prisoner a few minutes later.

Together with other members of the crew, he was taken to a dungeon in an old Hungarian castle. From there, the American prisoners of war were brought in a prison railroad car through Czekoslovakia and Austria on their way to Germany.

"When we came to Amstetten, Austria, the railroad yard had been bombed out, and the guards marched us around the yard to transfer us to another train," he said.

"Instigated by an S.S. man, some civilians attacked us and beat us up. When I saw a man with a rope, I became frightened that we were in for more than a beating, because it was not unusual for civilians to string up members of a bombing crew."

In the midst of the beating, a contingent of German soldiers came by. Among them was Hans Lobitzer, who, Mr. Baer said, led the soldiers in calming the civilians.

"He cited the Geneva Convention (about humane treatment of prisoners of war) and shouted that the war was almost over and that they could get in a lot of trouble for beating us," Mr. Baer recalled.

Under Mr. Lobitzer's leadership the soldiers managed to stop the beating and led the Americans to their artillery camp, where the company doctor patched the Americans up with his meager supplies, Mr. Baer said.

Mr. Baer said that at his request Mr. Lobitzer gave him his name and address on the condition that Mr. Baer would memorize it, fearing repercussions if the S.S. found the address on him.

From Amstetten the Americans were brought by train to Nuremberg to a prison camp, from which they were taken on a 150-mile forced march to Moosburg, as the war neared its end. The Moosburg camp was liberated by the American 14th Armored Division.

After the war ended, Mr. Baer wrote to Mr. Lobitzer to thank him, and a correspondence began in English that has lasted 30 years.

"To help them survive, we sent packages to Hans and his wife, Angela, and their tiny son, Harald, with food, needles, thread, seeds and clothing," Mr. Baer said.

"When we visited them, we found that not only do they still have all my letters, but they have almost everything we sent them. Hans's new wife, Claudia (Angela died almost four years ago) still wears a sweater we sent," Mr. Baer said.

"In my second letter I told him that I am of the Jewish faith, thinking it might matter to him. He wrote back and said it made no difference to him," Mr. Baer recalled.

An employee of Swissair, Claudia Lobitzer received a pass for several trips when she retired. The Lobitzers used the pass to visit the Baers in their Danville home for two weeks in May 1972.

This was the first time in 27 years the two former enemies met.

"Hans owns a phonograph record shop in Wels, Austria, and his contacts with Americans had been mainly with rich tourists," Mr. Baer said.

"He found common folks like us fascinating. He fell in love with hamburgers, tried all the American dry cereals, was delighted with our wildlife such as squirrels and bluebirds, and could not stop admiring mobile homes," he said.

Mr. Baer and his wife, Betty, returned the visit this month on their first trip abroad. They spent two weeks with the Lobitzers at their home in Wels and their cottage at Bad Aussee in the Austrian Alps.

Mr. Baer said the trip's highlight was attending the graduation from the medical school of the University of Vienna of Mr. Lobitzer's son, Erwin, who was named for Mr. Baer.

The two friends have some trouble surmounting the language difficulties, since each does not speak the other's language well, but the multilingual Claudia acted as interpreter when needed.

Mr. Baer said the Lobitzers showed the Baers Austria "from border to border" and introduced them to friends from all walks of life.

"The visit was such a success that I cannot find words to describe it," he said. "Hans's parting words were, 'We'll pick you up in Salzburg in two years. Don't bring any money for the stay, just come!' "

Next year Betty and Irvin Baer hope to give their 21-year-old daughter, Tobi, a trip to the Lobitzers' when she graduates from Illinois State University.

Mr. Baer said, "It was an incredible experience to ride down the Autobahn, side by side with my former enemy, and look up at the blue skies and think, 'Thirty years ago I flew up there with a load of bombs'."

June 1975

From Jail to the Pulpit

At age 13 Larry Simmons was incarcerated for three months in a reform school for taking part in an armed robbery.

At 18 he stabbed a man in a nightclub brawl.

Today, at 34, he is the charismatic and influential leader of a church and an educator of considerable reputation well on his way to a graduate degree.

Ironically, the violent act of the stabbing turned out to be the factor that turned the pastor of Greater Holy Temple in Urbana's North End away from the path taken by many of his childhood and boyhood friends who are now serving long jail terms or living lives blighted by hard drugs.

To avoid prosecution for the stabbing, Mr. Simmons joined the U.S. Air Force — a decision that changed his life in three fateful ways.

The Air Force imposed on him much-needed discipline; educated him as an instructor in the electrical system of aircrafts, thereby whetting his appetite for his later career in education; and, most importantly, stationed him at Chanute Air Force Base.

This neutral, geographical decision brought the lonely airman in his search for something more than solitary evenings of sitting on his bunk in the barracks with a whiskey bottle as company to Greater Holy Temple's inspiring pastor, the Rev. William A. Melker, and, through him, to God.

The Rev. Melker, who was widely known as "Brother Billy," died in 1974 at the age of 41.

"Brother Billy was like a father to me," Mr. Simmons said. "He and his wife, Shirley, almost adopted me. Soon after starting attending the church, I began to stay with them on weekends.

"The way he loved the Lord and the way he lived inspired me and changed my life."

The story of Larry Simmons begins in Aliquippa, Pa., a tough steel town some 20 miles north of Pittsburgh whose main claim to fame is its having spawned Tony Dorsett, running back for the Dallas Cowboys.

Here Mr. Simmons grew up in bonecrushing poverty as the oldest boy in a family of 15 children.

"I have seven brothers and seven sisters and was born on the seventh day of the seventh month," he said.

He was raised by his mother and his polio-stricken stepfather, never seeing his natural father until he was 13 years old.

His childhood memories include "eating some when the checks came in from welfare and less when they ran out," often subsisting on government surplus food, wearing cardboard soles in worn-out shoes and sleeping in a room with seven of his siblings, four to a bed.

"Christmas was all from the Salvation Army. We never got new toys and all our clothes were hand-me-downs," he said.

"Managing with so little did lend to a strong family relationship. We lived in maybe 23 or 24 different houses through my childhood, moving to escape the rent collector. Some of the neighbors called us gypsies.

"But moving from house to house so much made our family unit more central to us, and facing so many hardships together drew us siblings close together," Mr. Simmons said.

"We had so many memorable experiences. When my brothers and sisters and I get together and talk over old times, our sides ache with laughter."

The family closeness and the strictness of his mother and father kept the children in line until the age of about 12, when outside pressures took over, he said.

"It wasn't until I was 12 that I branched out into belonging to gangs. A lot of kids from broken homes moved into the project we lived in, and I began running with them.

"We'd go out and steal clothes whenever we needed them. If we had to have some sports equipment, we'd steal it.

"It was a tough town. You had to be a tough guy to walk the streets.

"At 13 I was picked up—deservedly—for armed robbery. I was sent to reform school and was there for three months.

"When I came out, it was back to normal—running with the gang, drinking, loving. I did a lot of bad things, stuff I don't do now.

"In spite of all this I somehow managed to graduate from high school at 18 and went to live with my real father in Buffalo.

"Soon after moving there I stabbed a guy in a nightclub after he had hit me on the head with a bottle. My friend who was with me grabbed me, held me back and hid the knife.

"They took me to jail in a paddywagon and kept me overnight but let me go the next day because they couldn't find the knife.

"The man I had stabbed put out a warrant for my arrest so I joined the Air Force to get away from the situation."

Mr. Simmons was first sent to Lackland Air Force Base in San Antonio, Texas. The following year he was able to choose where he wanted to be stationed and picked Chanute.

"I chose Chanute because it was near Chicago so that I could go to the big city and pick up my old life," he said.

But, through the mysterious workings of the God in whom Mr. Simmons now believes so deeply and whose teachings guide every aspect of his life, Chanute became instead the launching pad for the new direction in his life.

"They trained me to become an instructor in the electrical system of the aircraft and put me to work as an instructor," Mr. Simmons said.

"And it was while being at Chanute I found Brother Billy and his church."

An interdenominational church, Greater Holy Temple was founded by the Rev. Melker in 1965 after a large tent revival meeting that attracted the members who became the foundation of the church.

Mr. Simmons got involved with the church soon after its founding in 1965, when he was 19, and served as its youth director under the Rev. Melker.

He has pastored at the church since last November but became the church's official pastor last April, succeeding the Rev. Verdell Jones.

His original involvement with the church was triggered not only by Brother Billy and Mrs. Melker but also by the members of the congregation.

"The love the people in the church had for me helped make me change my ways. In childhood Momma made us go to church but the people there seemed like fanatics or phonies to me. I went only out of obedience. But the people here were different — so wonderful, so giving," he said.

The current congregation numbers about 150 people.

Mr. Simmons's pastorate is a full-time job although it allows him time for his graduate studies. His duties include preaching and conducting services and the adult Sunday school, hospital visits, counseling and the overseeing of educational programs.

He is aided by an assistant pastor, Robert Smith, and nine church members who serve as ministers.

Among the church members are one of Mr. Simmons's sisters, Sandra, a bus driver, and one of his brothers, Ronald, who works at Western Electric Co.

Many of Mr. Simmons's siblings have joined churches through the influence of his example, he said.

"All of my brothers were in the gang life in their teens. Today all of my siblings are doing fine. Almost all are married. None are in jail; none are hooked on hard drugs. Most of my brothers got away from the bad life by joining the Navy," he said.

The church places strong emphasis on education, Mr. Simmons said.

"We have a daily summer teaching program which is heavy on the three R's and includes crafts and sports.

"During the school year we have a three-hour Saturday school which emphasizes remedial instruction in addition to the Sunday school which concentrates on Bible study.

"This fall we are going to start a tutoring program in mathematics and reading during the week as well, helping the children with their school homework. I hope to get volunteers from the University of Illinois to help with this.

"We want to give the kids the best chance possible. Our church believes in investing efforts and time in children. We believe education is the key to life — along with a strong religious belief."

Mr. Simmons also works with released prisoners employed in the community through the State of Illinois' Urbana Community Correctional Center.

After leaving the Air Force in 1967 Mr. Simmons was employed by the Western Electric Co. in Champaign for a year.

Then, encouraged by the Rev. Melker, he decided to educate himself further and attended the University of Illinois on the GI Bill, graduating with a bachelor's degree in elementary education in 1973.

After graduation he was a fifth-grade teacher at Yankee Ridge School for five years. A trophy given him by one of his classes at the school, inscribed "Mr. Simmons, World's Best Teacher," holds a place of honor in his pastoral study side by side with a trophy for winning the welterweight championship at Chanute.

He is now working toward a master's degree in educational administration at the University of Illinois.

Simmons met his wife, Doretha, during his junior year at the university. Mrs. Simmons is from Chicago and attended the university, majoring in education, through the Special Education Opportunity Program, popularly called "Project 500." She is now a second-grade teacher at Bottenfield School.

The Simmonses have two children, Larry, 7 — "We call him The Champ! He has so much self-esteem," Mr. Simmons said — and Dionne, 5, about whom Mr. Simmons said, "She won't be outdone by anyone. Her brother is going to have his hands full keeping ahead of her."

They expect their third child in January.

"I spend a tremendous amount of time with my kids," Mr. Simmons said.

"They are at the age when they dream. When The Champ says, 'I can top O.J. Simpson's record some day,' I say to him, 'Yes, you can.' I don't break his dream.

"I believe that they, and the children I taught at Yankee Ridge and the children in our church, are the future, and you have to let them lead the way."

August 1980

The Earth-Father

A few days before Jerry J. Uhl's annual turkey roast took place last week the Urbana bachelor said cheerfully that he expected "somewhere between 75 and 150 people" to attend, depending on the weather.

As it turned out, the weather was perfect — warm and sunny with a light breeze — and an estimated 115 guests gathered in Professor Uhl's yard to partake in the feast.

Even if another 35 guests had come, there would have been plenty to eat for everyone. One-and-a-half of the eight turkeys, each weighing between 22 and 24 pounds, were left at the end of the party even though many of the party-goers had returned to the serving table for second and even third helpings.

An experienced giver of large parties, Professor Uhl, who teaches mathematics at the University of Illinois, had stocked his refrigerator with back-up supplies consisting of five chickens.

The evening after the turkey roast he partook in a "rump party" held at the home of friends, where the chickens were grilled and served as the main dish together with some of the left-over turkey.

Professor Uhl cooked the eight turkeys on four covered grills (his own and three borrowed grills) placed on the driveway to his home.

He said he picked the unfrozen birds up at the market at 7:30 a.m. on the day of the party and had finished preparing them for cooking and fired the grills by 9:30. The first four turkeys cooked from 9:30 until 1 or 2 p.m. As he took them off the grill, he wrapped them in aluminum foil and allowed them to rest until serving time about three hours later. He placed the second batch of turkeys on the grills as space became available.

As each of the first four turkeys was unwrapped at the party, it proved to be the rich color of finished maple with crackling crisp skins and juicy and still hot interiors. Some of the second batch were smoked with the addition of watered woodchips to the fire and were the color of mahogany.

Beaming like an earth-father in his visored cap, Professor Uhl did all the carving at a table in the driveway. He appeared to take great pleasure in heaping turkey on the plates of his friends as they passed by him in a steady stream.

An assortment of salads, vegetable dishes, breads and desserts had been brought by the guests who also contributed kegs of beer and six-packs of soft drinks.

Among the party-goers was Al Lazer, an old friend of Professor Uhl's, who had flown in from his home in Pittsburgh to attend the giant barbecue.

The turkey roast was the second such annual party given by Professor Uhl. He has also in the past held a party featuring a 120-pound roast pig and each year hosts a football party for from 85 to 90 guests at which he serves 35 pounds of bratwurst cooked with 30 pounds of sauerkraut and provides two 16-gallon kegs of beer.

A man with a great gift for friendship, Professor Uhl last fall held a gigantic birthday party for 2-year-old Georges Saab to ensure that the little boy would start out his life in the United States with plenty of clothing and toys. The boy was rescued from war-torn Lebanon by his father, Elias, a graduate student in mathematics at the University of Illinois, who made a perilous journey to bring the child out of Lebanon.

A measure of Professor Uhl's friends' regard for him is the recent birthday gift of a church pew which was bought for $10 and refinished by three married couples, and the fact that two friends put in the labor to turn his living room into a recreation room with a long bar.

Professor Uhl's house is as cozy and as snugly fitted to his needs as that of Mr. Badger in "The Wind in the Willows."

Five Smithfield hams hang in the kitchen which is decorated with a collection of beer coasters; the den with its big stone fireplace and comfortable furniture is conducive to study and philosophical thought; and the recreation room with its many mementoes of American railroads — "Purchased, not stolen," Professor Uhl stressed — is a wonderful setting for a party.

He has been a railroad fan since the days when he traveled from his native Pittsburgh to William and Mary College in Williamsburg, Va., for his undergraduate studies.

For a number of years in the early 1970s he arranged for members of the mathematics department at the University of Illinois to travel to the yearly January meeting of the American Mathematical Society in a private sleeping car which for some of the trips served as the group's hotel at the destination point.

The trips went to San Antonio, Texas, Las Vegas, Nev., and Dallas, Texas. For the latter trip, Judy McCulloh, a specialist in folklore and the wife of a University of Illinois math professor, prepared sheets of folk songs appropriate to the region the train passed through.

Professor Uhl's most recent train travel was a two-week trip in England and Ireland from which he returned four days before the turkey roast.

Professor Uhl, whose mathematical specialty is measure theory, received his doctorate at Carnegie-Mellon University in Pittsburgh. He has lived in Champaign-Urbana since 1968.

His first book, "Vector Measures," on which he collaborated with Joseph Diestel of Kent State University, will be published soon by the American Mathematical Society.

His recipe for the preparation of 184 pounds of succulent turkey meat follows.

ROAST TURKEYS

8 turkeys, weighing 22 to 24 lbs. each
½ c. salt
2½ (4.37 oz.) jars of coarsely ground pepper
40 onions
240 cloves
cooking oil
3 (1.75 oz.) jars of caraway seeds
1½ (0.62 oz.) jars of rosemary
1 (0.5 oz.) jar of basil
6-pack of beer

Wash the turkeys inside and out by hosing them down with a garden hose outside the house. Dry with paper towels.

Throw a small handful of salt and the same amount of coarsely ground pepper into the cavity of each turkey and rub it around well. Cut the peeled onions in half and stud each half with three cloves. Place 10 onion halves inside each turkey.

Coat the outside of each turkey liberally with cooking oil. Sprinkle the outside of each turkey with a liberal amount of caraway seeds and a smaller amount of rosemary and basil. Coat the turkey well with coarsely ground pepper.

Cook the turkeys on covered kettle grills (one turkey to each grill) for 3½ to 4½ hours or until done. The juices should run clear when the turkey is pricked at a joint. The fire should be as hot as you can get it. (Uhl used 50 pounds of charcoal to cook the eight turkeys). A drip pan should be placed underneath each turkey.

The cook drinks the 6-pack of beer during the cooking.

When the turkeys are done, wrap them in aluminum foil and let them rest for at least an hour before carving.

Makes 140 servings.

July 1977

THE MANY WAYS
WE LIVE NOW

Long-Distance Commuters

By car and by train, by inter-city bus and private and commercial plane, in the broiling sun of midsummer and in subzero winter weather, they travel from their hometown to another city to do their job.

They are the long-distance commuters who travel from Champaign-Urbana to a faraway place as a matter of course.

Many commute every workday from Champaign-Urbana to cities like Springfield (approximately 180 miles round trip) and Charleston (100 miles round trip).

Others make weekly trips to far-off places in Illinois or undertake regular periodic journeys to Chicago or New York as part of their jobs.

For others, long-distance commuting to places like Peoria, Iowa City and San Francisco is a short-term project, usually lasting one semester.

"Commuting can become a little wearying now and then, but there are so many advantages — such as good schools and the many cultural offerings and entertainment events here — that my wife and I have chosen to stay in Champaign," said Harold W. Bradley, Jr.

Mr. Bradley has commuted by car to his job as an instructional television specialist in Springfield for more than four years.

Since Mrs. Bradley is not employed outside of her home, the Bradleys often have discussed the possibility of moving to Springfield, but the attractions of the Champaign-Urbana area always have weighed too heavily, Mr. Bradley said.

Many of the commuters see the twice-a-day trip in positive terms and value the time spent commuting as an opportunity to be alone and do some quiet thinking.

"I don't mind the drive at all," said Irvin D. Baer, manager of Fairchild Camera in Champaign, who has commuted the approximately 38-mile (one way) distance to his job from his home in Danville for a total of 13 years.

"Although many people commute from Danville to Champaign-Urbana and I probably easily could get into a car pool, I prefer to go by myself so I can control my own time. I just think, listen to the news and make decisions. I enjoy watching the scene change month after month and, being a photographer, often stop and take pictures along the way," he said.

Sue Woods of Urbana, who commutes four times a week to her job as an instructor in health education at Eastern Illinois University in Charleston, said, "I find the driving time regenerating. I approach it as an hour I have to myself, out of reach of others. Otherwise it would become a burden."

Mrs. Woods's husband, Raymond, manages the Thinnes Service Station and Oil Company in Champaign. She has commuted to Charleston since last August.

George H. Elder of Champaign is one of 43 employees of U.S. Industrial Chemicals in Tuscola who live in the Champaign-Urbana area and commute daily to the plant.

Mr. Elder has commuted to his job as an operator in the process department at USIC for 20 years, the last seven from Champaign, the first 13 from Villa Grove. His wife, Alice, is a teacher at Central High School.

"Even if my wife wasn't working, I would not consider moving to Tuscola," Mr. Elder said.

"I like Champaign real well and I also think that if the plant was shut down, it would be hard to sell a house in the town where the plant is located."

Sheila Goldberg of Champaign is one of many local people who commute to Bloomington or Normal. She has driven the 63 miles to Normal twice a day five times a week since 1972 to perform her duties as an assistant professor of child development at Illinois State University in Normal.

This semester she plans to cut the driving down to four round trips a week by staying over in Bloomington one night weekly, she said.

She prefers to drive alone rather than join a car pool in order to broadcast over and listen to her CB-radio, which she acquired originally as an aid in case of emergency and now enjoys for the socializing it affords. Her CB handle is "Chantilly Lace."

A surprisingly large contingent of Champaign-Urbana citizens commutes daily to Springfield. In addition to Mr. Bradley, the contingent includes George Dee Roth and Paul Sparks of Champaign, among others.

The three men have formed a car pool in which Mr. Roth currently participates two or three times a week when his job as director of planning for the Governor's Council on Developmental Disabilities demands that he work in Springfield.

The remaining days of the week he takes the train the 128 miles to Chicago for the job, usually staying overnight in Chicago if the trip is for more than one day.

"When I commute to Chicago, I read and work on the train. On the drives to and from Springfield, I enjoy the companionship with the other members of the car pool, but otherwise I consider the 1½-hour driving time wasted," he said.

He has been a daily commuter to Springfield since June 1975 and expects his new split schedule to last six months after which he again will commute solely to Springfield.

A former principal at Jefferson Junior High School, Mr. Sparks has commuted to Springfield daily since last August. He is assistant to the ombudsman for the State Board of Education, Illinois Office of Education.

Mr. Bradley also works for the State Board of Education in his job as an instructional television specialist. In addition, he is producer and host for a public affairs television program, "People Beat," produced by Channel 12 in Springfield and shown locally on television station WICD, Channel 15, on Sunday nights, and does features for a radio program on black community life, "Eastside Beat," produced by WSSR-FM National Public Radio.

He shares an apartment in Springfield with a former Champaign resident and stays there overnight a few nights a week to cut down on the time spent on the road, he said.

Last semester Tony Peressini, professor of mathematics at the University of Illinois, left his office by midafternoon one day a week and flew in a university-owned small plane to Rolling Meadows, a northern suburb of Chicago. He taught a three-hour extramural class held at Rolling Meadows High School and returned on the plane to Champaign, arriving at midnight.

Professor Peressini, who lives in Champaign, has taught similar extramural classes for the university during seven or eight semesters.

On the weekly plane trips last fall he usually shared the plane with four other University of Illinois faculty members who taught similar classes in the Chicago area. The plane flew into Palwaukee Airport.

The five courses taught by Peressini and his travelmates were among 131 off-campus courses taught last semester by University of Illinois faculty members, according to Robert L. Johnston, head of Extramural Classes.

Most of the courses were given weekly throughout the semester while others were given for shorter periods, Mr. Johnston said. The locations of the courses varied from the Rock Island-Moline and LaSalle-Peru areas to Quincy and East St. Louis. The classes are part of an ongoing program of the extramural office.

The faculty members travel by university-owned plane to distant locations and by personal or university-owned car to nearby locations, he said.

Among the commuters who make periodic trips for their work are Sandra K. Watanabe of Urbana. A family therapist on the faculty of the Family Institute of Chicago, Mrs. Watanabe now commutes to Chicago "about a dozen times a year" but before the birth of her son, David, 20 months ago she commuted to Chicago once a week, according to her husband, Daniel, an associate professor of computer science at the University of Illinois.

Mrs. Watanabe was vacationing in Honolulu this week, so the information about her commuting was furnished by Professor Watanabe.

When the couple first moved to Champaign-Urbana six years ago, Mrs. Watanabe commuted once a month for a year to Boston to attend board meetings of the Boston Family Institute of which she was one of the founders, Professor Watanabe said.

During the years when she commuted weekly to Chicago, she would go on to Minneapolis on approximately every third trip, Professor Watanabe said. Mrs. Watanabe now is mainly involved in private practice in Champaign-Urbana, he said.

The employer of Kitty Mastny of Champaign is the H.W. Wilson Co., a leading publisher of reference books, making it necessary for Mrs. Mastny to commute to New York approximately every six weeks.

The mother of three children, Mrs. Mastny works from 25 to 40 hours a week in her home for the publishing firm as a researcher and writer. She currently writes biographies for a Wilson periodical, "Current Biography."

Mrs. Mastny, who earned a Ph.D. from Columbia University in medieval history, worked for the Wilson company while living in New York from 1970 until she and her husband, Vojtech, an associate professor of history at the University of Illinois, moved to Champaign in August 1975. She started her long-distance work for the firm six months after her arrival here and does her commuting by plane.

Some long distance-commuters do their traveling for a limited time, usually a semester. Among these are Mary Sleator Temperley, Karin Dovring and David Sides.

Right now Mrs. Temperley of Urbana is spending two weeks in Peoria starting a course in English for 19 Japanese bankers at Bradley University.

After the intial two weeks are over she will commute by car to Peoria three times a week to teach the course.

She is the mother of three children and the wife of Nicholas Temperley, professor of music at the University of Illinois.

Mrs. Dovring of Urbana commuted once a week to Iowa City for eight weeks last spring to teach a course for graduate students in her specialty, international communications.

The wife of Folke Dovring, professor of land economics at the University of Illinois, she commuted by bus, leaving Sunday and returning late on Wednesday night.

She said she chose the bus over airplanes out of fear of being stranded by bad weather and not arriving in time for her first class.

Mrs. Dovring is writing a textbook on international communications for journalists in collaboration with the president of the Institute of Comparative Social and Cultural Studies in Washington, D.C., Lorand Szalay, and flies to Washington approximately once a month for conferences with Mr. Szalay.

The commuter traveling the farthest is David Sides, visiting research associate professor in architecture at the University of Illinois, who totaled 4,000 miles a week for a while.

During the last four months of 1976, Mr. Sides flew from Champaign to San Francisco every Tuesday, spent the week as a consultant for the Energy Research and Development Association at Lawrence Berkeley

Laboratories, returned to Champaign by plane during the weekend, prepared his class at the University of Illinois during Monday and taught the class Monday night.

"I lived in perpetual jet lag," Mr. Sides said. "The worst thing about the commuting, though, was that I couldn't keep my digital watch straight!"

He lives in Champaign with his wife, Dorothy, a real estate broker, and the couple's two sons.

"I worked in the Cal-ERDA project to develop a computer program for architects and building officials to analyze energy consumption of buildings in preparation for new federal standards for approved energy budgets for all non-residential buildings," Mr. Sides said.

"It was sufficiently enticing and challenging work to make me spend a lot of time on airplanes."

January 1977

A Fair and Impartial Jury

Watching the selection of a jury brings to mind Walt Whitman's words, "I hear America singing".

In no other place does the panorama of a community's life unfold as during the questioning of prospective jurors.

Members of the various occupations, from cook to farmer, shirt presser to college professor, student to executive, file by, all laying bare the structure of their lives, their possible prejudices, their hobbies and interests, and their most deeply held convictions.

All these, along with almost forgotten transgressions of the law and tenuous family relationships, are brought out through the painstaking selection of a "fair and impartial jury."

During my recent two weeks of duty as a petit juror at the Champaign County Courthouse, the first day-and-a-half were given over to the selection of the jury for the trial for the murder of Greg Williams, a black University of Illinois football player shot during a fraternity house party.

I later sat through the picking of four other juries and was chosen for two of them.

Of the 175 jurors called for the session, 52 were questioned for the Williams case. For the other cases, an average of 20 jurors were questioned.

In its repetitiveness, the questioning is undoubtedly boring to the judges, bailiffs and clerks, but for a one-time juror it was fascinating.

It reminded me of the Hans Christian Andersen tale in which the princess obtains a magical pot that informs her what everyone in town eats for dinner. Listening to the jurors' answers, you may not learn what people have for dinner (though you often do during the recesses), but you find out just about everything else about their lives.

Would you be surprised to learn, for instance, that with a few exceptions, all the people questioned for the Williams jury either have firearms in their homes or have no objections to others possessing them?

Or that if my number had been pulled, I would have been only the third person in the group who attended University of Illinois football games last fall?

Other facts emerging were that hardly anyone had been the victim of a mugging or a hold-up, but many had had their homes burglarized.

Because many teachers and college professors had been called to serve earlier in the year and received deferments to June, the great number of people involved in education in Champaign County seemed even larger during this session. Three of the jurors and one of the alternates chosen for the Williams case were college professors.

Among all the jurors called for this session by lottery from the lists of registered voters, only two were black, both women. Neither of these women was retained on any of the juries for which their number came up in the five cases I watched.

One of the questions asked for the Williams case, in which the four defendants and the victim were black, was about racial prejudice.

Almost everyone said that a person's creed, color and so on would make no difference to his or her judgment. A couple of female jurors, appearing deeply troubled and embarrassed, did answer that this might influence them and were immediately excused.

Family relationships were illuminated by questions about whether anyone were related to people in the legal and law enforcement field.

Some jurors revealed that they had relatives who were lawyers or judges, usually in other states, and many were related to members of the local police and sheriff's departments. Interestingly, almost all of those with local relatives said they saw the relative in question — usually a brother-in-law or cousin — maybe once a year.

The question whether the juror had ever been involved in a lawsuit was answered in the negative by the majority.

For the few who had, the disclosures of youthful offenses usually ending in having been put on probation or of divorce suits instituted and later dropped were made with controlled anguish, leaving an impression of old wounds having been reopened.

Possible sexism directed against women was explored by one of the defense lawyers in the Williams case, Paul H. Vallandigham, who was to be assisted by his lawyer wife, Marian Kurata.

Mr. Vallandigham asked the jurors if they had any prejudice against woman lawyers or against women maintaining their maiden name after marriage. He found no one admitting to any such prejudice.

The many fine threads that unite people in towns the size of Champaign and Urbana came to light in questions exploring whether the juror knew either the lawyers or other jurors.

The positive answers included responses such as, "Yes, I have coached the daughter of (one of the defense attorneys) on a softball team" and "I once pushed the car of (one of the jurors already seated) out of a snow bank."

The upward social mobility of American life came through in the cases of a number of middle-aged jurors whose grown children have employments of higher prestige and earning power than their parents. An instance was a high school teacher with a son who is a major in the Army and another son who is a lawyer.

The limited employment opportunities for school teachers at present were shown by the number of people who had worked as teachers and were now in other lines of work, such as a male teacher now a clerk and a female teacher now an Avon representative.

Another reflection of the current economy was the fact that a truck driver said that, to avoid losing income, his schedule during the weeks of jury duty would be to make a round trip to Chicago with his rig every night and catch a few hours' sleep in the cab of the truck at either end.

The questioning of jurors for a driving-while-intoxicated case later in the week revealed that the great majority of the jurors had nothing against drinking and would themselves take a drink.

The two exceptions were a member of the Baha'i faith and a woman who said that she and her husband had made a commitment not to drink a number of years ago. Both were excused.

The questioning for this jury and for another case involving a traffic accident showed that almost everyone had been involved in at least one automobile accident.

This was another question that tended to reopen wounds since several jurors had lost relatives in car accidents.

It was entertaining to observe how the jurors picked up the courthouse jargon as the days went on.

People who on the first day had answered the question, "Have you ever sat on a jury?" by saying something like, "Yes, eight years ago. A car hit another car" would by the end of the two weeks respond in this vein, "Yes, Your Honor. This week. Criminal case. DWI." (DWI stands for Driving While Intoxicated).

The relationship among the jurors also changed as time went on.

Aside from the 14 jurors (12 regular and two alternates) for the Williams case, who were seen only going back and forth between their courtroom and their jury room for the entire two weeks, most of the jurors were chosen for two or three cases usually lasting one or two days.

During these cases as well as during the waiting periods, relationships sprang up. I spotted mild flirtations, deepening friendships between horticulture fanciers, exchanges of opinions between people reading the same books ("Jaws" and "Fear of Flying" were the most prevalent), worried conversations between women with small children at home, hard-nosed, quasi-legal discussions of past cases, and, sometimes, someone crossing to another bench to avoid talking to someone else.

Like everybody there, I got tired of the frequent recesses, the repetitious questioning and the hard benches. But, over all, it was a fascinating opportunity to peek into other people's lives.

July 1975

X-rated Experience

Serving on a jury can best be described as an X-rated experience—it is exasperating, exhausting and exhilarating.

After serving on two juries during my recent jury duty at Champaign County Courthouse, my main reaction is one of unlimited admiration for the conscientiousness and serious attitude with which the jurors approached their task, and a deep respect for the American judicial system.

Sure, there were lots of giddy moments, marked by jocular threats and dreadful jokes, but they were a natural way of letting off steam during the hours of concentration on what all the jurors saw as an awe-inspiring task: the reaching of a fair verdict.

Strange paradoxes developed. For instance, one of the cases involved a criminal charge of robbery, while the other was a civil case growing out of a fairly minor automobile accident.

Each case finished up shortly before midnight. In one case, the deliberations began at 11 a.m. and ended in a hung jury. In the other, deliberations began in early afternoon and resulted in a verdict.

The final decision in one case came after a lone hold-out bowed his head and folded his hands for five minutes of prayerful consideration before his last vote, while the other 11 stayed silent and motionless in their seats.

When the final vote was tallied, the hold-out bent over his Bible for several minutes, while a female juror broke into tears and was comforted by a fellow juror.

Although there were many points during the deliberations of each jury when diametrically opposed views were voiced and argued over, the second jury ended its deliberations with smiles and handshakes all around. When its members met for fresh duty the next morning at 9:30, most of them gathered together in a cohesive little knot with cries of delight at seeing one another.

The paradoxical fact was that the jury which reached its verdict with such agony of tears and prayer, was the one for the civil case, while the jury, that later reunited like old friends, was both the one unable to reach a verdict and the one dealing with the criminal charge in which a guilty verdict would send a man to jail.

Even stranger, in the civil case the major decision—whether the plaintiff was entitled to an award or not—was made affirmatively in one hour, while the thrashing-out of the size of the award took up the remaining eight hours.

The award ultimately agreed on was in the neighborhood of $11,000.

When one considers that this amount included both the loss of earnings so far and the projected loss of future earnings of an unmarried, fortyish woman with a fifth-grade education whose only possible livelihood was shown by the testimony to be physical labor, and who, the jury agreed, had indeed injured her back in the accident, the settlement certainly could not be said to bear any relationship to the stratospheric figures awarded by some juries in accident cases that one reads about.

The voting of the jury on the criminal case followed an interesting pattern.

The voting on the 10 secret ballots spread over about 10 hours followed a curve that began and ended with five guilty — seven not-guilty votes with a peak of 10 guilty — 2 not-guilty votes.

As the arguments of fellow jurors swayed one or the other, the balloting went 5 to 7, 7 to 5, 9 to 3, 10 to 2, 10 to 2, 9 to 3, 6 to 6, 5 to 7, 4 to 8, and 5 to 7.

It took deduction to figure out that the two votes for not-guilty on the 10 to 2 ballots were those of people who never changed their votes.

This was because this jury contrasted with my preconceptions that each jury member would early in the game make his or her belief known for an open discussion of the pros and cons of the case.

Instead, one of the unwavering voters for not-guilty and several of those convinced throughout of the accused's guilt never did state their conviction in the discussion, and their attitudes could only be inferred later by review of the voting.

A lot of the debate was led by those who changed their minds through the deliberations. One dynamic young man got the discussion out of many deadlocks by casting himself, as he termed it, as the devil's advocate and then, with equal forcefulness, arguing the opposite view of the evidence.

It was a surprise for most first-time jurors to find that we were unable to see a transcript of the testimony to clear up points, where the jurors remembered it differently. We were told to go on what we remembered to the best of our recollection.

Another rude surprise was to find out how hard it is to be accepted as a hung jury.

In the criminal case, the foreman sent a message to the judge at various points of the deliberations to say that the jury was hung, and about an hour before the final dismissal the jury filed into the court room in toto to report on its inability to reach a verdict.

Each of these instances were met by the admonition to keep trying.

The dynamics of jury deliberations are fascinating. On neither of the two juries did I see any sign of voting blocks developing along the lines of being the same sex or of the same background, whether blue-collar or university-affiliated.

The jurors thought independently and voted their consciences, and it was only in the course of deliberation that people began to fall into affinity groups based on their thoughts about the case.

Jury duty puts an adult into a restrictive situation reminiscent of being in high school. Whether you want to or not, you must be in a given place, either the courtroom listening to evidence or the jury room deliberating, at a given time.

While the testimony unfolds day by day, you must not read or hear about it in the news media or discuss it with anyone, even though your mind may be overflowing with thoughts about the case.

When deliberation runs into the evening, you cannot call home to tell your family so, but must ask the bailiff to do so for you.

For meals, the jurors are marched in a tight little group to a nearby restaurant under the surveillance of the bailiff and may not stop and greet an acquaintance on the way.

In the restaurant, the jury group is seated away from others. One evening a woman had through the bailiff asked her husband to bring her eye glasses. The husband was allowed to come only to the entrance of the restaurant to hand the glasses to the bailiff.

I ended up getting three free meals during the course of the two juries I was on, all at the same buffet-style restaurant. I can imagine that a jury sequestered for any real length of time might get a little tired of the food!

The aftermath of the jury duty stays with you for a long time. In common with several fellow jurors whom I have run into later, I dreamed every night for a week about the cases I had been on, holding forth in brilliantly persuasive arguments that bore no relationship to my actual halting statements in the jury room.

September 1975

Vantasy on Wheels

The time-honored American love affair with the automobile has found a new object: the humble, boxy, slab-sided delivery van.

Decorated on the outside with an infinite variety of subjects ranging from Colorado sunsets and eerie moon landscapes to ladies in various stages of undress, vans have been outfitted with richly accoutered interiors.

Their furnishings include all the comforts of home — refrigerators, television sets, arm chairs, reading lights and upholstered benches and tables.

One local van is paneled with weathered barn siding and has an elevated sleeping area in back made to look like a hayloft. Some vans are equipped with water beds, and others have jewel-box interiors of tufted velvet, paneling and stained-glass lamps.

Although some outsiders view customized vans with suspicion — "sin bins" is one of the most printable nick-names applied to vans — local van fans bristle at this attitude.

"The sexy image of vans is wrong. Vans are family rooms on wheels, an extension of yourself as personal as your clothes," said Larry Dykes of The Van Shop in Champaign.

"They are middle class people's motor homes," said Rod Moseley, whose paintings adorn the exteriors of many local vans. "I see them as a combination of the pioneers' covered wagon and a spaceship."

"Little kids love them. Vans provide a terrific opportunity for families to do things together," Mr. Dykes said.

Mr. Dykes believes that a coming trend will be to customize vans for use as traveling offices that can be converted to recreational vehicles for weekend use. He is planning such a combination for a customer who sells fire alarms.

The shop's average cost for a personalized van, fully equipped and customized inside and out, varies from $7,200 to $7,500.

"Of course, the sky's the limit if someone really wanted to go to town," Mr. Dykes said.

"I have owned and customized 10 to 15 vans for myself, and I have never done the same thing twice," said Mike Shaw, Mr. Dykes's partner in The Van Shop. "I get an idea while doing one van and try it out on the next one."

Mr. Dykes agrees. "You can reach a peak on quality, but you always can better yourself on ideas," he said.

He said that while "personal usage" vans are manufactured by the big car companies — about a third of Chevrolet's van production is customized at the factory — the big companies have a limited number of designs available.

In contrast, he said, his shop plans and executes the complete design to the customer's specifications.

Mr. Dykes's own van is a candy-apple red three-quarter ton with a 302 horsepower V-8 engine.

He decorated its exterior with a broad band of shimmery grey paint smoked with an acetylene torch into abstract patterns. The interior features black velvet, white paneling and a black-and-white shag rug.

Mr. Dykes and Mr. Shaw are president and secretary of the 6-month-old ChamBana Van Club, Ltd. which numbers among its members the owners of about 18 customized vans.

Many vans are customized by their owners. Ed Keller, who attended Urbana High School with Mr. Dykes and Mr. Moseley in the mid-1960s, caught the van bug this year and turned his one-ton 1975 stripped

Chevrolet van into a palace on wheels in a scant four weeks with the help of his wife, Vicki.

"We worked until midnight every night to get it ready for the Truck-In of the National Street Van Association in Bowling Green, Ky., in late July," Mr. Keller said.

The Kellers' efforts rated an eight on a scale of 10 in the judging of interiors at the truck-in which attracted more than 5,000 customized street vans from 49 states including Hawaii.

"If I had had time to make the cupboard doors close completely, I might have gotten a 10," Mr. Keller said ruefully.

An upholsterer at Beck's Country Shoppe who moonlights as a carpet layer, Mr. Keller outfitted his van with 3½ inches of styrofoam insulation on the walls and ceiling. After putting in 1-by-2-inch furring strips of wood, he covered the walls with inside-out wood paneling to provide a base for wallpaper and carpeting.

The floor and parts of the walls are covered with 24 yards of shag carpet in the colors of an erupting volcano which tie in with the exterior which was painted by Mr. Moseley with a primeval scene of erupting volcanoes and dinosaurs.

Large yellow flames decorate the front and other side of the van.

Dinosaurs cut out of carpeting ornament interior areas wallpapered in a luminous orange print, and Mr. Keller made a white plastic cover with a red dinosaur applique for the spare wheel.

The ceiling, doors and seats are covered with 22 yards of red velvet tufted with white buttons. The diamond-tufted ceiling alone has 380 buttons.

Mr. Keller put in two port-hole shaped windows with curved glass on the sides and a vent window in the ceiling.

He has added three benches to form a U-shaped sitting area in the back around a slate-covered table. The benches double as storage space and are equipped with red velvet pillows reversing to white plastic for practicality.

The table and back bench can be removed to make space for transportation of large items, and Mr. Keller plans a system of lowering the table top to fit between the benches to serve as a sleeping area.

The couple's son, Ed II, 6, has his own black mushroom-shaped stool.

The van is equipped with power steering and brakes, air conditioning, AM-FM radio, eight-track tape player, refrigerator and mag wheels.

The Kellers have reason to believe that van fever is catching.

"Everytime I return after having parked it somewhere, there are 20 people gathered around it waiting to ask me questions," Mr. Keller said.

Although van owners usually give their chariots fanciful names like Vantasy, Moby Van, Chiquita Vanana and Van on the Run, Mr. Keller has been too busy working on his vehicle so far to baptize it.

August 1975

Found by Fame and Fortune

You have labored long and hard in your chosen profession. One day Dame Fortune turns her smiling face towards you and bestows on you some of her gifts—fame or money or both. What happens next?

Judging from the experiences of a handful of local people, the fruits of fame can be bitter or sweet.

For Carolyn Haddad, the author, and Frank Gallo, the sculptor, the responses to their initial breakthroughs generally were on the negative side.

"It was a big jolt, not a good experience at all," Mrs. Haddad said. "At the beginning people are very nice. Then when they realize you are going to continue being successful they become very nasty.

"You become the target of a lot of nasty comments and get many calls from people who just have to tell you what so-and-so said about you. You find the friends you had before have disappeared. Almost all the friends I have now are new ones."

Professor Gallo said, "The response I noticed most was that people were hostile to me. You seem to lose friends or people you thought were friends. People seem separated from you. Maybe it is that people don't think you deserve it—that you are not that good."

For others such as Judy Eckert, the author, becoming suddenly well-known was a warm and rewarding experience.

"The greatest reward of all has come from readers who have taken the time to write about how they have applied the contents of my book to their own lives," Mrs. Eckert said.

"Another great reward for publishing on a nationwide scale has been the opportunity to meet and share ideas with professionals in my field and interviewers in the media. Instant feedback certainly recharges an isolated author's batteries."

The third most gratifying facet has been talking to "lots of people who saw me on TV or read the local articles and called and wanted the formula for writing a book," she said. "Of course, there is no formula," she added.

For others such as John Bardeen, professor emeritus of physics and the only person to win two Nobel prizes in the same field, and Dee Brown, agricultural librarian emeritus at the University of Illinois and author of "Bury My Heart at Wounded Knee," honor and fame made no great difference.

"I can't say it made an enormous difference," said Professor Bardeen.

"I get a lot more mail, something I'm not too fond of answering, and many more invitations to give talks and participate in conferences. But my work has gone on about the same as before, and on the local level it has made little difference."

Dee Brown said, "I don't think I have noticed anything different. I don't consider myself that well-known. I did get lots of mail (after the appearance of 'Bury My Heart at Wounded Knee') and it took a lot of time to answer it. A lot of people call you up for information so it does intrude on your privacy a little bit.

"But that's about it. It didn't make any difference to my close friends."

Mr. Brown's new book, "Hear That Lonesome Whistle Blow: Railroads in the West," was published this week.

Kenneth Appel and Wolfgang Haken, the two University of Illinois mathematics professors whose proof of the century-old, Four-Color Theorem made headlines around the world last July, have reacted in different ways to their fame.

"I have found the whole thing sort of unnerving," Professor Appel said. "It's the sort of thing that makes your parents happy but I have not enjoyed it particularly.

"When one meets new people they treat you differently than before, not as oneself, and I do not enjoy that. Locally I've received warm comments from my friends, but I have found that neither added or detracted from my feeling."

Among the tangible results, Professor Appel said he has received between 200 and 300 requests for reprints of the paper, been invited to give about 10 colloquiums, and has been recommended by his department for a full professorship.

Professor Haken, on the other hand, said he has found the world-wide response "certainly very nice."

"At age 48 one doesn't expect to have that many new things happen to you. It has been an exciting change but on the other hand I am happy the peaktime is over," he said.

"I gave 17 colloquium talks during the fall semester, most involving traveling. Every time the audience seemed entirely different, and I found the response and reaction very interesting and enjoyable."

He and Professor Appel received a lot of correspondence after the announcement of the proof and many requests for articles, all but two of which they turned down.

With all the time required to talk to science writers from journals and magazines mainly in Japan, Western Europe and the United States, Professor Haken said he had not had enough time to get his own work done.

"It doesn't bother me for one year but I am very glad to be back to normal," he said.

A prolific writer, Mrs. Haddad is now working on her eighth novel. Her first, "The Moroccan," was published in the fall of 1975 and will come out in paperback this December. The book has been translated into Dutch, and a movie company has picked up an option to film it.

Her second book, "Bloody September," has already been published, and her third, "Operation Apricot," is scheduled for publication.

She said about the reaction to the publication of "The Moroccan," "It was a shock and a surprise to me that the book was successful. I never wanted the attendant glamor. The many snide comments I got were very painful to me. I have adjusted now — you have to, otherwise it can destroy you. I finally said to myself, 'To hell with them.' It still comes as a surprise to me when someone makes a nice comment."

Frank Gallo said he first noticed a reaction to his emerging fame after he was chosen to be one of 12 American artists representing the United States at the Venice Biennale in 1968.

He sent some of his life-size epoxy-resin sculptures of human figures which stood out against the prevailing trend to abstract art at the time, he said.

"In art terms it was like getting the Nobel Peace Prize," he said.

He said the hostile response of many people he knew surprised him.

"I was so dumb I went around telling everyone. I didn't get the response I wanted, and I finally realized that no one was going to stroke me. I'm so greedy, I not only want the recognition, I also want people to love me," he said with a laugh.

"Around the community, among people who were not competing with me, the response was very nice. The banks in particular were much more friendly about giving me loans for the very expensive supplies I use," he said.

The warmth of the community response increased as he made the sculpture of Raquel Welch used as a Time magazine cover and portrayed Barbi Benton, the actress-girlfriend of Playboy publisher Hugh Hefner, he said.

Published last November, Judy Eckert's book, "The Joy Around You," has sold in the neighborhood of 100,000 copies as an original Dell paperback.

To publicize the book, Mrs. Eckert made four television appearances, appeared on many radio talk shows, and was interviewed by newspapers in Bloomington and St. Louis as well as by the two Champaign-Urbana daily newspapers.

The response to this was an interesting phenomenon, she said.

"People recognized me at the supermarket, at restaurants and the post office and would say things like, 'Oh, you're the one who wrote the book,'" she said.

This recognition, together with the letters from readers and the calls from people wanting advice, "gave me a perspective on what people living with real fame, like Alex Haley and Gail Sheehy, have to deal with," she said.

She said she occasionally has run into jealousy "from other writers who feel diminished by another person's success. But most people just are happy for you."

Now working on a book about "the joys of motherhood," she has received (and refused) many requests to give talks and has been contacted by companies wanting her to work for them "on everything from greeting cards to coloring books," she said.

Professor Bardeen received the Nobel Prize for physics in 1956 and 1972.

Other than the increased correspondence, he said he has found the only drawback to his fame to have been its occasional interference with the kind of lectures he would like to give and the talks with other scientists he would like to have.

Since his retirement from the university in March 1976 he has been able to accept many more speaking invitations than before, he said. He recently visited India and Japan.

"I found on this trip, as I have found on others, that my being a celebrity, so to speak, didn't give me as many opportunities to talk to individual scientists as I had hoped to," he said.

"Also in some cases where I had wanted to talk about recent developments in what I'm working on, I would have to gear my talks at a lower level because many students and younger faculty not in the field would attend.

"And sometimes the press of time and engagements would leave me less time to talk physics than I'd like to have. But this is only true of trips abroad, not in this country.

"In general, my work goes on just about the same. I don't feel any different here than anybody else."

Where Do I Know You From?

Have you ever found yourself greeting a familiar-looking person in the supermarket with a big smile, only to realize in the next aisle that it was someone you knew only from television commercials?

As more and more commercials for local companies are being produced in Champaign-Urbana, this kind of experience has become more common.

"I get the sensation that a lot of people look at me when I get on a bus. They seem to have the feeling they know me but they can't recall from where," said Edward F. Douglass, whose bearded visage may be familiar to many from his appearances in television commercials for Arby's Roast Beef Restaurants and Carter's Moving and Storage produced by Penta Corporation.

"A lot of people I meet around town apparently think it was me in the commercial but are not sure enough in their own minds to come up to me and ask. People with close ties to me either through work or social life usually will comment on the commercials, many with amusement and some even with admiration," he said.

Mr. Douglass is assistant manager of radio station WILL and a lecturer in radio and television in the College of Communications at the University of Illinois.

"Some people have asked me if it is appropriate for me to appear in commercials, and I have had some japes implying I'm selling my soul to the Devil, but I don't know whether these were in jest or serious. It has occurred to me that some of the ambivalent comments may have sprung from envy," he said.

Annilee Shaul of Champaign is used to having a stranger look at her and say, "You look familiar," and then having another stranger volunteer, "Of course, she is the Eisner lady."

The blonde housewife who resembles the movie star Cybill Shepherd made a series of commercials for Eisner Food Stores three years ago. The commercials were produced by television station WCIA, Channel 3, and were shown frequently both locally and in Decatur, Bloomington and Indianapolis for several years.

"The nicest part about the commercials was to have out-of-town friends and relatives recognize me," Mrs. Shaul said. "For instance, once at Homecoming an old friend from Indianapolis called me up, and a friend in Bloomington wrote me after seeing me on TV."

Mrs. Shaul still is recognized by young people who appeared on a show for children, "The Popeye Show," which she conducted on Channel 3 10 years ago, she said.

James Hurt, professor of English at the University of Illinois, has made 55 commercials for Rantoul Motors during the last three years.

Although he is disguised in the commercials in a loud, checked coat, a polkadot bow tie and a wig with the hair standing straight up, he is universally recognized as Cousin Buddy, his television character, wherever he goes, he said.

"The strangest thing that happened to me was once when I had just arrived at the airport in Paris and was waiting for my bags, and someone came up and said, 'There's Cousin Buddy,' " he said.

"It turned out to be someone from here who had been on the same plane. But for a second I thought, 'How depressing to think that Cousin Buddy followed me to Europe!' "

Professor Hurt, who also has made television commercials for Illinois Power Co., filmed three of the Cousin Buddy commercials during a sabbatical stay in London, using Big Ben, Westminster Abbey and the Tower of London as backgrounds for the clown's antics.

He also plays string bass in a dance band on Saturday nights.

"Lots of places we play, particularly in Rantoul, we get requests for me to do a Cousin Buddy commercial. So I get up in front of the band and do the patter," he said.

He said that although his children have mixed feelings about being known as Cousin Buddy's children at school, he has never received any derogatory comments about his starring in the commercials.

"The only people who mention it all joke about it," he said.

May 1977

The Best Party in the World

The best kind of party in Champaign, Illinois, the United States, the western hemisphere, the world and even the universe is a slumber party.

This was the consensus of five little girls who participated in a birthday slumber party.

Slumbering, needless to say, receives lowest priority on the agenda at these parties which have become almost a childhood tradition. The girls did just about everything else but slumber until they fell asleep around 3 a.m.

Behavior spanned from mirroring adults at the beginning and end of the party to the wildest gaiety.

The four 10 and 11-year-old guests arrived almost simultaneously about 10 minutes ahead of the 6:30 p.m. starting time and settled down demurely in a circle around the living room coffee table.

With backs straight and knees pressed together, looking like their mothers at a P.T.A. meeting, they exclaimed politely over each gift as it was unwrapped.

This contrasted with previous birthday parties when uninhibited exclamations about a certain gift being "yicky" might have been heard.

Called to dinner, they filed into the kitchen and daintily spit their chewing gum into the wastebasket before going to the table.

It is safe to say that many hostesses would be ecstatic if their adult dinner parties generated the wild laughter and lively repartee this group did while wolfing down two pizzas, a considerable amount of potato chips and a modest number of fresh carrot and green pepper sticks.

Even before the ice cream and meringues made their appearance, the girls started Indian-wrestling while fastidiously keeping their elbows out of the left-over pizza crust.

After the meal, five pizza-filled stomachs were given a hearty bouncing on the dining room floor in a game called Indian Circle.

The unwise assertion of one girl that "I am not ticklish" set off a successful joint effort on behalf of the other four to disprove the statement.

Still giggling, they tumbled upstairs like puppies to the birthday girl's room where a tennis ball was used in noisy games of hide-the-ball and keep-away.

This quickly gave way to a contest of who could kick the highest during which one contestant whammed her knee into her nose.

The resulting nosebleed was stilled by the resident mother — the man of the house having seen great advantage in leaving one day early for an out-of-town meeting.

While the nose-bleeder recuperated and the other four did their best to rearrange every item in the birthday girl's room, jelly beans and small foil-wrapped chocolates were hidden in the rooms on the main floor.

Equipped with brown lunch bags for the booty, the girls assembled in a quivering mass at the entrance to the living room.

At the word "Go," they turned into a blur of shapes, stripping the room of candies with the efficiency of five small vacuum cleaners.

Bags in hand, they swept on down to the basement playroom, while one methodic soul lingered behind and made a final, futile check of the premises.

Once in the playroom, they unrolled their sleeping bags and changed into night clothes, raising false hopes in the mother since the actual sack-out time came some five hours later.

In a quest for new scenery, the party moved upstairs to the second floor again. The sound of weeping, followed by a rollicking chorus of "Happy Birthday," turned out on inspection to signify another attempt at high-kicking, this time resulting in a bruise near the birthday girl's eye.

"They tried to cheer me up by singing 'Happy Birthday'," she explained between sobs as therapeutic kisses were applied by mother.

By 10:30 p.m., the party settled down in the playroom for the rest of the evening.

While devouring immense quantities of soft drinks and candies, the girls gave each other back rubs and styled each others' hair with combs and brushes.

Meanwhile two of the girls telephoned absent friends. "Don't worry, she never goes to bed until 11," one said.

Having transformed each other with new hair-styles, they decided their faces also needed redoing, and eye shadow, mascara and lipstick were raided from a bathroom.

The results were displayed to the mother.

"Look, I'm a movie star, va-va-va-voom," said one while parading around.

A period of playing "Twister," "Trouble" and a hockey game was interrupted by free-for-all pillow fights and tickling bouts.

At midnight, the mother went to bed after telling the girls to follow her example. Therefore, the events of the last three hours of the party must be narrated by the birthday girl.

"We played with Barbie dolls and finished up the candy and drank a lot of water," she said the next day.

"Then we got into our sleeping bags and turned out most of the lights. We had little discussions about all sorts of things, like people we know and TV shows and books.

"Nobody fought with nobody—not ever.

"One funny thing was that although I'd asked everyone to bring their favorite records, we never listened to them or turned on the TV. I guess we were just too busy having fun."

The next morning, after being awakened at 7:30, they staggered up from the basement, looking like middle-aged conventioneers after a particularly raucous convention.

After orange juice and cereal, they collected their sleeping bags and piled into the car to be taken home and, for two of them, to take part in a 9 a.m. softball game.

The party was over, and the house suddenly seemed uncannily quiet.

May 1975

Long-Distance Marriage

In this four-part series on work separation, 17 couples are featured. Listed in alphabetical order, the couples are:

A. Owen Aldridge and Adriana Garcia di Aldridge. Mr. Aldridge is professor of comparative literature at the University of Illinois. Mrs. Garcia di Aldridge is assistant professor of Puerto Rican studies at City College of the City University of New York. Their work separation is now in its seventh year. The couple has no children.

Robert M. Atkinson II and his wife, Melba. The Atkinsons maintained a work separation for three years ending in August 1974 while he obtained master's and doctor's degrees in industrial administration at Carnegie-Mellon University in Pittsburgh. During this time Mrs. Atkinson was director of financial aid and placement at Forest Park Community College in Missouri. The couple's children were 8 years old and 8 months old at the start of the work separation.

King W. and Sandra Broadrick-Allen. Mr. Broadrick-Allen is professor at the University of Illinois and director of the honors program. For the first 18 months after the couple's marriage in July 1975 Mrs. Broadrick-Allen served as acting president of Garland Junior College in Boston while Mr. Broadrick-Allen continued his duties at the University of Illinois. Mr. Broadrick-Allen has grown children from a previous marriage.

Paul and Marilynne Davis. For the last four years Mrs. Davis has held successive administrative positions in three Chicago suburbs. She is currently village manager of the Village of Richton Park. During this time Mr. Davis has continued to work in his position as news director and co-anchorman at television station WCIA, Channel 3. The couple's three children are between the ages of 13 and 16. The children lived with Mr. Davis until last September and now live with Mrs. Davis.

Paul and Susan Drake. Mr. Drake is associate professor of history at the University of Illinois and director of the center for Latin American and Caribbean studies. Mrs. Drake graduated from the University of Illinois law school in 1978 and has since January 1979 held a position with a public interest law firm in Washington, D.C. The first three months of 1979 Mr. Drake carried out a research project in South America. Since last April he has worked in Washington. He now lives in the couple's Champaign home while Mrs. Drake continues to live in Washington. The couple's two children will remain with Mrs. Drake in Washington.

Robert and Judith Drescher. Mrs. Drescher is director of Champaign Public Library and Information Center. Mr. Drescher is assistant director of the Illinois Valley Library System in Pekin. Their work separation has lasted 18 months so far. The couple has no children.

Gary and Mary Fritz. Mrs. Fritz has been coordinator of the multi-cultural program at Martin Luther King School in Urbana since 1973. During the six years that she has held the job Mr. Fritz has lived in other towns, first working as director of teacher education at Blackburn College in Carlinville and then for the Illinois Office of Education. After this he received a Fulbright senior fellowship to Mexico. He now serves the United Methodist Church in Pawnee as minister. The couple has six children, three of whom were in college when the work separation began. The three younger children have lived in various groupings with each of the two parents. At present one child lives with each and the third lives on the University of Illinois campus.

Ted and Jan Gill. Mrs. Gill is an accountant at the University of Illinois and lives with her parents in Urbana. Mr. Gill is a landscape architect who works in St. Charles, Mo. The work separation has lasted 18 months so far. The couple has no children.

Paul and Marcella Grendler. Mrs. Grendler has lived in Champaign for 2½ years. A renaissance historian, she is in the last year of a three-year project of preparing a catalogue and guide to a collection of Italian research materials in the Rare Book Room in the University of Illinois library. Mr. Grendler is on leave as professor of history at University of Toronto and lives with his wife and children in Champaign while on an appointment to the University of Illinois Center for Advanced Study. The first year Mrs. Grendler was here Mr. Grendler lived with the children, now aged 11 and 14, in Toronto. The following year the younger child lived with Mrs. Grendler in Champaign and the older accompanied Mr. Grendler on a research project in Italy for the year. Next August Mr. Grendler returns to Toronto and Mrs. Grendler may stay in Champaign to attend library school.

Carl and Genevieve Hass. Since 1977 the couple has lived together in Kankakee. During the previous five-year period Mrs. Hass continued in her position as a teacher of ninth-grade English and drama at Urbana Junior High School while Mr. Hass lived and worked in Kankakee where he is chairman of the social science department at Kankakee Community College. The couple's three sons were old enough to have moved away from the family home during the work separation.

James R. and Phyllis Tilton Hurt. Mr. Hurt is professor of English at the University of Illinois. Mrs. Hurt taught at Bowling Green University in Ohio during the 1978-79 academic year and has since September been director of the Michigan State Opera Theatre at Michigan State University in East Lansing. Of the couple's three children one is away at college, and the two younger ones, aged 14 and 18, live with Mr. Hurt in Champaign.

Gary and Susan Kelley. The Kelleys are both biologists. He is assistant professor of biology at Utah State University in Logan, Utah. She is chairman of the life science division at Parkland College. They have lived in different cities ever since their marriage 6½ years ago. Mrs. Kelley lived in southern California for five years before starting her position at Parkland last August, while Mr. Kelley lived in Utah. The couple has no children.

Frederick K. and Susan A. Lamb. The Lambs are both physicists. He is professor of physics at the University of Illinois; she is a visiting assistant professor of physics at University of Missouri, St. Louis. Their work separation has lasted 18 months so far. The couple has no children.

David and Jeanine Lindstrom. Mr. Lindstrom is executive director of the University YMCA in Champaign. Mrs. Lindstrom is coordinator of women's studies and assistant director of liberal and professional studies at Stephens College in Columbia, Mo. The work separation has so far lasted three years. The couple has three children of which the youngest, age 11, lives with Mrs. Lindstrom and the two older, aged 13 and 14, live with Mr. Lindstrom.

Christopher Martin and Ellen Everett-Martin. Mr. Martin is producer of the 6 o'clock news at television station WCIA, Channel 3. Mrs. Everett-Martin works as a teacher at Lincoln Park Cooperative Nursery School in Chicago. The work separation began in August, and Mr. Martin expects it to continue for a while. The couple's 4-year-old son lives with Mrs. Everett-Martin.

Vojtech and Kitty Mastny. Mr. Mastny is professor of history at the University of Illinois and spends Monday through Thursday of each week during the academic year on the campus. Mrs. Mastny is manager of development for a private non-profit organization, the International Management and Development Institute, in Washington, D.C. She has held this job for 18 months. During the first year of this period Mr. Mastny was on leave from the university and lived in Bethesda, Md., in the family's permanent home. He commutes weekly from Bethesda to the University of Illinois. The couple's three children live in the Bethesda home.

Robert and Diane McColley. Mr. McColley is professor of history at the University of Illinois. Since early September Mrs. McColley has taught renaissance English literature as an assistant professor at Rutgers University in Camden, N.J. The couple has six children of whom one is away at college and the other five, aged 8 through 19, live with Mr. McColley in the family's Urbana home. Mrs. McColley's position is on the tenure-track and the couple expects the work separation to be of long duration.

He's Here; She's There

Summaries of three local married couples' life-styles:

She teaches in New Jersey, he is a professor at the University of Illinois and runs the household for five of their six children.

She is the village manager of a Chicago suburb, he is the news director of television station WCIA, Channel 3.

She is the director of Champaign Public Library, he helps direct the regional state library system in Pekin.

They are part of a relatively new phenomenon—married couples separated geographically by their work.

Call it long-distance marriage, two-city marital living, commuter marriage or work separation, this phenomenon involves a life-style in which married couples live in different cities on a long-term basis in order to pursue their careers.

Contrarily to what some skeptics might surmise, it involves married couples with strong, enduring marriages and no thoughts of divorce.

Work separations have become a stronger trend as the job market, particularly for academics, has grown tighter, more women have obtained advanced academic degrees and the number of two-career families has increased.

Although the trend has grown steadily—in 1974 this reporter after months of inquiry was aware of five couples in Champaign-Urbana who were or had been work-separated as compared to 26 now—it will not be charted in the 1980 census.

The census will have no provisions to ascertain the number of married couples who live in different cities, according to Dorothy Whitson of the U.S. Census Bureau promotion office, Sweetland, Md.

For the 17 couples featured in this article, the length of their work separation ranges from more than six years to about five months.

At least one member of each of the 17 couples was interviewed. One member of each couple (except one couple, the Atkinsons) is or was based in Champaign-Urbana during the work separation.

For four of the couples the work separations are now concluded although for one of the couples it may begin again next fall. In the remaining 13 cases the work separations are going on now.

At least nine additional couples in Champaign-Urbana maintain current work separations but either were not reachable for interviews or did not wish to be featured in the article.

Nine couples who have chosen work separations for a period of less than one year (mostly for academic sabbaticals) will be featured in the third article of this series.

The decision to give up all the benefits of living on a day-to-day basis with their marriage partner—and, in many cases, with their children— and to accept the rigors of loneliness and commuting and the expense of maintaining two households was not an easy one for any of the 17 couples featured in this article.

But, in each case, the need for each partner to fulfill himself or herself through their careers overrode other considerations.

The assessment of how the arrangement works out varies from "absolutely superbly" (A. Owen Aldridge) to "terribly difficult" (Jan Gill).

Mr. Aldridge described his marital work separation, now in its seventh year, as "a beautiful arrangement."

"I feel I have the best of both worlds," he said. "My wife has an apartment in Greenwich Village, and I have a house here. We spend the summers here together and I commute to New York on weekends about twice a month.

"The expense of commuting is great but I consider it cheap in relationship to the advantages, both intellectual and personal, that I get from it."

Judith Drescher, Mary Fritz, Susan Kelley and David Lindstrom also view their work separations in very positive terms.

"For us it works out fine," Mrs. Drescher said. "We are both very busy and very involved in our careers. This arrangement gives us both time to work very hard during the week and take some time off over the weekend."

The Dreschers own a house in Champaign and Mr. Drescher rents a small apartment in Peoria — a typical arrangement for work-separated couples. They commute to be together every weekend and, occasionally, during the week as well for social engagements.

They are one of six of the 17 couples for whom the need for a work separation was accentuated by the fact that the couples work in the same field or closely related fields, making employment harder to obtain either because of unavailability of jobs or nepotism rules.

One advantage of being in the same field is that the couples often can meet at professional conferences and workshops. Mrs. Drescher, Mrs. Kelley and King W. Broadrick-Allen, among others, all mentioned this opportunity to meet at professional meetings as a facet of their work separations which made the arrangement easier.

Mrs. Fritz sees one of the great advantages of her commuter marriage as the fact that her maintaining a home in Champaign-Urbana has created a base for the family's children while they attend the University of Illinois.

In addition to her job as coordinator of the multi-cultural program at the King School — a program she designed and wrote the proposal for — she is pursuing a doctorate in education at the University of Illinois, "more for recreation than for anything else," she said.

She views her work separation in wholly positive terms with the sole exception of "the huge telephone bills."

"As a working mother who goes to school, I think I would keep busy every minute of the week if we all lived together," she said. "This way, when I go home to Pawnee to my husband every weekend, I am a 100 percent mother and wife for 48 hours and do not touch my work. The funny thing is when I am in Pawnee I talk about Champaign-Urbana as 'home' and vice-versa."

The Kelleys' work separation began immediately after their marriage 6½ year ago.

"When I got married, I had a traditional marriage in mind and the thought of living apart never even crossed my mind," Mrs. Kelley said. "But we were unable to locate jobs in the same city. This kind of arrangement is not for everybody but it has worked very well for us.

"We share the commuting, usually adding a vacation day to a weekend, and see each other every five or six weeks. When we are together it's like a honeymoon all over again."

Each of the Lindstroms travels to see the other every month, so that the family is united every other week, and they talk on the phone several times a week.

"We have found during the last three years (of work separation) that our relationship has changed, in many aspects for the better," Mr. Lindstrom said.

"We find when we are together that the quality of the relationship has been enhanced to a great extent. We have stopped playing many of the games we played when we were living together. It is a separation of kind but there are still all the commitments that were there before, particularly all the relational commitments," he said.

"I have a certain awareness that our relationship would not have endured without this arrangement. With both of us being professionals, we each need to pursue our careers. If I had stayed in Columbia, I would have had bitternesses about being forced to move, and if Jeanine had come here, she would have felt the same way. Instead, being in a commuter situation has affected our relationship for the better."

He stressed that he sees the negative aspect of the work separation as being its cost in phone bills and commuting expenses.

The majority of the 17 couples view their work separations with mixed-to-positive feelings. Their attitude is perhaps best crystallized in Paul Davis's statement, "It's second best—it's not ideal."

Mr. Davis said about his four-year work separation, "It's better than separating and not as good as living together, primarily because of the children. You don't do it unless you have to.

"It has some very nice benefits. I have an interesting wife and I have a lot of friends who don't have interesting wives. Neither of us is dependent on each other for the wrong reasons. We stay married because of emotional ties to each other and not because of our functional relationships."

Mr. Davis commutes weekly to be with his wife and three children. Until last September the children lived with him, and Mrs. Davis commuted here once a week.

"The most fascinating thing to me," Mr. Davis said, "is that no one sees anything wrong with me living here and going home weekends but people were highly critical of my wife when she did the same thing."

He cited the cost of dual housing, gasoline for commuting and phone calls as the major problems of a work separation.

"One good thing is that it does give you some time to be alone, which is valuable, but the cost is a bit high when you are alone four nights a week," he said.

"But all in all, it's definitely second-best."

Sandra Broadrick-Allen said about her now-concluded work separation of 18 months, which came immediately after her and her husband's marriage in 1975, "We managed but neither of us was too fond of it."

She said, "We did the best we could. I wouldn't say it was satisfactory but, on the other hand, it was not a great trauma.

"We were each involved in our work and gave each other a lot of professional advice. We had continuing communication — but life was much better when we were able to be together.

"I think we were lucky in that we had never lived together before. I think it would be a lot harder after you had established patterns of living together."

Mrs. Broadrick-Allen said she took some teasing from the students at Garland Junior College, a women's college, of which she was acting president.

"They would say, 'Dean Allen, you've got it in reverse. The common trend is to live with the man and not be married — not to be married and live apart from him!' " she said.

Some of the couples look upon their work separations with emotions varying from resigned acceptance to outright despair.

"It's a very hard career decision to make," Christopher Martin said. "The distancing is wearying. It is difficult — particularly not seeing your child on a daily basis. You recognize the growth of your child in two-week increments rather than in daily increments."

Marcella Grendler said, "I wouldn't want to use too many jolly positive words about it. It's a well-known middle-class truth that being a single parent isn't much fun for anyone.

"The first year I almost didn't exist as a domestic person. When you are used to cooking for four, making a bologna sandwich for yourself is a switch. I missed the nest-making that goes into caring for three other persons," she said.

Genevieve Hass said she and her husband never liked their work separation too well although it lasted five years.

"I missed the chit-chat in the evening, the reviewing of the day's events," she said.

"Our social life became a limbo situation. I felt it was very hard for us to have a social life on weekends when my husband was gone so much and didn't make social contact with people in Champaign-Urbana during the week.

"During the week I found I was very much alone in the evenings. I never developed the knack single women have of building up a social life alone.

"From a financial point of view it was a good thing that we lived apart, but I wouldn't like it as a continuing life-style."

Many of the longtime married couples credited the length of their marriages with providing a base of shared memories and profound stability that makes the work separations workable. Concomitantly, they voiced concern for young, recently wed couples attempting work separations.

Not surprisingly, the strongest comments against work separations as a life-style come from members of two young couples, Jan Gill and Susan Lamb.

Mrs. Gill described her 18-month work separation (out of two years of marriage) as "terribly difficult."

She said, "It's bad enough not being together but the driving on weekends is also terribly boring."

The Gills drive to see each other every weekend.

"The work separation is a lot harder for my husband because he is living alone and I'm living with my parents and do have people around me," Mrs. Gill said.

Mr. Gill has been looking for work in the Champaign-Urbana area ever since their marriage, she said.

"I would never do it this way again. I would either postpone getting married or have the job situation all straightened out beforehand," she said.

Frederick and Susan Lamb's work separation has lasted 18 months so far.

"I do not consider it permanent because it is such a wasteful and painful way to live," Mrs. Lamb said.

"My attitude is that it is a necessary evil at present. The real evil is in society, a society that would like people to have stable families and yet does everything to discourage them," she said.

The Lambs had been married seven years when their work separation began. They commute to see each other every other weekend.

"It's a terrible strain to have two bases, moving back and forth between them. Many people I know who are doing this, particularly on the two coasts, say it makes them feel schizophrenic," Mrs. Lamb said.

"The tax situation is very penalizing. You are taxed as a couple but your expenses are those of two single people with the cost of commuting added."

The effect of the work separation on their children was a major consideration for the 10 of the 17 couples who have children under 18 or, in the cases now concluded, had children under 18 at the time of the work separation.

Five of the couples have no children. Mr. Broadrick-Allen's children from a previous marriage and the Hasses' children all were grown by the time of the work separations.

Mr. Lindstrom said, "We have found that as long as my wife and I are comfortable in our relationship, that transmits itself to the children. They tend to see our relationship as the norm and others as unusual."

"Our children have done very well," Paul Davis said. "We have always raised them to be self-sufficient. They are good starters and good finishers and get high grades in school."

Robert McColley, who lives in Urbana with five of the family's six children while Mrs. McColley teaches in Camden, N.J., said emphatically, "I see absolutely no evidence that the children are behaving differently than before Diane left."

His children now pitch in more with household duties, he said.

"Kids can become much more self-reliant than most American kids today are permitted to be," he said.

Most of the couples have found the reactions from relatives, friends and acquaintances to be interested and non-judgmental.

"Generally speaking, the men are not particularly interested but the women are very curious about how it's working out and take a very upbeat approach," Mr. McColley said.

"We have never been exposed to any innuendoes," Mr. Aldridge said.

Others, however, have been at the receiving end of negative remarks.

Mrs. Fritz said, "Sometimes people accuse our daughters of having divorced or separated parents."

Mrs. Lamb related, "I got a Christmas card from a friend which said, 'The marriage of everyone I know who has done this is on the rocks.'"

"In a lot of the feedback we get from other people there is an underlying suspicion that something has to be wrong," Mr. Lindstrom said.

Phyllis Tilton Hurt, Mrs. Drescher and Mrs. Kelley all voiced their opinion that a work-separated person often tends to be a better bargain for his or her employer than other employees.

"I have plenty of time to devote to my job because I don't have to go home and cook dinner," Mrs. Drescher said. "I see it as an asset to employers—during the week it is all work."

Considering the growth in the trend locally and nationally (almost all the couples interviewed knew of couples in other cities who are work-separated), it seems safe to predict that the 17 couples have chosen a life-style that will become increasingly prevalent in the future—if the energy crisis does not worsen.

"I think the energy crisis will not allow it to continue much longer. Airfares and gasoline for car trips have gone up a lot in the 1½ years we have been commuting," Mrs. Lamb said.

But the interest in and need for work separations is intense.

"I have a lot of women ask me how it works out for me," Mrs. Drescher said. "I translate that into that they would like to do the same thing. I run a lot of mini-workshops in corners!"

A Sense of Calling

A profound commitment to their professional callings keeps Diane and Robert McColley 700 miles apart geographically.

But an equally strong commitment to each other and their six children, nurtured by 21 years of marriage, keeps their relationship healthy and strong in spite of their geographical separation.

The McColleys' work separation began last September when Mrs. McColley started a tenure-track job at Rutgers University in Camden, N.J., as an assistant professor teaching renaissance English literature.

She was chosen for the job from a field of 136 applicants.

Meanwhile Mr. McColley, a professor of history at the University of Illinois, runs the family home in Urbana for five of their children, aged 8 to 19.

Mrs. McColley earned her Ph.D. in renaissance English literature from the University of Illinois in 1974 when her youngest child, Robert, was 3 years old. Since then she has hunted without success within driving distance from her home for a tenure-track job in her field.

When the Rutgers job came up, she and her husband thoroughly discussed the advantages and disadvantages of accepting the position. They decided the professional opportunity was too good for her to pass up.

The decision was made easier by the fact that Mr. McColley always had done a large share of the household duties.

"When we were first married, Robert was a graduate student and I taught high school. His time was more flexible so he made breakfast and did the vacuuming," Mrs. McColley said.

"When the babies came, he continued to help a lot. Later, when I went to graduate school, I don't think I would have been able to complete my studies if Robert hadn't done at least half of the housework."

Now that Mrs. McColley lives in a small apartment in Camden, near Philadelphia, Mr. McColley still is in charge of most of the household chores, including the laundry and breakfast.

He is aided by three of the couple's daughters, Teresa, 15, and the 13-year-old twins, Carolyn and Margaret. Teresa cooks supper, Carolyn does some of the food shopping and Margaret helps her father with the cleaning. The twins also are in charge of the dishes.

The oldest child, Becky, 19, is working her way through the University of Illinois and lives at home. She and young Robert also pitch in with the household duties.

The sixth child, Susanna, 18, is a student in the honors pre-medical program at Northwestern University, as well as a philosophy major.

"I think we maintain minimum standards of sanitation but it just isn't very elegant," said Mr. McColley, whose conversation often is marked by a dry, understated wit.

"I am very proud of my family for the way they work together," Mrs. McColley said. "They are getting along fine which is bad for my ego but good for my conscience.

"I don't feel nearly the anxiety for them that I thought I would."

She was interviewed during one of her monthly visits to the Urbana home.

The McColley children's initial reactions to their parents' work separation ranged, Mr. McColley said, "from 'Go get them, Mom!' from the oldest to a certain amount of skepticism from the youngest."

The older children continue to be very positive and young Robert's skepticism has abated as he and his father have drawn closer together in the pursuit of manly activities such as painting and carpentry work, Mr. McColley said.

He described the children as "bright, ambitious kids with large extracurricular commitments including church work."

The McColleys are active in Emmanuel Memorial Episcopal Church, where both parents and four of the children sing in the choir.

"I see absolutely no evidence that the children are behaving differently than before Diane left," Mr. McColley said.

In addition to monthly visits and long holiday vacations, Mrs. McColley will spend summers here doing research in the famous John Milton collection at the University of Illinois library.

She wrote her doctoral thesis on the 17th Century poet's "Paradise Lost" and has just finished a book manuscript entitled "Milton's Eve."

She said that by living apart from her family to pursue what she describes as her "sense of calling," she sees herself acting out the thesis she set forth in her dissertation and book.

"There is a striking parallel between the work I am doing and the life I am living," she said.

"Milton's 'Paradise Lost' is the first and perhaps the only representation of the Book of Genesis that shows Adam and Eve obeying the commandment to dress and keep the garden which stands for callings of many kinds.

"The question I have been working on is whether Eve ought to have left Adam for a short while to do some work of her own. Or, in other words, whether woman as well as man was created, in Milton's words, 'sufficient to have stood, though free to fall.'

"I think that Milton does show her sufficient and gives to her his own argument for liberty and responsibility. I didn't imagine when I began, though, that this pattern in Milton would touch so closely on my own life."

Mr. McColley views the work separation as being harder on his wife than on him.

"I have seen her off and on since 1958 and will continue to see her in the future," he said.

"It's a harder decision for her to give up the day-to-day life with the children who will grow up and be gone after a while."

Mrs. McColley said, "I am terribly lonely, of course. I have never lived alone before in my life except for one semester as an undergraduate when I had a room at International House in Berkeley.

"During my first weekend in Camden, I laid down and cried. I couldn't believe I had actually separated myself from my family. It was shocking to me."

But, as she became involved with her work and found the family managing well, both on her visits and through frequent phone calls, she came to terms with the move.

"I love my work and I love my family. Now I have the best of both worlds," she said.

"A job means more than money and status. I think there is a deep need in the modern world for the kind of coherent view of life that renaissance literature offers and therefore I feel I have the opportunity to participate in truly important work.

"My husband shares this sense of calling and has encouraged me to follow it."

Mr. McColley specializes in American history, particularly the Jefferson era and the early history of slavery.

The family has made its home in Champaign-Urbana for 19½ years.

Mrs. McColley has taught almost every semester while working towards her doctorate and during the five years following. She has taught, among others, at Milliken University in Decatur, Wesleyan University in Bloomington, Parkland College, University High School and, mainly, the University of Illinois.

One of the twins, Margaret, said she could envision herself living in a work-separation arrangement when she marries if the circumstances call for it.

"Lots of times I wish she was home, just to kind of be there and take us shopping. But we can basically run the house, and we are doing fine," she said.

"Now that Mom has lived alone, she is a lot happier when she's home," Teresa contributed with a teasing grin at her mother.

The children will visit their mother in Camden from time to time. Early in her stay young Robert and Becky visited her there.

Mr. McColley said about the duration of his and his wife's work separation, "We are both more apt to be job hunting in five years than we are now.

"Careers have an ebb and flow to them. I've gone several years without publishing one of those exciting books that make those with jobs decide to offer you a senior position.

"This doesn't mean that I'm immobilized but that the only way I could move now would be to accept a chairmanship at a school whose history department would be considerably below that of the University of Illinois.

"I am not keen on this. The history department here is a very good place to get the kind of work done I like to do. And I consider Champaign-Urbana an unusually good place to raise children in this day and age."

He said about his work separation, "Marriage shouldn't be less than eating and drinking and sleeping together but it ought to be a great deal more. We both take marriage very seriously. It is for life, as it says in the wedding ritual. I think this makes living apart easier for us.

"The kind of thing we are doing can be done from very conservative premises — seeing marriage as a long-lasting and very serious commitment — as well as from very modern ones.

"We are not in the same situation as those married six months or three years. Having been married 21 years there is an enormous part of memory. Your wife has become part of yourself. Even when she is not around you know what she would say in a certain situation and even pretty much what she is doing at the moment."

Temporarily Apart

While long-term work separations are or have been a permanent life-style for at least 26 local married couples, many couples in Champaign-Urbana have accepted this way of life for shorter periods.

Short-term work separations usually are undertaken by academics for the duration of a sabbatical or other leave and last less than one year.

Not surprisingly, at least one member of each of the nine couples interviewed for this article is or was employed by or studied at the University of Illinois.

Two of the short-term work separations are going on now while seven took place in the past.

Short-term work separations are more frequent than the long-term ones and are likely to become even more prevalent.

They are apt to increase in number as more women are employed and find it inadvisable or impossible to leave their jobs. Inflation also makes it an increasing financial hardship for those on sabbaticals to bring their families with them.

Being finite in duration, the work separations are not seen as a great hardship by the couples interviewed.

"You miss something and you gain something," Karma Ibsen-Riley said.

"You miss the closeness of the traditional nuclear family but you gain the kind of professional freedom my husband and I feel is vital."

Mrs. Ibsen-Riley is an actress, director and playwright who has had two of her plays performed locally during the fall. She also works as a bartender at Grunts in Campustown. Her husband, Thomas J. Riley, is an assistant professor of anthropology at the University of Illinois and has done anthropological research in the Marshall Islands and, now, in Hawaii since June. He will remain in Hawaii until August.

The couple has three children, aged 4 to 11, who live with their mother here.

The work separation is not the first for the couple. Mr. Riley studied on a grant at M.I.T. in Cambridge, Mass., for six months a year ago and has been away on research projects of three or four months' duration before then.

Mrs. Ibsen-Riley and the children visited him in Hawaii for four weeks recently. Mr. Riley telephones the family here about every two weeks.

"It works out pretty well," Mrs. Ibsen-Riley said. "The major problem is to get enough help to take care of the children. My friends have been a tremendous help.

"As for missing each other, we are both too busy to get lonely."

The second ongoing work separation involves Dora and Tasos Apostolidis, a Greek couple. Mr. Apostolidis continues to teach mathematics at a high school in Greece while Mrs. Apostolidis is doing research for a year in the University of Illinois mathematics department while on leave from her teaching position at the University of Salonica.

The couple has no children. A visit by Mrs. Apostolidis during the University of Illinois Christmas break to her husband will be the only time the couple sees each other until August.

Lennart and Ulla-Britt Backstrom also were separated by the Atlantic Ocean during their work separation. A visiting professor of veterinary clinical medicine at the College of Veterinary Medicine at the University of Illinois, Mr. Backstrom preceded his wife and three children to Urbana by seven months, arriving at the university in January 1979.

Mrs. Backstrom, a teacher of French, stenography, typewriting and dancing in the couple's native Sweden, said about her work separation, "I worried a lot at first."

"I think it is good for a woman to gain the self-confidence of managing things alone. So many women will become widows. It is very good to find out that you are stronger than you think."

Eugenia and Nicholas Petridis were work-separated during the academic year of 1977-78. Mrs. Petridis was working toward her Ph.D. degree in Byzantine history at the University of Illinois while Mr. Petridis was organizing a department of mathematics at University of Crete in Heraklion, Greece.

The couple has no children and lives in Charleston, where Mr. Petridis is a professor of mathematics at Eastern Illinois University and Mrs. Petridis continues the research for her doctorate.

Short-term work separations also have been maintained by Douglas and Danielle Hilson, Neal and Rozann Rothman, Dennis and Judy Rowan, Wendell and Dorothy Williams and William and Pearl Goodman.

Mr. Hilson, who is chairman of the graduate program and professor of art in the University of Illinois art and design department, spent the 1979 spring semester in New York on sabbatical to paint and establish a gallery connection.

Mrs. Hilson, who is assistant to the head of the department of political science at the University of Illinois, remained in Champaign with the couple's two children, aged 5 and 10.

The Hilsons traveled every third week to see each other, taking turns commuting.

Each of the Hilsons kept a journal during the work separation.

"We each wanted to record our thoughts to see how and if we changed while being apart," Mrs. Hilson said.

Rozann Rothman commuted by airplane from Washington, D.C., to carry out her duties as an assistant professor of political science at the University of Illinois during the 1979 fall semester. Her husband, a professor of mathematics at the university, is on leave of absence from the university for one year to work for the National Science Foundation in Washington as a project director.

The couple's youngest child, who is 15, lived with her father. The two oldest children are grown and on their own. During the current semester Mrs. Rothman is working in Washington on a research project partially funded by the National Endowment for the Humanities.

Judy Rowan stayed in Champaign-Urbana during the 1977 spring semester while her husband, a professor of art at the University of Illinois, taught at the Manoa campus of the University of Hawaii. Mrs. Rowan is an editor in the university's office of public information. The couple has no children.

Dorothy Williams, coordinator of the University of Illinois news bureau in the office of public information, and her husband Wendell, a professor of physics and ceramic engineering at the university, have maintained two work separations.

The first, in 1974-75, lasted one semester after which Mrs. Williams and the youngest of the couple's two daughters joined Mr. Williams in Washington, where he spent the year as energy coordinator in the division of materials research at the National Science Foundation.

The second, in 1977-78, lasted a year while Mr. Williams was section head for metallurgy and materials in the same division. In each case Mrs. Williams continued in her job here, taking leave during the second semester of the first work separation.

"I think you have to have a very strong marriage to survive the kinds of strains it puts on the marriage," Mrs. Williams said.

"I felt I got a lot of veiled glances and a lot of 'Is Wendell planning to come back?' from people who should have known better."

During one of the work separations Mr. Williams supervised a $14 million research project for the National Science Foundation.

Pearl Goodman continued in her job as a teaching associate in the University of Illinois division of English as a second language (she is now an instructor) while her husband spent the academic year of 1972-73 as director of the Office of Urban Systems in Washington.

Mr. Goodman is a professor of urban and regional planning at the University of Illinois. The couple's two daughters were in college at the time of the work separation.

Mrs. Goodman said, "Initially it was exhilarating. I felt liberated after so many years of family responsibilities, and I enjoyed my freedom and the excitement of airport life—flying to Washington for the weekend.

"Then, after a couple of months, I began to feel emotionally let down and vaguely dissatisfied as well as physically fatigued from all the travel.

"When the year was over, I was grateful, as though I had gone through some sort of endurance test which I had managed to survive."

Long-Range Effects

What are the long-range effects of a work separation on a family?

Excellent, according to Melba Atkinson who looks back on her three-year work separation from a five-year perspective.

"It worked out for the best for our family," she said.

Her husband, Robert M. Atkinson II, lived in Pittsburgh from September 1971 until August 1974 while she lived in St. Louis with the couple's two children.

The Atkinsons are one of at least 26 local married couples who are maintaining or have maintained work separations. They are the only couple of the 17 interviewed for this series in which one of the partners is not or was not based in Champaign-Urbana during the separation.

During the Atkinsons' work separation Mr. Atkinson earned master's and doctor's degrees in industrial administration at Carnegie-Mellon University in Pittsburgh. Mrs. Atkinson remained in her job as director of financial aid and placement at Forest Park Community College in Missouri.

Their children, Kimberli and Robert III, were 8 years old and 8 months old when the work separation began.

After the family was reunited, it moved to Urbana as Mr. Atkinson started his current position as an assistant professor of business administration at the University of Illinois.

The Atkinsons' decision to live apart temporarily came about when Mr. Atkinson, who already had a master's degree in business administration from Washington University in St. Louis, decided to pursue further graduate study at Carnegie-Mellon.

After assessing Pittsburgh as a place to live, the Atkinsons decided that the employment opportunities for Mrs. Atkinson and the schooling for Kimberli were better in St. Louis.

During the three years Mr. Atkinson flew to St. Louis four times a year to visit his wife and children. The family also spent one summer vacation traveling together.

Mrs. Atkinson and the children never got to Pittsburgh during the work separation because of the cost.

The family kept in close touch by telephone and the Atkinsons encouraged Kimberli to call her father whenever she wanted to.

"The monthly phone bills ranged from $62 to $125 but it was worth it," Mrs. Atkinson said.

Both the adults were so busy during the living-apart period that they scarcely had time to miss each other, Mrs. Atkinson said.

Mr. Atkinson said, "Being separated never bothered us. It was really no different from when I was in the service as a first lieutenant in Vietnam.

"It all comes down to being willing to defer your rewards."

Mrs. Atkinson said, "The end was harder for me than the beginning. The last two or three days I felt as if I was going to fall apart."

Today the family is thriving and no ill effects of the work separation are evident at any level, she said.

Two new members of the family, Heather Marie, 3, and Robin Renee, 2, now toddle around the Atkinsons' home in Urbana and play with the family's Siberian husky, Misti.

After some years at home while the two new daughters were tiny Mrs. Atkinson has returned to having outside employment and works as a clerk at the Urbana Police Department.

Mr. Atkinson continues to find his university work challenging and stimulating and, like Mrs. Atkinson, Kimberli and Robert, enjoys being a member of a complete family again.

Young Robert is now 9 years old and is involved in his school work and Cub Scouting with soccer and football as his major hobbies.

"He is really close to his father," Mrs. Atkinson said. "He used to rely on me for everything but now he thinks his father is the greatest.

"He is a very independent child who can take care of his own meals when necessary."

During the work separation Kimberli provided a lot of the care for her younger brother and willingly gave up many extra-curricular activities to help her mother, who frequently worked 10 to 12 hours a day.

Kimberli made up for lost time after the family was reunited, throwing herself into participating in chorus, creative dance, cheerleading, gymnastics, Girl Scouts, Gra-Y, softball and hospital volunteer work.

PORTRAITS IN COURAGE

She also has been working on improving her diving at Crystal Lake Pool and recently performed a back flip for the first time.

"I like challenges. Doing the same stuff over and over involves no risk," she said.

Becki wears her artificial leg only for cross country skiing, using her crutches for sports such as running and a special toe clip on the pedal of her bicycle.

Buoyed by her fervent religious faith, she sees the effects of the loss of her leg not as a hindrance but as having provided her with a special form for freedom.

"In high school, before the operation, I had standards for always having the perfect look, perfect clothes, perfect hair and makeup, perfect behavior," she said.

"I always failed to reach that level of perfection. When I lost my leg I could relax. It gave me freedom to be who I am, to be who God meant me to be.

"It made me realize that I never could be physically perfect. Yet I don't feel I am ugly. Losing your leg does not make you ugly.

"Now I am unique. I can't be compared with anybody. I can't be stereotyped.

"If I had had all my stock in my looks, losing my leg would have ruined me.

"But I believe in eternal life. I am going to die anyhow someday. So 17 pounds of me have already died. It is not important.

"I appreciate my body more than I did before. I realize my body is vulnerable and is not going to last, and that is why I am putting my trust in something that will last. Putting my trust in something eternal, in God, I know I won't be disappointed."

Her acceptance of her handicap is not the norm for handicapped people, she said.

"My belief in Christ is why I did not get bummed out about it," she said. "But I have been in contact with a lot of amputees who have let their handicaps ruin their lives, among them a beautiful girl whose legs were paralyzed in a Jeep wreck and who refuses to leave her house.

"Last winter I competed in the Midwest Handicap Races for skiers with about 60 other amputees. They did more partying and more sleeping around than other students do. They seem to feel life has ripped something away from them and want to grab everything back they can."

It is precisely in order to motivate other handicapped people to improve the quality of their lives that she plans a career in therapeutic recreation.

"I want to give handicapped people through athletics another area of success so they can feel better about themselves. And I want to work on emotional therapy as well," she said.

lives in Vevey with her husband, and this summer she has journeyed to California to visit her boyfriend, Brian, a student at UCLA.

She and Brian met during their attendance at the Intervarsity Urbana conference last Christmas. Each considers the other "pretty special," she said, but continues to date other people.

Right now the big excitement in Becki's life is the imminent arrival of a sophisticated new prosthesis which features a hydraulic knee.

Becki plans to call the prosthesis "Harvey" and says she looks forward to having a brother for her present prosthesis which she with typical insouciance has named "Harold the Hairless Wonder."

She wears Harold — who is a treasured inhabitant of her girls' dormitory at Taylor and frequently referred to by the other girls as "the guy living on the fourth floor" — about 16 hours a day during school days.

At home she prefers to hop around on one leg, unencumbered by Harold.

This habit once led to an incident which illuminates the way Becki has aided everyone around her in accepting her handicap.

When Mrs. Conway a few months after the amputation asked Becki not to hop around the family home on one leg but to use her crutches because the sight of her hopping tore her father up emotionally, Becki's answer was loving but firm.

She said, "Mom, if Dad's having problems, that's because he isn't accepting me as I am. This is me. I have only one leg. And Dad needs to accept it.

"No, I won't use the crutches."

August 1980

2nd Place, Illinois UPI 1980 feature contest (with "Crawlspace Castles" and "The Abandoned Farm")

Widowhood in Mid-Life

Four Champaign women, ranging in age from mid-30s to late 40s, reacted in different ways to the shock of their husbands' sudden deaths.

Two of the women have been widowed for four years, one for 18 months and one for only a few months.

"I survived by living one day at a time," said Kitty Williamson. "The fact that my husband died so suddenly, as if God had reached out of the sky and plucked him away, made me realize that I have no power over my destiny.

"Strangely enough, realizing how fragile and precious life is is what gave me strength to go on—that and my religious faith and the children."

Mrs. Williamson has three sons aged 6, 10 and 13. She was widowed in January when her husband, James, became ill and died within minutes, possibly of the Port Chalmers flu.

She said, "If someone had told me six months ago that this would happen to me, I would have said, 'I'll crawl under the bed and never come out'. I know I could wallow in self-pity and ask myself what will happen to me in two years, in five years, but you have to have faith that things will work out and face each day as a new adventure.

"Losing your husband is like having a baby: there is no way you can understand what it is like until it happens to you."

Mrs. Williamson stressed the importance of helping children express their grief. She did this by including her children in making funeral arrangements and letting them know that she was grieving.

"Children know you from your actions," she said. "If you keep a stiff upper-lip and hide your true feelings, they may interpret it that you don't really care that their father died.

"I got a lot of strength from the outpouring of concern immediately after Jim's death. My advice to others would be to go to the house of the survivor immediately, even if only for a few minutes, or to send a card right away.

"The concern shown helps the grieving person. Also, it lets him or her say without words, 'I'm all right, I'm functioning, don't be afraid of me'. It makes the first trip to the supermarket that much easier for him or her."

Jane Shoemaker felt differently.

"After my husband died (of a heart attack in 1971), a stream of people came to visit me," she said. "I felt during the first day that he was still a little bit there and was slowly slipping away, and I would have preferred to be alone although I understood their good intentions.

"If people want to help in a crisis situation, you almost have to let them take over, and I did not like to let them do that. But in the days following I did appreciate the concern and presence of my friends. In this mobile

"My husband had done all the grocery shopping, but I learned to market. Today I claim to be the town's top bargain hunter!

"Although we had a wonderful life and a perfect marriage, it was a great source of agony to me that my husband made all the family decisions alone, even buying a new car without telling me about it.

"Now I feel capable of handling everything. I discuss many decisions with my children to teach them how to handle the decision-making that I was so unprepared for.

"I find that the small decisions are sometimes the biggest headache to make."

Jane Shoemaker said that during the first two years of her widowhood she would ask herself how her husband would have handled a decision and act accordingly. She has five children. The three youngest, at home, are 6, 16, and 18.

"My husband had handled our financial affairs, and I did find it hard to take over. Something about the trauma of death tends to fragment your thinking," she said.

Mrs. Beberman and Mrs. Williamson had both been in charge of their families' financial affairs and handled vacation planning and most decisions involving the children.

"Jim and I counseled each other and discussed the decisions, but basically I was what I would call a matriarch," Mrs. Williamson said.

"I already did everything, took care of home repairs and family finances and the children, and drove my husband everywhere since he did not drive," said Mrs. Beberman. "It would have been twice as hard when he died, if I had not been used to handling everything.

"Even so, I was in a state of shock for a long time after his death after 24 years of marriage. It was a full year before the impact really hit me."

All four women decided to stay on in the community where they had lived with their husbands. The women all live in Champaign.

"I think it is important that my three sons stay on in their schools and the familiar house and neighborhood," Mrs. Williamson said.

"When you are widowed, parents will often suggest that you move close to them. I did not want to do that because I reason that it takes two to three years to settle in a new community as a couple, and as a single I would expect it to take five or six years."

Mrs. Beberman said, "My husband had provided for us through life insurance, university retirement, veteran's benefits and Social Security.

"The result was that I had a feeling of complete freedom, but I didn't know what to do with it. We were in England for a year's stay when Max died, and I was torn between staying there and returning to Champaign. I decided to return to Champaign mostly for the children's sake."

The economic effects of the death of the breadwinner can be crushing. While the other three women said they are reasonably well-provided for,

Mrs. Smith's husband carried no life insurance and had invested heavily in the stock market which lost considerable ground after his death.

"The money has dwindled since my husband's death," she said. "It seems like it runs through my fingers like sand. There is so little coming in and so much going out, with four children to support.

"Death is too expensive. The final expenses and the cost of the attorney are so high, although I hasten to say that my attorney has been of invaluable help to me.

"But the financial loss is too high. Losing your husband is already an irreplaceable loss that should not be coupled with financial hardship and worry."

Although Mrs. Beberman's situation is different, she concurs.

"When you and your husband build up savings together through your marriage, and you then have to pay inheritance tax on the fruit of your joint labor, it is like being stabbed in the back all over again," she said.

Couple-Oriented World

Elizabeth Beberman, Jane Shoemaker, Kitty Williamson and Mrs. Smith are among the nearly 10 million widows in the United States.

Among the problems widows face after the immediate ordeal are living alone in a couple-oriented world, making new friends, dating and finding a job.

"When you consider how many women are ultimately going to become widows, married women would do well to think about what it will be like," said Mrs. Beberman.

"The hardest for me was to adjust to living in a society based on couples, where I was no longer wanted after my husband died.

"The old Indian custom of burning the widow on the husband's funeral pyre was at least honest. In modern American life, widows are pushed outside the mainstream in many ways.

"You frequently feel that people write off both partners in a marriage when the husband dies.

"I find that my friends today are a completely different group than when my husband lived, although we had an active social life and entertained a great deal.

"Most people seem to feel that if they have you for dinner once as a widow, that is it.

"For parties, people sometimes include a few widows, but, considering our number, not very many. It is much easier for widowers because there are so few of them that they are much in demand.

"The result is that you slowly build up a new circle, almost all composed of other single people.

"You are limited in where you can meet men. Bars are out, because most people assume that unaccompanied women are there for the sole purpose of a sexual pick-up.

"The old advice about meeting through church groups and clubs does not work very well.

"In my opinion, the best thing that has happened to singles in Champaign-Urbana is the singles gathering at the Levis Center on the University of Illinois campus every Friday night.

"It is a way for people with similar problems to meet under relaxed circumstances."

Jane Shoemaker said, "I feel my social isolation has been as much my own fault as that of my friends. I do find myself ill at ease with couples.

"It is important for a widow to remember how many widows she included socially when she was married. Remembering that should make you more tolerant.

"I have never felt that I was thought of as a threat to the marriage of friends. I think that is a tale widows like to believe in.

"There are very few single men around after age 35 to 45. I know I did not meet a single man the first nine months after my husband's death.

"The important thing in re-entering social life is not to show self-pity. You do tend to be tearful at first, but it is important to overcome that and to learn to talk about your husband easily. This can aid you in easing back into the couple-oriented society."

Mrs. Beberman said, "When you do begin to date, it embarrasses your kids. The first time I went out on a date, the children sat me down and instructed me in the proper behavior on a first date. Now they wait up for me at night and ask me if I had a good time."

Mrs. Beberman and Mrs. Shoemaker both have re-entered the job market.

Although she was qualified to teach elementary education and music in grades one through nine, Mrs. Beberman could not find a teaching job and became a proof-reader and typesetter instead.

"Hunting for a job is rough," she said. "The fact that I can hang storm windows, bake bread and sew a dress did not get me anywhere in the job market."

"Being employed is the single greatest asset you can have," said Mrs. Shoemaker, who works as a secretary. "It gives you an identity of your own as well as income."

She said she was apprehensive during her job hunt, since she had not worked outside her home for many years. Mrs. Shoemaker suggested women continue working after they are married so that, should the husband unexpectedly die, they do not have such an adjustment to make.

Help during the transition period can be found in many places. Mrs. Smith said that her friends and neighbors gave her "terrific support." She also attends group counseling sessions at the Family Education Association and has joined Parents Without Partners.

Mrs. Williamson said that Catherine Marshall's book, "To Live Again," was of great help to her. She termed Lynn Caine's book, "Widow," "almost a textbook of what not to do."

"Mostly my friends have helped me," she said. "It seems like the right person has constantly arrived at the right time to give me aid. I do wish that an organization of widows existed."

Mrs. Shoemaker said that she credits her counsellor at the Psychological Clinic at the University of Illinois with "a great deal of my hanging on and managing."

The four women advise married women to become full partners with their husbands in all aspects of running a household and to develop their capabilities as much as possible.

They suggest that women strive to be fully informed about their families' financial affairs and be aware of where tax records, life insurance policies and investment certificates are kept.

They all stressed the need for a will and the designation of a guardian for children, in case both parents should die.

They urge married women to finish high school, college or vocational training to have a marketable skill.

Several of the women underlined the importance of asking advice from as many professional sources as possible if widowed and not holding back from fear of seeming ignorant.

Mrs. Beberman said, "Everyone should be prepared for widowhood because it can, and does, happen overnight."

May 1975

Small of Stature, Big on Courage

Cathy Yeager packs a lot of courage and pluck into her small body.

While many other 12-year-olds fret about getting a vaccine injection at their yearly medical check-ups, Cathy submits without a wince to three weekly shots which aid her physical growth.

And while most of her schoolmates at Edison Middle School probably have to put up with some of the teasing that is a hallmark of behavior among junior high school-aged children, Cathy has developed an extraordinarily tough hide all over her 3 foot 11 inch tall body to combat the merciless and relentless teasing by some contemporaries that is her daily lot.

Cathy is a hypopituitary dwarf whose growth before the discovery in the late 1950s of the successful results of the administration of human growth hormone (HGH) would have stopped at four feet.

Instead, through three weekly injections of HGH given year round until Cathy reaches 16 years of age, she and the Michael Reese Medical Center team of doctors in charge of her case expect that she will reach somewhere between 4 foot 7 inches and 4 foot 10 inches as her adult height.

For the first 2½ years of the 4½ years during which Cathy has been treated with HGH she, along with other children in the United States being given the hormone, received injections for only eight months of each year because of the shortage of HGH.

HGH is an extract from human pituitary glands obtained by the National Pituitary Agency from total autopsies performed by pathologists across the country and from individuals who specify that their pituitary gland be donated for this purpose after their death.

During the last two years Cathy has received HGH three times a week on a yearly basis.

In addition, her dosage has been doubled since her growth has not been as rapid as the team of doctors first had hoped.

During the first years of treatment Cathy received the extract from between 120 and 200 human pituitary glands every year. It now takes between 240 and 400 glands to provide the yearly extract.

Research to produce the extract synthetically so far has been fruitless.

The pituitary gland is an organ a little larger than a pea that lies beneath the brain at the base of the skull.

The cost of her treatment is about $10,000 and is borne by the NPA.

Cathy is the daughter of Bob and Judy Yeager of Champaign, who also have a 13-year-old daughter, Jenni, who is 5 foot 5 inches tall.

Mrs. Yeager is director of Champaign County Crime Prevention Council and also takes classes in business administration.

Bob Yeager is a private consultant in the field of computer-based education and teaches a course on the subject at the University of Illinois.

Cathy's condition was discovered in a school checkup by the public health nurse when the family moved to Champaign seven years ago.

Cathy weighed seven pounds at birth and developed normally during the first three years of life. Although her growth lagged behind for the next several years, the Yeagers were assured by their doctors in Chicago where they then lived that she would soon "catch up," Mrs. Yeager said.

When the HGH treatments began when Cathy was 7½ years old, she was less than 3 feet tall and had weighed 29 pounds for 2½ years.

After 18 months of treatments she had grown seven inches and gained seven pounds.

Today, after three years further treatment, her height is between 3 feet 11 inches and four feet and she carries 42 pounds on her perfectly proportioned frame.

The medical team at Michael Reese in Chicago, which is headed by Dr. Lynne L. Levitsky, director of the pediatric division of metabolism and endocrinology, originally hoped Cathy's height might reach 5 feet but is now talking about 4 foot 7 inches to 4 foot 10 inches as her adult height.

For Cathy, her small size appears to have fueled a fierce determination to live a full and active life in which obstacles exist only to be overcome.

Blessed with sensitive and intelligent parents and a delightful older sister, she has a full schedule as a seventh-grader at Edison and the carrier of a daily newspaper.

Cathy and Jenni each plan and cook dinner one night a week (two nights during summer vacation).

The two girls care for the animal population in the Yeager home which Cathy ticked off as currently including "a dog, a rabbit, a squirrel, a canary, trillions of fish and guppies, and nine gerbils — the mother, father, five babies and two babies from the previous litter."

Among her hobbies are bicycling, skateboarding, photography and collecting animal posters.

Her career aim is to become an interior designer, she said.

For most of her endeavors her small size presents no problem but she does face some hurdles in the family kitchen and in classes such as shop and home economics because of the height of kitchen counters, appliances and of the shop work tables.

In her own kitchen, she is adept at pulling out drawers to make a ladder and has accustomed herself to walk on the kitchen counter to reach overhead cabinet shelves and the freezer compartment.

"Last year in shop, all the tables were three and one-half feet off the ground and it was hard for me to saw and hammer so the teacher made me a stool. This year home ec is really bad. I can reach the stove but I can't see into the pot and I can't reach the water faucet. I am too embarrassed to use a chair to stand on because of a boy in the class who makes wisecracks," Cathy said.

The constant wisecracks and teasing were hard to take last year when she entered Edison after finishing her grade school education at Washington School.

"Last year I was really down in the slumps. I barely knew anybody and in my homeroom there were whole bunches of people sitting at both sides of me who just ignored me," she said.

"Of the kids who knew me everybody teased me. I never wanted to go to school last year.

"This year is much better. Not all of the kids are 5 feet 9. A lot of them are 4 or 5 feet tall in my group. But some kids still tease me a lot.

"There are kids who tease to mean it, and those who tease for fun. I try to avoid the bad teasers as much as I can.

"I've worked out some self-defense. I am supposed to go to the teacher and tell her right away but I never do because then the kids would call me Sissy or Chicken. I walk away and go over to my friends who are bigger than I am," she said.

William Sippel, principal of Edison, said, "Cathy does very well. She is very well adjusted and has a terrific attitude socially and emotionally. She fits into our school and situation fine."

Cathy lights up when she talks about her best friend, Kelly Schaefer.

"We are just sort of made for each other. We help each other as we go along. Kelly has a seeing problem and we help each other through hard times.

"We have quarrels but five minutes later we are laughing our heads off together. We are just like sisters. I don't think anything will ever break off our friendship," she said.

October 1978

1st Place, Illinois AP 1979 life style contest

199

The Three Musketeers

August 16, 1979. A day of sunshine and gentle breezes. A day to gather in the backyard, iced tea tinkling in glasses, lazily enjoying the bursts of color of flowers and the hum of bees. A day to watch a grandchild toddle in pursuit of a butterfly, chubby hands reaching out toward the fragile, fluttering toy.

August 16, 1979. For the men and women gathered at Temple Baptist Church in Champaign, a day of bleached faces, muffled sobs, hands stretched out to clasp other hands in silent communion. A day of brief, wordless embraces — of sorrow shared.

August 16, 1979. A day marking the final chapter in a saga of suffering, endurance, nobility of spirit, steadfast love, faith in God and — above all — of friendship.

For the third time in less than six months the parishioners of the small church and their young minister are gathered to mourn the death from cancer of a man who has been an irreplaceable mainstay of the church for many years.

Sustaining them in their sense of loss in this monstrous coincidence is the memory of the magnificent friendship the three men felt for each other and the way they supported each other through their years of agony.

They also are nourished by the same rock-like religious faith that was so integral a part of the three men's lives.

The three men were Lawrence E. Bailey, who died Feb. 25, 1979, at the age of 63; James G. Shelton, who died April 3 at the age of 62; and Moyle S. "Moe" Williams, who died Aug. 14 at the age of 57 and whose memorial service is being held.

Termed "three pillars of the church" by the minister, the Rev. John A. Thomason, the men called themselves "The Three Musketeers."

It is an apt description of a friendship in which the men visited and telephoned each other frequently throughout their periods of illness and carried out their intense involvement with the church, as often as not through mighty arguments about church policy decisions between Mr. Shelton and Mr. Williams with Mr. Bailey acting as peacemaker.

The friendship extended to and included their wives, Opal Bailey, Marguerite Shelton and Mary Williams. Through the many hours of grieving and struggling to come to terms with their loss, the women have continued to counsel and comfort each other.

For Mr. Bailey and Mr. Williams, the journey that ended in 1979 began in 1962, the year when for each of them diagnostic surgery revealed they had cancer.

Mr. Williams went on to undergo a total of 24 surgeries ranging in seriousness from minor to very major including the amputation of a leg in

1964. His last years were marked by increased suffering through which he managed to continue his church work and carry out his duties as association director of the University of Illinois Cooperative Extension Service.

Mr. Bailey's illness went into an eight-year remission following the initial surgery. Beginning in 1970, he was treated with radiation and chemotherapy and after 1975 he underwent surgery many times.

He retired from his position as manager of central stores at the University of Illinois in 1975 after having worked his way up through the ranks through 38 years of employment. His last years were filled with month-long hospital stays with many periods in the intensive care unit.

Mr. Shelton was diagnosed as suffering from cancer after major surgery in November 1977. After a hospital stay of 2½ months, his health seemingly improved for about 10 months and he was able to lead a near-normal life. During the last three months of his life, his illness grew increasingly worse and he was hospitalized several times.

He retired from his job as a teacher of earth science at Rantoul Township High School, where he worked for 17 years.

During World War II he served as a glider pilot in the European Theater.

Mr. Shelton's death was a particularly hard blow for Mr. Williams, who almost seemed to have a premonition of the instant of his friend's death.

Mary Williams relates her husband was seated in his room in the family home when she and the couple's only child, the Rev. Anne Kessen, came in to tell him Mr. Shelton had just died.

Mrs. Williams said, "Moe said, 'I knew it. I'd been praying for all of us and it was as clear as could be that Jim had died and no longer needed my prayers. But I am going to continue to pray for Marguerite and her family.' "

Mrs. Williams added, "Moe was not given to flights of fancy so I found this very moving because he knew almost the exact time of Jim's death."

The brotherhood of "The Three Musketeers" showed itself in many ways.

"My husband was an ag major in college and taught vocational agriculture for many years," Marguerite Shelton said. "Moe (who had a doctorate in agricultural economics) and he shared an interest in agriculture as well as in the church.

"They were both very strong-willed and strong-minded persons who would have many fierce discussions both about the church and about agriculture which always ended up with their hugging each other."

In their illnesses the three men were great supports for each other.

"They encouraged and supported each other through everything," Marguerite Shelton said.

"It was our custom to go to the hospital to visit Moe after all his surgeries and he and Mary did the same for Jim."

Mr. Bailey was too ill to make visits by the time Mr. Shelton fell ill but Mr. Shelton would visit him, and the two families stayed in constant touch by phone, Mrs. Shelton said.

"Dad had such respect and admiration for Mr. Bailey and felt so for him because he suffered so much," the Rev. Mrs. Kessen said.

In a talk to church members given four months before his death, Mr. Shelton spoke about his gratitude for the example in fortitude Mr. Bailey had presented to him.

In spite of his precarious health, Mr. Bailey had repainted the trim on his house in the spring of 1977, and when Mr. Shelton decided his own house needed painting during the summer of 1978, although he did not feel well, he drew on Mr. Bailey's words about his undertaking.

"I get out and work for about half an hour, then I come in and rest awhile. Then I go back and do a little more and then I rest for awhile. It's pretty slow but I'll make it," Mr. Shelton quoted Mr. Bailey as having said.

With these words as inspiration, Mr. Shelton proceeded to start on his paint job.

He said in the talk to the church members, "After I finish a section and step back to look at it and see the improvement in appearance, I say, 'Thank you, Lawrence, for helping me paint our house.' "

An extra measure of poignancy for the church membership, which numbers about 250, and for the Rev. Thomason, who is serving his first pastorate at Temple, was added by the fact the minister delivered a series of sermons on death and dying on the Sundays from March 11 through April 8.

The sermons had been planned for the pre-Easter season for a long time and had been in preparation for several months but the timing—starting two weeks after Mr. Bailey's death and ending on the Sunday following Mr. Shelton's death—made them both an extraordinarily painful and cathartic experience for the pastor and the church members.

The congregation is made up mainly of young couples, many of them graduate students at the University of Illinois, and the loss of three major older figures within the church was almost more than the parishioners could bear, the Rev. Thomason said.

"Our congregation is so unaccustomed to death and dying," he said. "Those three funerals were the first and only funerals that have ever taken place in our sanctuary."

The cornerstone for the sanctuary was laid in 1970.

"We are used to losing members who move away but not in such a dreadful and final way," the Rev. Thomason said.

Lawrence and Opal Bailey were among the 17 persons who founded the Champaign church in 1950. Mrs. Bailey is now the only active person from this group still living in Champaign-Urbana. The Sheltons were members of the church for well over 20 years, and the Williamses joined the church a few months after moving to Champaign in 1963.

All three men contributed to the church in untold capacities, as deacons, teachers and committee members. They were all men who could wield a hammer or a paintbrush to spruce up or remodel the church with the same fervor with which they involved themselves in church policy decisions.

Mr. Shelton, a master craftsman and artist, designed and handcrafted the five beautiful stained-glass windows that dominate the sanctuary.

The windows portray major Christian symbols — the ship, the chalice, the cross and crown, the open Bible and the dove.

The Rev. Thomason summed up the three men by describing Mr. Bailey as "a genuine spiritual leader, a calming influence and one of the great continuity figures of both his church and his community," Mr. Williams as "tempestuous and volatile, a man who always came clean with his feelings and never held a grudge — a wonderful man," and Mr. Shelton as "quieter than Mr. Williams but just as firm in his convictions" and "a creative genius."

"They were giants," the Rev. Mrs. Kessen said. "That any church should have one man like that is amazing but three at one time. . . ."

The Rev. Mrs. Kessen was ordained as a Southern Baptist minister at the church in May 1979. She was 22 years old at the time and is, as far as can be ascertained, the first woman in Illinois to become ordained as a Southern Baptist minister. The moving ceremony of her ordination marked the last time her father was able to leave the family's Champaign home.

The Rev. Mrs. Kessen is a second-year student at Vanderbilt Divinity School in Nashville, Tenn. She plans to work as a hospital chaplain counseling terminally ill patients and their families after her graduation — a choice inspired by her father's long illness.

Her husband of three years, Michael, is working on his master of divinity degree at Vanderbilt and also works in the Office of Development there.

The Rev. Mrs. Kessen and the Sheltons' only son, James, have been close friends since childhood. The young James Shelton also has chosen the ministry as his vocation and is a student at Northern Baptist Seminary in Lombard. His wife also has chosen a career involving nurturing. She is employed as a public health nurse.

Mr. Shelton also is survived by two daughters, Marilyn Benton of Irvine, Calif., and Joyce Taylor of Westminster, Calif., and four grandchildren.

In the Bailey family, seeing a parent suffer for so many years from a devastating illness has had the opposite effect from the one on the Rev. Mrs. Kessen and young James Shelton. Mr. and Mrs. Bailey's only daughter, Sheri Morrill, is a registered nurse but has chosen to pursue a career in real estate rather than in nursing, "perhaps because of all the suffering she saw her father go through," Mrs. Bailey said.

Mr. Bailey also is survived by two sons, Phillip, an Urbana businessman, and Larry, an attorney in Seattle, Wash., and eight grandchildren.

For Mrs. Bailey, the period surrounding her husband's death was made even more painful by the fact that her daughter's husband was transferred to Fort Worth, Texas, from Champaign at that time, and the young couple was in Fort Worth looking for a house on the day Mr. Bailey died.

In the Williams family, the 95-year-old father of Mr. Williams died a week after his son's death without having been told about the loss of his son.

The three women left behind—who cared for their husbands through their purgatory of pain with such steadfast devotion and quiet strength that it would be presumptuous to attempt to describe their gallantry—all have rebuilt their lives with a supreme act of will.

They have been greatly aided in this by the loving support of the church members and the Rev. Thomason, who have constantly encouraged and aided them emotionally, all three women said.

"The members of Temple responded beautifully to each family's needs," Mary Williams said. "The congregation at Temple is a warm, responsive group of people with John (Thomason) leading the pack."

Marguerite Shelton said, "John Thomason did such a magnificent work of art in writing the funeral sermon to fit each man's personality and lifestyle. We love him so much. He is so young but so capable."

Mrs. Bailey, who had moved with her husband to a house in Mahomet he had designed for their retirement less than a year before his death, sold the house and moved back to Champaign-Urbana to be close to the friends of a lifetime.

For the last three months she has worked part time for Sears Roebuck & Co., where she had worked full time for about 18 years as lingerie manager, retiring in 1973.

Mrs. Shelton taught vocal and general music in the Villa Grove school system and then in Rantoul. She served Temple as music director for 22 years.

About a year ago she started a music group for children in grades four through six called Champaign-Urbana Civic Junior Singers and is currently writing the lyrics and music for a musical history of Champaign-Urbana that the group will perform in May.

She continues to live in the family home in Urbana that Mr. Shelton filled with countless examples of his craftsmanship including hooked rugs, stained glass and pieces of furniture.

Mrs. Williams had worked as a saleswoman at VanLaw Carol's in Champaign for years before her husband's death and returned to work there in November.

She continues to live in her Champaign home surrounded by the garden that was one of her husband's great interests.

The Baileys, Sheltons and Williamses all were given the full facts about the men's illnesses from the beginning. The three women all expressed their gratitude for the openness and possibility of sharing that this knowledge gave them.

"We have never hidden anything from each other and Anne or from family and friends," Mrs. Williams said. "It helped that we always were able to talk everything over."

Marguerite Shelton said, "Being able to talk completely honestly with my husband about the course of his illness and the approach of his death made it so much easier for me.

"It gave me a sense of peace and actual rejoicing that this closeness should be ours and that it enabled the three men to support and encourage each other so much."

Anne Kessen's words about her father might stand as the epitaph for all three men.

Quoting Dylan Thomas's poem, "Do Not Go Gentle into That Good Night," she said, "My father followed the teaching of that poem.

"He fought every moment for extra time, yet never doubted he was going into that good night. And when he left, he left with dignity."

February 1980

HAPPY FAMILIES
ARE NOT ALL ALIKE

Dare to Do

Irmgard Haken sees motherhood as her life's work.

"Anyone can fill a job in the working world but I am the only one who can mother my children," she said.

"When my children leave home I at least can say I did one thing right, and if I didn't teach, didn't use my Ph.D., so what did it matter compared to that? I feel my children would not have turned out quite the same if I had left their upbringing partly to babysitters.

"Mainly I try to provide a base from which they can work and feel safe and dare to do things."

She added, "Of course, you never know if someone can make something of his or her life."

So far the parenting provided by Mrs. Haken and her husband, Wolfgang, a professor of mathematics at the University of Illinois who won world renown last summer as co-solver of the century-old Four-Color Problem, appears to have enabled their six children to dare to do a great deal with their lives.

The second youngest, Rudolf, 11, is in the news now since he will conduct his own composition, "The Animals Which Escaped From the Zoo," at two youth concerts and one kinderkonzert of the Champaign-Urbana Symphony this week.

A fifth-grader at Washington School in Champaign, Rudolf started writing music at the age of 6 and already has a foot-high stack of compositions to his credit.

He won first prize for "The Animals" and second prize for his Symphony No. 0 at a composers' contest held at Eastern Illinois University in Charleston earlier this month.

His oldest brother, Armin, 19, graduated from the University of Illinois last summer as a Bronze Tablet Scholar and received Highest Distinction in his major, mathematics. Now a graduate student in mathematics at the University of California at Berkeley, he will return to the University of Illinois in August to finish his graduate work.

He plans to make the trek from California to Champaign the same way he made it last summer, by bicycle.

The oldest Haken daughter, Dorothea, 18, is a junior at the University of Illinois majoring in computer science. She worked as a grader last semester and, in the months before her father and Professor Kenneth Appel announced their solution to the Four-Color Problem, together with Armin and the brother next to her in line, Lippold, put in many hours of hard work checking the computer computations used to solve the problem.

Now almost 16, Lippold is a junior at University High School with a strong interest in computer science. He won first prize for a project in

Irmgard Haken and her youngest son, Rudolf

which he taught a computer to write music at the Engineering Open House at the University of Illinois.

The second-oldest daughter, Agnes, 13, is a subfreshman at University High School. Her favorite hobby for several years has been working at a local riding stable where she helps out and is rewarded by an opportunity to exercise the horses.

The youngest daughter, Armgard, 9, is a third-grader at Washington School. Like all her sisters and brothers she takes violin lessons. She is the favorite musical partner of Rudolf, who has written a great number of violin duets and violin-and-piano duets for himself and Armgard to play.

All six children are bilingual. Professor and Mrs. Haken grew up in Germany and came to Champaign 15 years ago and consider it imperative for the children to learn their parents' native language.

Mrs. Haken said that although she feels it is nice for the children to have a second language, the main reason for teaching the children German has been her and her husband's conviction that children should know the language their parents spoke as children.

The family speaks only German in the home—"I do not answer if the children speak to me in English," Mrs. Haken said. A large library of German books has helped the children familiarize themselves with the language.

The three older children received daily after-school lessons in German from Mrs. Haken when they were younger and have each spent 1½ months in Germany at some point, staying with their grandparents and attending German schools.

Asked how you go about raising such a high-achieving brood of youngsters, Mrs. Haken said she is a proponent of children getting plenty of sleep, learning self-discipline through daily music practice, getting exercise through running, bicycling and backpacking, learning self-reliance through taking some trips on their own, and not having a television set in their home.

She said about TV-watching, "I think the worst you can do to children is to support the normal human laziness.

"If a child is bored it will soon look for something to do. I think it is important that children make things happen and don't sit back and have things happen to them."

All the Haken children take music lessons and must practice for at least an hour a day. Mrs. Haken encourages them to do their practice in the morning before school and has them tape-record their practice sessions so that she can spot-check the tapes.

She does all the transcribing of Rudolf's compositions—virtually a fulltime job in itself.

The older children commute to their schooling in the University of Illinois campus area from the home in western Champaign on bicycles or, occasionally, unicycles.

The family spends its vacations on backpacking trips, and, in earlier years, the youngest child was carried on Mrs. Haken's back. Everyone helps carry the two-person tents and supplies. Among the areas the eight Hakens have explored together are the Appalachian trail, Grand Canyon, Havasu Canyon and Isle Royale in Lake Superior.

The three older siblings have hiked the Appalachian trail alone together, and in 1974, when Armin and Dorothea were 16 and 15, the two of them made a bicycle trip of several thousand miles through Germany.

Playing and listening to music is another favorite pursuit. The living room houses a grand piano and a harpsichord and clavichord, built from kits by Professor Haken and Armin. Rudolf has his own piano in his bedroom. All the family members also are constant concert-goers.

To balance the family budget in order to purchase musical instruments for the children and pay for concerts and music lessons (Rudolf alone has five lessons a week), Mrs. Haken has become a great bargain hunter in food stores and has in addition developed many low-cost, highly nutritious menus.

For many years she has made a yearly trip to a grain elevator to buy wheat and soybeans. Last fall she bought 700 pounds of wheat and 60 pounds of soybeans.

She grinds the wheat with a hand-grinder and uses it to bake a flavorful bread which the children affectionately have named "Elephant Toenail Bread."

She uses the soybeans in a variety of ways, in casseroles, ground up for patties, and cooked whole. She also buys bananas in bulk when they are cheap, dries them in the oven and cuts them into dice for a high-energy food for the backpacking trips.

With Professor Haken keeping working hours from early morning to 10 p.m. virtually daily throughout their marriage, almost all of the upbringing of the children has fallen to her.

"But I knew this about him when we married, and I have never minded," she said.

She added that her husband, an expert woodworker, has made almost all the furniture in the family's home and is an accomplished repairer of musical instruments and bicycles.

Like her husband, Mrs. Haken earned a Ph.D. in mathematics in Germany, but nine sinus and eye operations lengthened the period needed to obtain the degree so that she has never used it.

"By the time I got my degree, Armin was born and I wanted to concentrate on bringing up our children," she said.

Child Prodigy

At the ripe age of 11 Rudolf Haken has studied violin for four years, piano for three, and flute and music theory for two.

During the last five years the child prodigy has created a huge stack of compositions, among them "The Animals Which Escaped From the Zoo" and his first symphony, Symphony No. 0.

A bouncy, outgoing child with sparkling blue eyes and freckles, he explained he numbered the symphony No. 0 in order not to be embarrassed later in his career by having the work included in the official tabulation of his works.

"And when I write my next symphony, I will call it Symphony No. Double Zero," he said.

Among his other works are trios for piano, flute and violin and for viola, flute and violin, each 50 pages long, and a 60-page long string quartet. He has written many violin duets for himself and his youngest sister, Armgard, 9.

For "The Animals" Rudolf wrote out the scoring for the 30 different instruments in pencil, and his mother did the copying in ink. "My duty is to see that he doesn't overwork himself," Mrs. Haken said.

A fifth-grader at Washington School, Rudolf spends four to five hours a day on music. He has five private music lessons a week, two in theory, one in violin, one in piano, and one in flute, and also studies cello and oboe at school. Much of the time left after lessons and practice is spent improvising at the piano.

He does most of his composing in the early morning hours when his five siblings have not yet started practicing their musical instruments, arising at 4 or 5 a.m.

He said his favorite composers are Mozart, Beethoven, Handel and Tchaikovsky but was loath to discuss modern composers.

He did admit to disliking Arnold Schoenberg's music, adding, "You can put that down because he isn't living anymore, so it won't hurt his feelings!"

March 1977

A Tractor Finds A Home

A 1936 John Deere tractor pulling an old grain wagon filled with laughing children is a common sight on some streets in southwestern Champaign.

The outfit belongs to Norris and Margaret Hansell, who acquired the tractor in 1964 from a junk yard in Belvidere for $60, figured at $1 a hundred pounds for scrap metal.

It took the family two years to clean up the rusting machine and replace missing parts.

Since then, the tractor has become such an integral part of the family's life that they brought it on a flat-bed trailer from Illinois to Concord, Mass., for a year's sabbatical at Harvard.

The tractor was the major consideration in selecting a house in Champaign when they arrived two years ago.

"We picked this house because it is on a cul-de-sac near open fields and has a perfect storage for the tractor," Mrs. Hansell said.

Although mainly a hobby, the old tractor has its practical uses.

When the Hansells moved six miles from Evanston to Wilmette in 1971, they used the tractor and farm wagon to transport all their possessions except filing cabinets.

They were provided with police escorts and moved everything in five or six trips. The tractor has a maximum speed of six miles per hour.

It also serves as an auxiliary power system.

"Its 10,000 watt generator manufactures enough power to keep the furnace and lights going for us and a few neighbors," Dr. Hansell said.

"We also use it to pull our snow plow or a chain of sleds ridden by children. Unlike others, we are hoping for lots of snow and power failures this winter," he said with a smile.

But mainly the tractor serves as "a children-clustering activity," Dr. Hansell, a psychiatrist, said.

"Ten minutes after we start the engine, the wagon is full of children ready for a ride around the neighborhood and to nearby fields," he said.

"Adolescent boys and girls like to learn to steer it, and when it is parked outside our house, they use it as a sort of club house."

"It's a terrific help for Cub Scout and birthday parties," Mrs. Hansell added.

The Hansells have four children, Charles, 17, Walter, 16, Ruth, 13, and Gerald, 10, who help keep the tractor in shape.

Dr. Hansell is professor of psychiatry at Northwestern University Medical School, lecturer in psychiatry at Harvard Medical School, attending psychiatrist at Champaign County Mental Health Center and a member of the staff of Mercy Hospital.

Mrs. Hansell is a teaching assistant in the astronomy department at the University of Illinois with a master's degree in science.

Dr. Hansell also owns a model collection of about 200 diecast aluminum tractors and farm machinery pulled by tractors. He described it as a collection representative of different makes for each model year since 1940.

Dr. Hansell said he became interested "in machines that made the prairie bloom" when he played in his grandfather's farm implement store in Pennsylvania during his childhood.

The interest was rekindled during a five-year period he served as zone director for the Illinois Department of Mental Health in Rockford and met many farmers while setting up mental health districts.

One of these men told him about the tractor in the junk yard.

"When I first saw it, it was rusty and had flowers growing out of it," he said.

"We took it apart in our garage, and for two years it was spread out all over the floor. With the help of the neighbor children, our children and we scrubbed for many hours to remove tons of grime and rust."

Since parts were no longer available, getting the tractor to the running stage required many hunts through junk yards all over northern Illinois and southern Wisconsin for spare parts.

"That was the part the children liked best," Mrs. Hansell said.

"Finally we put it all back together with the whole neighborhood watching," Dr. Hansell recalled. "I turned the fly wheel, the engine went 'put-put' on the first try, and everyone cheered!"

The valves had been ground and the magneto remagnetized at an implement company in Belvidere, which later made the iron work fittings for the snow plow and the farm wagon.

Guided only by photographs of the fitting places on the tractor, a craftsman made the snow plow fittings while the Hansells and the tractor were in Massachusetts.

On a trip to Rockford, Dr. Hansell picked up the plow and brought it to Concord in a rented truck to find that it fitted perfectly onto the tractor.

The farm wagon was built in the 1930s in an iron shop near Sublette on a 1929 Model T Ford chassis and was acquired by the Hansells in 1967.

The wood panels and doors had rotted, so the couple took careful measurements before removing the wood and had new pieces cut and milled to specifications at a lumber yard. They retained the old iron hinges.

Dr. Hansell said he chose the 1936 John Deere tractor because it was the first one to be mass-produced.

"In the early '30s, John Deere and International Harvester developed similar models and sold more than 100,000 in various series until 1942," he said.

"The average buyer of these tractors was replacing a two-horse team. It is a simple machine, designed to be repaired with the help of an instruction book by its user."

He said the tractor is designed to eliminate the need for a battery, fuel pump and water pump.

The tractor and wagon carried several thousand youngsters on rides at the Wilmette Centennial Fair in 1972. It also took part in the 4th of July parades in Champaign-Urbana in 1973 and 1975 and appeared at the centennial parade in Philo.

It has won first prize in a tractor pull for machines 35 years and older.

"Basically it's an absurd hobby," Dr. Hansell said. "But you have to have some absurdity in your life to stay sane the rest of the time."

October 1975

A Family's Chain of Love

In a gigantic chain forged by love and family solidarity that stretches all across America, they come from faraway states and nearby counties to be together. From May through September thousands of family reunions are held on weekends, a large proportion of them in the Midwest, which has the additional pull of its central location.

In public parks and small backyards, on farmsteads and in city apartments, family members gather to exchange news, admire the new babies, exclaim at the growth of the teen-agers, sit at the feet of members of the oldest generation as they recount family history and, once more, bring that special pie first made by Grandma.

Most of all, they are pulled to the family reunion to share nostalgic memories and by a need to reweave and strengthen those indefinable ties that hold a family — and America — together.

Ola Winterbottom leans over and gently wipes lipstick marks off the cheek of her oldest sister, Demarce Bowlin.

"By now no one has any lipstick left on their lips," she says with a smile.

Most of the lip coloring has been deposited on the cheeks of Mrs. Bowlin, at 88 years of age the matriarch of the E.B. Neal family, which is holding its family reunion.

The old lady whose sight is greatly diminished is seated in a chair next to the registration table where each family signs in. Smiling and indefatigable in spite of the humid air and temperatures hovering in the high 90s, she receives the homage of each family member as they take turns to embrace her, holding their faces within inches of hers as they identify themselves.

The Neal reunion, one of 11 family reunions held in Hessel Park and one of several scores held in Champaign County on this Sunday in August, is taking place for the 59th time.

Coming from 11 states — California, Oregon, Washington, Arizona, Colorado, Minnesota, Missouri, Wisconsin, Michigan, Indiana and Illinois — 131 of the 388 family members recorded in the family archives have gathered to break bread together and renew the already close ties that bind them.

Throughout the Hessel Park pavilion, which Mrs. Winterbottom reserved in February, five generations are reveling in each other's company.

Uncles in visored caps are joking with gangly nephews, toddlers with moist tendrils of hair clinging to their foreheads are wending their way through a forest of legs, newly married in-laws are introduced to their spouse's favorite childhood playmate and older women are poring over faded family photos and daguerreotypes.

Outside on the grass, family groups seated on blankets guard the sleep of babies as they survey the softball game in which several generations of Neals are engaged.

In one shady corner of the pavilion seven sisters, daughters of one of seven sisters, are gathered around their mother, hands touching and faces lit with tender smiles.

"Don't you just feel the love? That's what holds them together," says Mrs. Winterbottom, herself one of the seven sisters who make up the oldest generation of the Neal family.

And indeed the love within the Neal family is an almost tangible quality. The feeling of goodwill and freely expressed warmth in this family is so strong even an outsider, a reporter allowed to attend the gathering, is constantly swept up into embraces, held by the hand or elbow or given an occasional kiss.

The 121 families that contain the 388 Neal family members are the descendants of Ephriam Bradcutt Neal (1866-1940) and his wife, Desona Lee Snow Jones (1872-1922).

The family has deep roots in the United States. Mr. Neal's ancestors arrived in 1712 from Ireland and through Desona Neal the family traces its lineage back to Stephen Hopkins, who came over on the Mayflower.

E.B. and Desona Neal started out their married life in Kentucky and also lived in Texas and Tennessee before settling in Illinois in 1914.

They had 10 children, the seven daughters who still survive and of which Mrs. Bowlin is the oldest and Mrs. Winterbottom the second youngest, and three sons, two who died in infancy and Bradley, who died in 1972 at the age of 79.

Mrs. Winterbottom keeps in a place of honor in her Champaign home a wooden trunk her father made for the family's move from Kentucky to Texas in 1891.

The trek was made in a covered wagon as part of a wagon train at a time when there were no roads or road maps.

The first reunion was held in Champaign in 1921, and the reunion has been a tradition ever since. Like many of her sisters, Mrs. Winterbottom has never missed a reunion.

Of the seven sisters who make up the oldest generation all but one are able to attend the 1979 reunion.

In addition to Mrs. Bowlin and Mrs. Winterbottom they are Rosa Clark, Coal City, the only one with five generations in her family; Daisy Ebert, Crawfordsville, Ind., who has a total of 118 direct descendants and their spouses; Ethel Dickens, Champaign; and Orpha Hampel, Champaign, who counts the smallest number of descendants — seven.

It is not for want of trying the seventh sister, Lois Hanson, is not present. The 75-year-old woman and her 80-year-old husband returned to their California home a week before the reunion from a 7,000-mile trip in a motor home to Alaska to discover they were unable to get airplane reservations to make it to the reunion in time.

This makes it the first time in 20 years Mrs. Hanson has missed a reunion.

Among the members of the second-oldest generation, all of Daisy Ebert's seven daughters and one of her sons are present. Like her mother, Mrs. Ebert had seven daughters and three sons, nine of whom are living.

One of her new relatives, Tom Langel of Portland, Ore., is attending the reunion for the first time, having married one of Mrs. Ebert's granddaughters, Libby Thompson, a year ago.

Like many of those attending, the Langels planned their vacation in order to be present at the reunion.

"For me it is a chance to get to love the people my wife loves," Mr. Langel said. "The older ones seem particularly special to me, maybe because one realizes they are not going to be here forever. You can learn so much from them and enjoy them.

"I think a family tie means a lot to people. It gives you a sense of who you are, a feeling of identity and continuity."

The Neal reunion is traditionally held the first Sunday in August. This year the hours of the gathering are from 8 a.m. to 4 p.m.

At noon, six picnic tables arranged in a long row are filled with a variety of homemade foods, each family having brought several dishes.

The food ranges from turkey, ham, meatloaf and lasagne at one end of the tables through baked beans, corn pudding, macaroni dishes and salads to gooseberry, peach and rhubarb pies.

One three-star item that quickly disappears is a family favorite, the egg noodles Ethel Dickens has arisen at 6 a.m. to prepare from scratch.

After everyone has eaten their fill and then some — occasional groans of contentment are heard from some of the men who are resting their legs seated on the low wall surrounding the pavilion — Orpha Hampel in her capacity of secretary-treasurer for the family conducts a brief business meeting.

Unlike many family reunions where prizes are awarded to those who have come the longest distance to attend, been married the longest or is the youngest father present, the Neal reunion contents itself with the announcement of facts about the changes in the family.

Since the 1978 reunion four weddings, one divorce, four births and no deaths have taken place in the family, Mrs. Hampel tells the family.

The Neal family members are equally easygoing about arranging the reunion. Mrs. Winterbottom and her husband, Russell, reserve the pavilion and make nametags and family banners. As for the rest, "everyone knows it is the first Sunday in August and each sister reminds her children and they remind theirs," Mrs. Winterbottom said.

When all is said and done, what is the best part about the reunion?

"Seeing people you haven't seen for a long time" — Delores Lang, Mrs. Ebert's youngest daughter, who has driven in from Colorado to attend her first Neal reunion in 10 years.

"Playing in the playground with your cousins" — Lisa Herzog, 7, Newmarket, Ind.

"Being with a group of beautiful people" — Jean Weber.

"Grandma Dickens's egg noodles" — Sonja Martnick.

"Being with the fantastic women of my mother's generation" — Dorothy Ostema, Loda, Mrs. Ebert's daughter.

"Just being happy!" — Mrs. Ebert.

August 1979

Lozar Shipping Lines, Ltd.

If a surrealist filmmaker wanted to stage a sea battle involving vessels from many periods, Charles Lozar could supply the ships.

Mr. Lozar keeps more than 20 boats in various stages of restoration and refurbishing in the garage and basement of his Urbana house. The boats were constructed in major movie studios for use in films.

Exquisitely detailed with miniature cannons, oarlocks and winches, the boats range in size from a few feet to 16 feet long.

His more than 20 non-studio ship models include a Dutch freighter bought in Holland and since restored and a Turkish freighter built by Mr. Lozar from scratch and equipped with a working steam engine.

The Dutch and Turkish vessels are mementoes of a year spent in Holland in 1965-66 by Mr. Lozar and his wife, Ginger, and of a trip around the world made by the couple in 1967-68. The trip lasted a full year and was supported by a Plym Traveling Fellowship.

Some of the models date back to when Mr. Lozar first fell in love with ships at the age of 10. He constructed these small models not from kits but by hand on the basis of photographs.

Mr. Lozar, who also owns another 25 boats kept in his parents' attic in Chicago, said he first began acquiring film studio models 18 months ago. He has bought most of his collection from Universal Studios.

Among the studio models are the longest boat in the collection, a 16-foot long World War II tanker used in "Tora, Tora, Tora," a tugboat from "Tugboat Annie," a barge from "Cleopatra" and a Mississippi paddle wheeler from "Showboat."

Mr. Lozar also owns a boat from "Ben Hur" made entirely of copper, a 14-foot steamer used in "The Sand Pebbles" and a pirate ship from the 1929 movie, "The Buccaneers," with light sockets behind each gunport activated by a keyboard to create the illusion for the camera of cannons being fired.

The pride of his collection is Admiral Nelson's flagship, the H.M.S. "Victory," built for an unidentified movie.

"Many of the ships have been stored at the studios for 20 years or longer, and no one remembers anymore for what movie they were built," Mr. Lozar said. "I often watch old movies on TV and study books on movies to try to identify some of my ships.

"The biggest problem was to move them here from California. I rented a truck with a 12-foot-long loading area, and since the "Tora, Tora, Tora" tanker is 16 feet long, I had to cut it in two to transport it.

"Before the trip, I dragged the tanker into our house in San Francisco. I was unable to turn it over because of its weight. When I ripped off the decks, I discovered 300 pounds of lead weights in the hull."

While repairing, repainting and generally restoring the boats, Mr. Lozar keeps them on wheels.

Most of the models were discovered by Mr. Lozar's parents during a tour of Universal Studios. He said he paid less than $200 each for eight models and that restored models are worth from $5,000 to $10,000 each.

"I love ships both from an architectural and artistic viewpoint. I would like to start a museum of movie model ships. Presently there is no such place in existence," he said.

Mr. Lozar has lived in Champaign-Urbana off and on since 1959. An architect working for the U.S. Army Corps of Engineers with a specialty in bio feedback, he received his master's degree from M.I.T. and a doctorate in urban design from a Dutch university during the year spent in Holland on a Fulbright scholarship.

The Lozars lived in Urbana before and after the trip around the world. Their stay here was interrupted by one year in California, where Mr. Lozar worked towards a second Ph.D. in architectural psychology from Berkeley.

Mrs. Lozar did her undergraduate work at the University of Illinois and received her master's degree from the university in oral interpretation.

She has taught in the communications department at the University of Illinois and has worked in dance, mime and children's theater as a director and performer.

Her most recent endeavor was aiding in the design and construction of puppets for Children's Theatre, Inc. of Champaign-Urbana's school and library shows this fall. The shows introduce school children to "The Nutcracker" which will be performed by the National Academy Ballet. She also was one of the three puppeteers.

Mrs. Lozar plans to start a puppet theater that would perform at children's birthday parties, but right now her time is occupied with caring for the couple's three children, David, 6, Troy, 3, and Carmen, 4 months.

She also serves as "almost a housemother" for students living in two houses owned by the Lozars on Oregon Street.

She may base her theater on puppets bought in Indonesia and Taiwan during her year of travel.

Mr. Lozar's purpose of the world trip was to explore the cultural implications of architectural styles. He applied his research to the design of disposable housing for underdeveloped nations.

The couple traveled more than 35,000 miles by plane, train, bus, car and ox-cart. Among other places, they visited Hawaii, Japan, Hong Kong, the Philippines, Malaysia, Thailand, Burma, India, Nepal, Afghanistan and many European countries.

At one point they joined up with an American art dealer who was traveling across India in a Land Rover with his wife and three children.

"It was a bit crowded," Ginger Lozar said. "The youngest child was 6 months old, and my unforgettable impressions of India are framed in my mind by drying diapers flapping around the windows."

Also unforgettable was "the endless trip," a six-week journey from Delhi to London in a ramshackle bus for which the Lozars paid $90 fare each.

The bus ran every two months and journeyed through Pakistan, Afghanistan, Iran, Turkey, Greece, Yugoslavia and central Europe.

The 24 occupants became "intimate enemies" by the end of the trip, Mrs. Lozar said.

"The women slept on the bus, the men underneath it or in tents, and the Australian driver and his girlfriend claimed the space underneath the radiator with their dog.

"When we stopped to eat, two passengers would be handed the equivalent of five dollars and told to buy and cook provisions for us all with that," she recalled.

Another travel memory is an 18-hour ride on a crowded train through Germany when Mrs. Lozar stood in the corridor holding a sitar acquired in India, while Mr. Lozar spent the entire trip in the lavatory — the only free space large enough to hold him and a huge boat model.

November 1975

The Baptism of Koula Giannopoulos

Firmly gripping 7-month-old Koula Giannopoulos by her chubby wrists, the Rev. Nicholas F. Voucanos lowered the baby three times into the silver baptismal font until the water reached her neck.

Her small nude body glistening with olive oil, Koula smiled beatifically through the immersions. Her tiny lips shaped into a contented "Ah" when Father Voucanos handed her to her godmother, Mrs. Peter F. Tomaras, to be wrapped in a white receiving blanket.

The immersions marked the high point of the hour-long baptismal service last Sunday in the Greek Orthodox Church in Champaign.

Before the start of the service, many of the approximately 60 friends and relatives of Koula's parents, Mr. and Mrs. Ted Giannopoulos of Champaign, kissed an icon hanging next to the entrance of the nave and crossed themselves before entering the pews.

The Sacrament of Holy Baptism in the Greek Orthodox Church is divided into two parts, the exorcisms and the baptism. With a few exceptions, the entire service was performed in Greek.

The service began as Father Voucanos walked to the wall opposite the altar together with Mrs. Tomaras with Koula in her arms and the two other members of the baptismal party, Mrs. Tomaras's grandson, Valorios (Val) Shaffer, 8, and Mr. Giannopoulos's sister, Rea Stathos.

Father Voucanos blew gently on Koula's face and made the sign of the cross, symbolizing his command to evil spirits to depart from the baby. He then read five prayers asking God-The Holy Trinity to remove any evil from the baby.

Repeating after the priest, Mrs. Tomaras as the baby's sponsor denounced Satan three times and declared three times that she now sides with Christ. The priest then recited the Creed of the church and with a prayer gave the baby her name.

The group then moved to the font in front of the altar for the baptismal service. While Father Voucanos blessed the font with a gold-covered Bible and read two prayers to sanctify the water in the font, Mrs. Tomaras and Mrs. Stathos undressed Koula at a nearby table.

While Mrs. Stathos held Koula, by now swathed only in a receiving blanket, Mrs. Tomaras produced an octagonal plastic bottle of Pompeian Olive Oil, which the priest blessed. After pouring some oil into the font, he annointed the baby on most parts of her body, dipping his hands into oil held by Mrs. Tomaras in her cupped hands.

The annointment symbolizes that the person being baptized already has attracted the mercy of God and is about to enter into the kingdom of salvation. The symbolism derives from the olive branch brought by the dove to Noah's Ark.

The immersions into the font followed, signifying the wiping out of original sin.

As Koula sat in her godmother's arms, Father Voucanos blessed her and cut three strands of hair from her head.

The haircutting symbolizes that the baby will be a servant of God. Its origin is the custom in ancient times of masters cutting the hair of their slaves after purchasing them.

While Val held back the wide sleeves of Father Voucanos's full-length black robe, the priest washed his hands with soap and rinsed them in the baptismal water. Meanwhile Mrs. Tomaras and Mrs. Stathos cooed softly as they dressed Koula at the table in her white baptismal gown, which had first been blessed by the priest, and covered her head with a close-fitting white bonnet.

Father Voucanos lighted a white candle held by a stick covered with pink tulle by touching its wick to one of three candles attached to the font. He then changed into a magnificent white robe with a gold center panel.

As Mrs. Tomaras held the still beaming Koula whose dark curls moist with olive oil peeped out from under her bonnet and Val carried the pink-tulled candle, Father Voucanos picked up a metal incense burner and swung it on its chain.

With the priest at one side of the font and Mrs. Tomaras, Koula and Val at the other, the party walked three times around the font while the congregation sang a hymn.

The circling of the font symbolizes the joy of the church over the saving of the baptized person's soul.

Using a second Bible, its gold cover ornamented with enameled icons, the priest read two selections from the Bible before blessing the baby and bringing the book to her lips to kiss. After Mrs. Tomaras and Val had kissed the Bible, the priest blessed Koula with a golden cross.

As he intoned the final prayers, Koula finally emitted her first whimpers of the ceremony, ceasing immediately when she was handed a small altar bell.

The service ended as Mr. and Mrs. Giannopoulos and Mr. Giannopoulos's father, Tasi, who had flown from Athens to attend the ceremony, joined the baptismal party to receive the priest's blessings and congratulations and kiss the cross, while Koula merrily rang the altar bell.

After the congregation had passed through a receiving line in front of the font to congratulate the family, each person attending received a white rosette on a pink ribbon ornamented by a tiny golden cross.

A dinner and dance to the music of a bouzouki orchestra from Chicago was held at the Ramada Inn after the ceremony.

The first dance was danced by a line formed by Mr. Giannopoulos and his father and sister. They were soon joined in the traditional Greek chain dance by friends and relatives of all ages, dancing joyfully to celebrate Koula's baptism.

November 1976

The Flourishing Floras

At first glance you would expect Chuck Flora to raise daughters in the mold of protected females, fluttering demurely below white parasols, proficient in needlework and watercolors, and politely aghast when faced with a power tool.

The very essence of a "man's man" — a wrestler in his youth, a camper and canoer, a man who stalks moose, deer and wild boar with bow and arrow, a flyer with the rank of flight instructor, a do-it-yourselfer par excellence — Mr. Flora might well have been expected to have imprinted his daughters with all the attributes of what in his formative years were considered ideal for a "feminine" woman.

Yet this man and his wife, the gentle Mary Lou, have managed to raise two daughters not only of mind-boggling academic and civic achievements but also with a rare degree of preparation for the demands of 1980s womanhood.

Academically speaking, the two multiflora blooms on the family tree, 18-year-old Denise and 14-year-old Sharla, have brought the Floras many accomplishments to make this Father's Day memorable.

To cover just the peaks, Denise graduated from Central High School two weeks ago with Highest Academic Honors for her five-point average.

She is a National Merit Scholar finalist, an Illinois State Scholar and scholarship winner, winner of the Rotary Youth Merit Award and chosen as the outstanding senior girl by the faculty for the American Legion Auxiliary Unit 24 Good Citizenship Award.

The latter award also was won by Sharla on her graduation recently from Edison Middle School, in her case for being the outstanding eighth-grade girl.

Sharla's academic awards for the school year also include a scholarship honor certificate for high scholastic achievement for choral music and Spanish, and certificates of merit for creative writing and her participation in the Advanced Computer Club.

But academic accomplishments are only part of the spectrum of the Flora girls' lives.

Chuck and Mary Lou Flora both believe in exposing their daughters to a wide range of activities. Coupled with the climate of trust and self-confidence they have provided through example and participation, this belief has made the stretching of wings the norm for their girls rather than a rare occurrence.

The range of activities in which Denise and Sharla perform with competency is truly breathtaking.

These girls can split a stack of wood, build a piece of furniture, help turn a stripped van into a camper and do just about everything around the house and yard except, Mr. Flora says with mock sternness, "clean out the garage."

They can play a wide range of musical instruments from the African thumb piano to the grand piano with Denise specializing in piano, guitar and banjo and Sharla favoring the guitar. Denise also composes and has had her ballads performed at concerts by others while Sharla loves to sing and is a member of several choirs and singing ensembles.

They can hit a clay pigeon with a shotgun and a target with a BB gun.

They know how to handle a canoe and a snowmobile, set up a campsite and hunt for Indian relics. A few weeks ago Sharla found an 8,000-year-old arrowhead on an early morning family excursion.

They love to ski and play volleyball and softball on their schools' teams and on the softball team of Champaign Park District which their father has helped coach several summers.

They both write poetry. One of Sharla's poems received honorable mention in a creative writing contest at Champaign Public Library. In 1975 Mr. Flora arranged for the printing of 100 copies of a 70-page book, "Reflections," containing a collection of Denise's poems written during the previous three years, as a surprise Christmas gift for her.

Denise teaches private lessons in guitar, piano and Spanish to earn pocket money. She improved her Spanish through contact with an exchange student from El Salvador, who lived with the Flora family for six months in 1979, and a subsequent visit to the student's home in San Salvador during Christmas break.

She leaves next week for a 40-day trip to Europe as a member of the People-to-People High School Student Ambassador Program. She will visit Austria, Hungary, Yugoslavia, Greece, Italy and West Germany and live for short periods with local families in Vienna, near Munich and in Athens.

The most recent family undertaking is a quick course in photography given by Mr. Flora to Denise to prepare her to take pictures on the trip.

Next fall Sharla enters Central High School while Denise begins a five-year program at the University of Illinois in a combination of engineering and liberal arts.

For the first four years of her university studies she is assured of $1,750 in yearly scholarship support — $1,000 through the Illinois State Scholar Program and $750 as a National Merit Scholar.

The two girls have been able to venture out into their many challenging endeavors because of their base in a home in which high standards, warmth and encouragement are almost tactile components.

This is a family whose recreation room in the basement as well as several other basement rooms are given over to materials for the family's many joint undertakings.

The recreation room is filled with sports equipment, photo materials, scrapbooks, photo albums and musical instruments as well as the hides and heads of animals brought down by Mr. Flora's bow and arrows.

A gigantic waterbed ("I told you girls to make sure you call it a water-sofa," Mr. Flora said, mindful of the equivocal image of waterbeds) was built by the family members and serves as an inviting spot for the four Floras to gather to watch television.

It is typical of the Floras that every winter they move the porch swing from the back porch at their home in Champaign — designed and built by Mr. Flora 19 years ago — to hooks in front of the recreation room fireplace, substituting firegazing en famille for the summer activity of Mr. Flora and Sharla using the swing as a perch for shooting BB guns at a target.

This is a family who greeted the student from El Salvador, who had never before seen snow, with a huge snowwoman in the front yard bearing a welcoming sign in Spanish.

It is a family that combats the busyness of their four schedules by making dawn excursions to Lake of the Woods, cooking breakfast over an open fire, romping with the dog and swimming, and returning to town by nine o'clock before the crowds arrive.

It is a family that guiltily but firmly reserves Christmas Eve for a dinner of pheasant or venison just for the four of them in front of the living room fireplace, taking out an evening to focus on each other in the midst of a busy season.

It is a family in which Mr. Flora has earned the authority to make an edict of No Dating Before You Are 16 and have it accepted without questions, yet also has the playfulness to make his daughters dissolve in laughter as he inspects the label of a newly acquired sweater and bemoans the fate of "all the little acrylics who had to give up their lives" so the garment could be made.

A Champaign native who spent four years in the Navy, Mr. Flora has worked for the University of Illinois for 20 years and is now supervisor of graphic design at the Printing Services, which produces the majority of the publications for the university ranging from personal calling cards to case-bound books.

Mrs. Flora manages the office for the Public Works Center of the City of Champaign, where her duties include keeping inventory, ordering parts and keeping the books for everything having to do with mechanical maintenance of all the city's vehicles including police cars, fire engines and snow plows.

She has been working outside her home for three years, preferring to stay at home full time until the younger daughter was in junior high school.

"Our whole philosophy in raising the girls has always been to reward them for trying, whether they win or not," Mr. Flora said.

"The things I have tried to teach them are the things my father taught me and still does—the common, everyday horse sense of life."

He credits his wife with the larger effort in bringing up the girls.

"Lou instilled a lot of their attitudes. She was always at home when they needed her and would take time to sit down and hear all about their day. Her availability, the readiness to play reading games and math games when they were small, the being there for all their later needs, made all the difference," he said.

As for his own contributions, he said he believes the girls gain freedom and independence through being competent in many areas.

"Every girl should know how to wire a lamp, handle a shotgun and deal with tools," he said.

He compares child-raising to flying an airplane.

"Anyone with average intelligence can fly an airplane. There is no magic to it at all.

"As one of my early flight instructors said, all it is is a bunch of minor adjustments on a continuing basis.

"The only time you get in trouble is when you either are too busy or when you ignore the fact that an adjustment is needed. Then you may find that a major adjustment is needed.

"And, fortunately, most of the work is done by the co-pilot!"

He added, "Sometimes I can't believe the way the girls have turned out — the fact that they don't bicker, the fact that we have such loving kids, such well-rounded kids.

"Yet, accustomed as I have become to their doing well, everytime they do something fine it's a marvel to me."

June 1980

Room for Four More

"We fell into the pattern of a family right away," said Jowann (Jo) Grotelueschen.

Two years ago Mrs. Grotelueschen and her husband, Arden, adopted four siblings from Canada.

The couple already had two children, Teresa, now 11, and Hans, 6. The four adopted children are Willie, now 10, Bonnie, 8, Tammy, 7, and Violet, 6.

They decided to adopt a child after their son, Drew, who came between Hans and Teresa in age, died of a brain tumor.

"It felt empty around here," Mrs. Grotelueschen said. "We knew we could never get another child to take Drew's place, but we all felt we would be happier and busier with more children."

The couple applied to Lutheran Welfare Services in Peoria, saying they would be happy to adopt siblings.

"We thought they might give us two," Mrs. Grotelueschen said. "One day the agency called and asked if we would be interested in four. I never thought twice but just said Yes. When my husband came home that evening from an out-of-town trip and said, 'Hi, what's new?', I said, 'Maybe you better sit down before I tell you'."

Mr. Grotelueschen came through like a trouper, in his wife's phrase, and the preparations for the multiple adoption began.

Ten months after the original application was made, the children flew in from Canada for an exploratory weekend visit, accompanied by a caseworker and one of their foster mothers.

Three weeks later, in July 1974, Professor Grotelueschen flew to the children's home town 500 miles north of Winnipeg with a friend in a borrowed plane and brought the children back.

The children, who had lived in various foster homes in groups of two, began calling the Grotelueschens Mommy and Daddy right away.

"The first few days were an uproar, but, all in all, it wasn't too traumatic," Mrs. Grotelueschen said.

The couple had discussed the adoption with Hans and Teresa throughout the proceedings and had taken them to most of the meetings at the adoption agency.

"We thought it important to talk about the disadvantages with Hans and Teresa ahead of time," Mrs. Grotelueschen said. "We explained they would have to share more and would not get as much attention from us as before. Both children are very gregarious, and everything worked out well.

"We felt it was imperative for Teresa to remain the oldest child in the family, and she did. Hans was the youngest before, and although Violet is younger and smaller than him, he still is the youngest boy."

While Hans and Teresa are blonde and blue-eyed, the four adopted children have an Indian great-grandparent or grandparent and have dark hair and eyes.

Mrs. Grotelueschen said that all six play happily together either as a group or several at a time without regard for who is who's original brother or sister.

"Many families on our street have five children each, and the children have a lot of playmates," she added.

The couple spent the three weeks between the adopted children's weekend visit and permanent arrival preparing their large Urbana house. They carpeted and paneled the lower level of the house and made it into a bedroom, bath, and recreation room.

Through the first months of being a family of eight, the Grotelueschens would discuss the problems of the day at a nightly session, which often included Teresa.

"We would talk everything over, trying to keep our sanity and just keeping our heads together," Mrs. Grotelueschen said.

"We had countless little things to iron out. We tried to deal with each as we went along and not to be overwhelmed with the bigness of it all.

"The biggest change has been a good one: there are far, far fewer exceptions to the rules like eating up your food, picking up your toys, brushing your teeth, and doing your household duties. And the children aid me by checking on each other."

All six children and Professor Grotelueschen help her with dinner preparations and after-dinner clean-up one day a week. This is also a time for her to be alone with each family member.

236

The children also help with the vacuuming, dusting and folding of laundry. Mrs. Grotelueschen sorts and distributes the clean laundry.

"We have a rule that whatever fits you, you wear," she said with a smile.

She handles all arrangements for medical and dental appointments and after-school lessons. A piano teacher comes to the house one entire afternoon a week and gives lessons to her and all the children.

"Our arrangement is that I run the house on a day-to-day basis, while Arden sticks to his office job and plans our future," Mrs. Grotelueschen said.

An associate professor of education, Mr. Grotelueschen is director of the office for the study of continuing professional education at the University of Illinois.

The Grotelueschens have nothing but gratitude for their opportunity to be the parents of six youngsters.

"One reason we were able to get the children was that the caseworker saw we had plenty of room," Mrs. Grotelueschen said.

"I am sure there are many families who would like to adopt four children but just don't have room for them."

June 1976

Two Years Later

Lightning had zeroed in on the pump house two days before, leaving the family without water.

Fifteen friends were expected for dinner a couple of hours later, making for 24 at the dinner table, and several of the guests would stay overnight.

But these pressures failed to ruffle Arden and Jowann (Jo) Grotelueschen as they concluded a tour of their country estate with a reporter.

Totally relaxed, the couple showed off their large log home and wooden barn, both erected since last fall, the pastures where 36 head of Black Angus cattle and five horses graze, the 3½-acre lake teeming with fish, the flourishing kitchen garden, the orchards and berry patches, all set in an idyllic landscape of rolling fields and dense woods partly bordered by the Little Embarras River.

The couple, who had lived in Urbana for many years, bought their country property near Oakland two years ago.

The farm is made up of two parts, 103 acres where the family lives and 77 acres one mile away.

Of the 180 acres, about 80 are in timber, 70 in row crops (corn and beans) and 15 are set aside for small fruits. The remaining 15 acres are taken up by pasture and the pond.

The family moved from its Urbana house last fall and lived in a rented house in Oakland while building the house and barn. It moved to the farm, which is called "The Patch," in April.

Professor Grotelueschen commutes to his office in Champaign at least four days a week. The drive takes him about one hour each way.

In addition to Jo and Arden Grotelueschen, the three-generational family includes Mr. Grotelueschen's mother, Hilda, and six children, Teresa, 13, Willie, 12, Bonnie, 10, Tammy, 9, and Hans and Violet, both 8.

The reason for the move to the country was a wish to undertake an endeavor which would involve the whole family working together, Professor Grotelueschen said.

"I lived on a farm in Nebraska for the first eight years of my life until my father died," he said. "Farming is in my blood."

"We were very happy in Urbana but I found myself getting more and more involved in women's clubs and organizations and felt it would be far more satisfying to live a life centered on working outdoors," Mrs. Grotelueschen said.

"The solitude you can find on a farm, working in the berry patches, kitchen garden or orchards or roaming around the woods and river, is a special joy to me," she said.

With many friends visiting and working on the farm on weekends, social contacts are plentiful, she said.

The Grotelueschens have always spent a lot of time with their children but with the move to the farm, family members work together more.

"The whole idea of chores is important in raising children," Professor Grotelueschen said. "The kids work hard, and we think this is good for them."

Among the children's chores are grooming and watering the horses, helping their father feed and water the cattle, and weeding and fruit-picking in the orchards and berry patches.

One child is in charge of caring for the dog and another takes care of the two cats, which Professor Grotelueschen calls "our Black Angus cats" because their color matches that of the cattle.

Everyone helps in the kitchen garden which is the special project of the elder and younger Mrs. Grotelueschen. The garden contains green beans, sweet corn, zucchini, green peppers, onions, tomatoes, Brussels sprouts, pumpkins, cantaloupes, watermelons and butternut squash.

"We could feed the world out of our garden," Professor Grotelueschen said with a grin.

The family has planted 40 cherry trees and 250 apple trees in addition to blueberry and strawberry patches.

Next spring they plan to plant more strawberries and apple trees as well as blackberries and raspberries.

The 70 acres in row crops are farmed by a neighbor but the remaining work on the farm, as well as much of the work involved in building the house and barn, has been done by the Grotelueschens.

Their equipment includes a tractor, disc, mower, fork and posthole digger. They chose a fairly small tractor to enable Mrs. Grotelueschen, a petite woman, and, later on, the children, to drive it.

They have been learning about farming on the job, getting advice from friends and neighbors and the senior Mrs. Grotelueschen.

"The system is: You see it, do it, teach it," Professor Grotelueschen said.

Jo Grotelueschen, whose background is in education, took university courses in soil nutrition and fertilization and in pest control while the family still lived in Urbana. Among the skills she has learned on the farm are pulling calves from a birthing heifer and performing artificial insemination on the cows.

The children also help with the cow breeding.

"We don't have to make a big deal out of sex education. The children learn from their chores with the farm animals," Professor Grotelueschen said, adding that he calls Bonnie "our heat detector," because it is her job to ascertain when the cows are in heat.

He designed the barn himself — "Probably the first wood barn built in the county in a long time with pole barns being so popular," he noted — and acted as his own contractor for the building of the barn and the house.

Many jobs were performed by subcontractors, but the Grotelueschens did a great deal of the work.

The house is built of pine logs which were shipped precut and numbered from Montana and erected by the log company. It has a complete English basement which holds a stone fireplace, a recreation room, the boys' bedroom and bath, a mud room and an extra room.

The main floor has a towering cathedral ceiling allowing space for Jo and Arden Grotelueschen's bedroom on a loft above the living room.

The living room is dominated by an open stairway leading to the exposed loft bedroom and a gigantic stone fireplace.

Both the living room and the large kitchen-dining room are furnished with country antiques. The dining area contains art works appropriate to the country setting including three farmscapes by Champaign artist Billy Morrow Jackson and a windmill sculpture by Nona Leeper of Champaign.

The main floor also has three bedrooms, one for Grandma Grotelueschen furnished in antiques, and two for the four girls, each with loft space for sleeping or play. Grandma and the four girls share a bathroom, and another bath is planned next to the master bedroom.

Also in the planning are two screened-in porches, one on cantilevered logs off the master bedroom, and one below, off the living room facing the woods. Another upcoming project is chinking with mortar between the logs.

The construction on the house began Nov. 1. In spite of severe weather, only four days' work was lost during the winter.

All the Grotelueschens love their new life shaped by the farm work and the lovely nature surrounding them and have perhaps enjoyed most of all the experience of becoming part of a small community.

The children attend school in Oakland and ride their bikes during the summer to the Oakland pool and to take part in softball and baseball games. They are members of 4-H groups.

Professor Grotelueschen is a member of the Lions Club in Oakland and both he and his wife cherish their early morning visits to Oakland where, Professor Grotelueschen says, "I can get hold of more people I need to talk to between 5 and 7 a.m. than I can during a whole day at the university."

The family has joined the closest Lutheran church, which is in Charleston.

Among the pleasures of country living for the family are the identification of 70 wildflowers since the beginning of spring and the sighting of ducks, geese and egrets on the pond.

The farm presents plenty of challenges, and three generations of Grotelueschens agree with Jo Grotelueschen when she says, "I love it! There is always so much to do but we have come a long way."

August 1978

SOME PERSONAL COLUMNS

July 4, 1976

Although 200 years does not seem like such a long time to me — my hometown in Denmark celebrated the 500th anniversary of its city charter in 1942 — the Bicentennial might be a good time for a naturalized citizen to take stock of her feelings about her adopted country.

Trite as it may sound, I guess my strongest feeling about America is gratitude for the freedom of speech and religion that we Americans enjoy.

Although the three other countries in which I have lived (Denmark, Sweden and France) were all democracies, I feel that the freedom extended to individual citizens is even greater here in America.

On an every day level, I appreciate the way that life in the U.S. is so hassle-free. For instance, when you move, your main responsibility is to tell the moving van company. In Denmark, every time you move, you must go to government offices in the town you leave and the town you move to and report your change of address.

And, although I am a fervent Francophile, I usually can subdue my most intense yearnings to be in France by focusing on the fact that it takes 15 minutes to cash a check in a French bank and a full day to get your identification papers in order.

American life is so efficiently arranged in most every day matters that you have more time and energy for essentials. I think our institutions and businesses work with less bureaucracy than in any other country I have lived, and that government agencies interfere less here than in these other countries.

What else do I like best about America?

In no particular order, I liked the public outrage over Watergate and the demonstration of the effectiveness of the system of checks and balances the Watergate aftermath indicated.

I like the fact that although disparities certainly exist in American life, a very large majority of the population has lives of great comfort and security.

I like the degree of classlessness in our society — the fact that you are not pigeon-holed by your speech or dialectical intonation, that, thanks to the ready-to-wear industry, clothing is not a means for dividing people visibly into categories, that the executive's son is as apt to have a newspaper route as the laborer's.

I like the dynamic tension generated in a society composed by many different ethnic groups. I think we are stronger and more interesting as a people because we bring so many different backgrounds to being Americans.

No matter how much I enjoy a visit to Denmark, I usually end it with a feeling of boredom caused by the homogenous ethnic and cultural background of the Danes.

I like — although that is too weak a word — the kindness and openness of Americans. I like the way Americans rush to help each other and people abroad when needed, whether the needy ones are farmers unable to bring in the harvest because of illness, tornado victims in a small town, or earthquake survivors in Guatamala.

I like the bigness of the country. When you grow up in a country one-third the size of Illinois, you revel in the hugeness of America and the feeling of unlimited physical and emotional space.

I like sharing a language with hundreds of millions of people.

I like the way Americans handle their cars. Perhaps Americans drive better and less aggressively than the French and Danes because car ownership has been widespread here for a much longer time and does not represent a sudden emancipation. Whatever the reason, most American drivers are enormously much more considerate and polite than Danish and French drivers.

I like the fierceness and extremes of our Midwestern climate — the violent thunderstorms, the brilliantly sunny days we occasionally get in January, the blessed relief when a week of tropically hot and humid summer weather ends.

I like the Midwestern landscape any time of the year — the rich black soil dormant in winter, the ocean-like expanses of freshly-disced fields in spring, the fields of corn as tall as a man in summer which make the roads seem like tunnels, the brilliant reds and yellows of the trees in fall.

I like fireflies, cheeseburgers, football games, porch swings, bumper stickers, country music lyrics, seeing an opossum in my back yard, the parade of high school bands to the stadium every fall, the smell of skunk on a summer evening, the warmth of people who say not Goodbye but Take Care.

In short, I like my adopted country.

Happy Birthday, America — and Take Care.

July 1976

Barbara Lessaris in Memoriam

Attempting in vain to save her youngest son, Barbara Lessaris died yesterday morning in a fire in her home.

Mrs. Lessaris was the center of two large, warm, Greek families — her own and her husband Pete's — and her death at 37, and that of her 9-year-old son George, will be felt most of all by them.

But in her years in Champaign-Urbana, she has become a treasured friend to so many people that the shock of her death reaches out in wide circles.

A woman of startling classical beauty, she had escaped the trap of trading on this. She was a woman of great warmth, compassion and gaiety which she combined with a hardheaded effectiveness in her many volunteer jobs.

In a time of discontent among women, she was unselfconsciously proud and happy to center her intelligence and energies on being mainly a wife and mother.

The family moved a few years ago from a modest, smaller house to the large house on Waverly Drive in which she and George lost their lives. She loved the new house with its swimming pool and filled the home with friends of all ages.

With tactful persistence, she spent countless hours working for organizations she believed in. She was benefit chairman this year and last for the Symphony Guild, and active in AAUW, Children's Theatre and the Greek Orthodox Church.

Most of all, she took pride in her Greek ancestry and in being part of the Greek community in Champaign-Urbana.

Among her friends, she was a source of light — the first to subscribe to a paper in which a friend's articles began to appear, the first to show up with a huge pan of baklava for an anniversary party, the first to care about and share both joys and sorrows.

No one can comfort adequately those left behind — her husband, her son, the two families, the countless friends. Perhaps it was for a time like this that Matthew Arnold wrote, ". . . for the world, which seems to lie before us like a land of dreams, so various, so beautiful, so new, hath really neither joy, nor love, nor light, nor certitude, nor peace, nor help for pain."

All one can do is remember the remark of someone at a recent party who intercepted a look between Barbara and Pete Lessaris and said wistfully, "If only I could bottle that look, I'd be rich in a world so short on love."

December 1974

A Technicolor Faith

Seeing "That's Entertainment" is a little like watching good home movies. The film is made up of excerpts from Metro-Goldwyn-Mayer musicals, the oldest from the first M-G-M musical made in 1929, the latest from "Gigi." The bulk is from the great decades, the 1940s and 1950s, when the American movie musical was one of the freshest art forms sweeping the world.

The home movie aspect is visible in the behavior of the audience who, the night I saw the movie, would whisper hurriedly to strangers to identify a player and laugh together indulgently at a young and skinny Frank Sinatra or a de-romanticized Clark Gable in a corny vaudeville routine.

Touching as it must be for a native American to see Judy Garland and Mickey Rooney at their freshest and Fred Astaire at his peak, I think it may be almost impossible to convey the Proustian impact this movie has on someone who grew up in Europe, and for whom American movies provided the first and all-pervading view of the New World.

Shortly after the start of World War II, American and English movies disappeared from the screens in countries occupied by Nazi Germany. For five years the only movie fare available in a country like Denmark, where I grew up, were Danish, Swedish, French and German films.

Consequently, when the war ended, a flood of great and minor pictures deluged the screens for an audience starved for a view of the United States and England, and with an immense good will toward the liberating countries.

I had just reached the age when I was old enough to go to the movies by myself when this deluge began. For the first six years after the war I, like many of my contemporaries, went to the movies several times a week.

The cost was minimal, the equivalent of 9 cents. Seating was either in the second balcony if any, or in the first four rows of the main floor.

Several years after the war, when I began to work as a reporter and received reviewer's tickets, I remember marvelling at the beauty of Leslie Howard and Veronica Lake as seen from the middle of the theater. The second-row seat enabled you to see the film all right, but the close-ups did look distorted!

Being the youngest reporter on the staff, I would get the last choice of tickets for the new films to arrive in town. A typical Monday or Friday night assignment would have the city editor at the local opening of "Sunset Boulevard," the police reporter at the latest J. Arthur Rank film, and me at a Western with George Macready and Sonny Tufts.

After the show we would head for the newsroom and bat out our reviews. No candidate for the front cover of the New York Times Book Review ever approached his assignment with more conscientiousness than we did.

What did we look for in American movies those first years after the five-year deprivation?

First of all, we listened. We all had studied English in school, invariably taught by teachers with Oxford accents, but to us America and the American pronounciation were glamorous. We scanned the Danish sub-titles quickly with our ears wide open and came out of the theater with the cadences of Henry Fonda's Nebraska speech or Humphrey Bogart's Eastern drawl.

We looked avidly for any sign of everyday American life, no matter how silly and superficial the movie. I remember clutching the hand of my companion whenever a bicycling newspaper boy would throw a paper onto a porch. To us this was a symbol of American life.

In the bathtub scenes which were prevalent in those innocent days, we would marvel at the clouds of bubble foam and delight in the fact that the soap would float instead of sinking as ours did.

We took in everything the film cared to reveal — no matter how fleetingly and unintentionally — about the way American cities looked, the clothes Americans wore, the foods Americans ate, the number of cars on the streets, the slang terms, the chewing gum, the saddle-shoes, the Coca-Cola.

The largest proportion of the films we saw were light-weight musicals with no pretension to portray the reality of life. We realized this while still taking in any revelation of everyday American life that might seep through stories about getting a show successfully on Broadway or about a bunch of sailors on leave.

Once in a while a movie would come along that dealt with life as it was really lived in the United States. Then we would return several times to absorb the details and texture. Such a movie was William Wyler's "The Best Years of Our Lives" about the problems of returning veterans.

But mostly our world was peopled, to our complete satisfaction, with the vigorous, glamorous movie stars who live again in "This is Entertainment:" Gene Kelly, Donald O'Connor, Esther Williams, Kathryn Grayson, Lena Horne, Debbie Reynolds — an endless parade of Americans, unscarred by war and post-war depression, and, to us, the very affirmation of the future.

September 1974

A Mother Is Many Things

A mother is many things.

Depending on the stage of her life, she is someone who sleeps with an ear cocked for a cry in the night after a back-breaking day of spooning in baby food, folding diapers, and leafing through Spock in a frantic attempt to identify red spots.

She is the peacemaker when fights over the ownership of a shovel erupt in the sandbox and the one who covers her refrigerator with paintings brought home from nursery school.

She reads the "Just So Stories" aloud at bedtime and says "Who's There?" and answers riddles for 9-year-olds going through the Knock-Knock joke and riddle stage.

She is someone who goes on long walks on rainy days to sail twigs in sidewalk gutters and who helps small recalcitrant hands write Thank-You notes on that dreadful day after the birthday.

She makes peanut butter-and-jelly sandwiches for a houseful of playmates and tries to get across the feeling that liver is a delicious, forbidden food offered as a reward for good behavior.

She answers questions about where babies come from as they are put to her, usually while maneuvering her car into a tight parking space and not, as she may have imagined in her younger years, during a cozy fireside chat.

She is someone who closes all the windows in the house on a hot summer's day before a son's rock band arrives to practice and who retrieves her favorite blouse from a teenage daughter's closet without comment.

She trains herself to focus her thoughts on the political primaries or the situation in Lebanon when the urge to say "When are you going to get a haircut?" or "Please clean your room before I forget the color of your rug" comes over her.

She is someone who realizes staying in touch with college-aged children means accepting collect phone calls and who welcomes them and their suitcases full of dirty laundry at holiday weekends with equal pleasure.

Throughout, she is someone who learns to let go, allowing fumbling hands to carry out a job she could do herself in a fraction of the time.

At the same time, she manages to keep an inner core of herself through the buffeting of the demands put on her.

She permits a young family to live through its own struggles and decisions and follows the grandchildren's development without saying, "Don't you think you should . . ."

In some instances, she is someone who has to watch a child live with a severe handicap. In others, in a heart-breaking reversal of the natural order, she has to see her child die and somehow find the strength to go on without letting bitterness permeate her life.

In most cases, she is someone who sees her grown-up children mature until it seems that they and she are all the same generation and share a deepening friendship.

But always, she is someone who loves and accepts and cares.

May 1976

The Return of a Native

Eight shiny 10-oere pieces in 12 days—that was my reward for simply bending over and picking up coins on the streets of Denmark during a late-October visit.

The fact that the 10-oere piece (value: two cents) is no longer apparently considered worth the effort to pick up by the Danes and is left for a visitor to collect says a great deal about the status of inflation in the small country.

To me one 10-oere piece has the additional significance of having constituted my weekly pocket money during a number of years of my childhood in my native Denmark. Ten oere in those pre-inflation days bought a large cone of hard candies or two cream-filled chocolate frogs.

But considering the prices the Danes pay today it is not surprising the 10-oere piece is regarded with disdain.

Here are some representative prices: $3.20 for a gallon of gas; about $12 for an LP record; $3.20 for a package of cigarettes; $1.70 for a beer or a pot of coffee or tea in a modest restaurant; 30 cents for a postcard; and 50 cents for a weekday Copenhagen paper.

Other Danish prices are $10 including tips for a lunch in a medium-priced restaurant (One open-faced sandwich with pickled salmon and a main dish of pork tenderloin with potatoes—no salad, dessert or beverage included) and $22 and $20 respectively for two of the season's bestsellers by Danish authors, both published European-style with soft covers and uncut pages.

Some of these prices, such as the cost of cigarettes and gasoline, reflect a large tax bite but most of the prices are simply instances of the high cost of living in Denmark today. All of the prices include a 20 percent tax—cigarettes and gasoline simply have additional taxes above that added.

Of course, a true comparison of Danish and American living standards would involve consideration of the Danish medical health insurance system, which makes health care virtually free for the majority of Danes, and the fact that the minimum wage is about $7.50 and that all jobs include four weeks paid vacation with an additional 10 percent vacation pay.

One should also take into account the income tax rate which is much higher than the American; the unemployment compensation which in Denmark stands at $15,000 a year; and the fact that an average teacher's salary in Denmark for a teacher with several years' experience is $24,000.

Granted that a valid comparison of prices and remuneration could only be done within the framework of a lengthy thesis on economy, you can still conclude that Denmark has become a very expensive place for American tourists.

Most of the prices listed were gleaned in my hometown, a city of about 50,000 with a healthy balance of industry and being the shopping center for an extensive farm community.

During my two days in Copenhagen I paid $25 for a ship cabin-sized room in a picturesque hotel housed in a renovated harbor-side 1804 warehouse near the center of the city.

Fair enough, you say, particularly since the price included a breakfast buffet. But wait—the price was a special late-fall weekend rate and the room during the tourist season rents for $54 for one person.

As someone who spent my first 19 years of life in Denmark and returns every three or four years to visit my family there, I find myself full of mixed reactions on my visits.

The homogeneity of the population—the enormous number of people you see on the street who obviously share the same ethnic background, leavened only by the faces of a few foreign workers from Turkey, Yugoslavia and Greece—has an oppressive effect on me.

I constantly find myself yearning for the stimulating and dynamic variety of ethnic backgrounds present in every state in the United States.

Walking around the streets of my hometown, where I as a young reporter knew a large proportion of the population, becomes a constant exercise of mentally stripping 20 or more years of age from the faces I see. By the time I have subtracted the signs of age from a middle-aged man or woman glimpsed on the street and realize who the person is, he or she usually is two blocks away.

While my spoken Danish remains flawless according to all reports, I find myself a virtual dinosaur in respect to direct address.

During the years I have lived in the United States the Danes have moved away from having two forms of direct personal pronouns, "du" for members of the family and close personal friends and "De" for everyone else. Instead they in most cases address everyone as "du."

I found myself jumping three feet, metaphorically speaking, and bitterly resenting what to me appeared as an over-familiar and intrusive form for address whenever strangers called me "du" on this visit.

It indicates to me that while we in English call everyone "you" the you is a formal form of address that needs to be tempered with the use of one's first name to become informal.

A few vignettes based on my visit:

—The anti-Americanism evidenced in the press and on television during my previous visits has largely disappeared. I got the impression that this has come about not so much from any greater respect and love for the United States but from a more intense concentration on local issues and a general turning-inward.

—The Danes have us Americans all beat as far as a non-fawning attitude towards celebrities and a relaxed view of nudity are concerned.

In Copenhagen I attended a performance of the Royal Danish Ballet in a rather small theater. Just before the start of the show the lovely young queen, Margrethe II, entered the royal box accompanied by her two little boys.

The audience rose, sat down and — to a man, it appeared — proceeded to gaze straight ahead at the stage to allow Her Majesty the privacy of enjoying the performance without being the object of stares.

The queen, by the way, is a talented designer and archeologist — the very model of what 1979 royalty should be like.

—The previous night I attended the gala opening of a new production of a 9-year-old modern ballet, "The Triumph of Death." An 80-minute work by Danish choreographer Flemming Flindt, it was highlighted by the presence of the Roumanian-French playwright, Ionesco (on whose play the ballet was based) in the audience and of a famous five-minute sequence in which almost all the female performers danced in the nude. As far as I could tell, the audience never batted an eyelid.

—I also stole one morning away from family visits in order to walk through some of the old parts of Copenhagen including Nyboder, a lovely neighborhood of yellow row houses built in the first half of the 17th century for sailors and their families by King Christian IV, and the classically beautiful square of Amalienborg, the residence of the queen.

As I crossed the square, I heard a strange sound from the sky. I looked up and saw high above me six wild swans flying in V-formation above the ancient city.

November 1979

254

Mother and Son Go to Europe

Bouncing around Europe on a winter journey as a mother-son act is great fun.

It is also extremely unusual, as my 22-year-old son, Mark, and I discovered on a three-week jaunt in November.

Nowhere, neither among the sparse number of tourists encountered on this trip, nor among the hordes met during earlier summer journeys which also included Mark's younger sister, have we ever come across a similar family combination of travel companions.

Yet, once you think about it, the advantages of traveling with your child are obvious, at least from the mother's viewpoint.

After all, during all those years of child-raising you have consciously and unconsciously imprinted your child with your own values and tastes.

Add to that the genetically conditioned similarity of temperaments and outlooks on life that you are apt to have, and you may find, as I did, that your own kid — in the final reckoning one of the major do-it-yourself projects of your life — makes the ideal travel companion.

And so, leaving my husband and daughter to care for each other for the duration, we set off on a journey of exploration and sharing.

We flew to Cologne (because fog deflected the plane from landing in Brussels) and returned from Brussels. Within Europe we traveled everywhere on the excellent trains with a first-class Eurailpass.

We spent two days in Germany; seven days in northern Italy, divided equally between Venice and Florence; five days exploring individually; five days in Paris; and one evening and night in Brussels.

During the five days apart, Mark visited Pisa briefly and spent the remaining time in Nice and Monte Carlo while I divided my time among Paris and three sites in northern France, Mont-Saint-Michel, Saint-Malo and Chartres.

Keeping the cost within reasonable bounds has become increasingly difficult on a European trip.

As recently as 1974 I paid $35 a day in a beautiful beach-front hotel on the Mediterranean in southern Italy for the two children and me.

For this money we got two rooms overlooking the sea, breakfast and a fine dinner. With another $5 for a picnic lunch and chair rental on the beach this made a daily $40 cost for three people for a paradisiacal life.

On the November trip we tried, like virtually all the travelers I know, to keep costs down, using Arthur Frommer's "Europe on $15 a Day" for lodging suggestions, limiting lunch to a sandwich, and seeking out modest restaurants for dinner.

Even so we never got below a $60 expenditure for the two of us (in Venice and Florence) and often hovered around the $100 figure (Paris and

Brussels) when we included theater or jazz concert outings.

We did benefit from an incredibly low transatlantic fare, paying only $345 each for the Chicago-Europe roundtrip on SABENA, the Belgian airline, which was introducing its new Chicago-Brussels run.

For the kind of trip Mark and I had agreed on, with its emphasis on museums, cathedrals and cultural events, traveling in winter has many advantages and some drawbacks.

The greatest advantage is the lack of tourist crowds everywhere.

This enables you to spend unjostled hours in front of the renaissance masterpieces in Florence, from the Botticelli paintings in the Uffizi to the poignantly unfinished Michelangelo sculptures that surround the so-very-finished "David" in the Academy.

It also makes it possible to travel without an itinerary since hotel accommodations generally are easy to get—a freedom we treasure greatly.

Another advantage is seeing the cities, which are overrun by crowds in the summer, pridefully and possessively regained by their own inhabitants.

A third is the enjoyment of a vast variety of weather, from brilliant sunlight on a Sunday afternoon in Paris in late November to snow on the Roman ruins in Germany's oldest city, Trier, on the second day of the trip.

The drawbacks are conditioned by the same factors which influence the advantages.

Winter weather and its accompanying slowing of the tourist stream from a flood to a trickle means that some excursions are not available.

For instance, the boat trips along the Rhine's castle-dotted banks and the excursions along the coasts of Normandy and Brittany from Saint-Malo—a ramparted town from which many buccaneers and explorers set forth—were discontinued for the season.

The main drawback is also brought about by the winter weather: you wear yourself out much more than on a summer journey.

The chance to rest up between bouts of museum-going and cathedral visits by sitting at a sidewalk cafe or a park bench is non-existent.

The sidewalk cafes are closed and it is too cold to linger on a bench.

When you add to that the clean but dismal rooms you end up with in low-priced hotels, which do not induce you to return for a rest during the day, you find yourself in a situation of being constantly on the go and ultimately exhausting yourself.

But the advantages, at least for us, far outweigh the drawbacks.

Consider these experiences:

—An hour at dawn in the Chartres Cathedral, watching the jewel colors of the greatest stained-glass windows in Christendom emerge slowly like developing Polaroid photos—the only people in the vast Gothic edifice the caretaker and a few worshippers, briefcases and shopping bags in hand.

—Twilight in the empty, winding streets of Mont-Saint-Michel as the high tide washes in around the 11th Century Benedictine abbey off the

English Channel coast of France. In summer these streets compress such a writhing mass of pilgrims and tourists that movement is impossible.

— A glorious concert by the French flutist, Jean-Pierre Rampal, in Florence, followed by a late-evening walk along the banks of the Arno with the Ponte Vecchio and all the glorious renaissance buildings flooded with electric light.

— An afternoon in the park at Versailles, the statues shrouded for the winter and looking like the figures in a dream sequence in a Fellini film.

— The constant motif of soccer, that most European of all sports. From the animated crowds that surged past our hotel windows overlooking the Grand Lagoon in Venice on their way back from a professional game to the improvised games played on a field below a Rhine castle and on a sandy strip of beach below the ramparts of Saint-Malo.

— The kindness of strangers everywhere — in particular all the kind people who obviously found the spectacle of mother and son traveling together charming and endeared themselves to me by telling me what a "merviglioso" and "magnifique" son I had!

January 1981

Signs of a Lifer

You have lived in Champaign-Urbana a long time when you

— Can no longer spell the name of that bubbly drink served at weddings without stopping to think first.

— Always say "over in Urbana" if you live in Champaign and vice versa.

— Don't look non-plussed when the driving examiner tells you to turn the wheels to the curb because you are parking on a hill—and the road looks perfectly straight to you.

— Refer to the Kenney Gymnasium at Springfield and Wright as the Old Men's Gym.

— Concentrate the week's errands into the 1:30 to 4:30 p.m. period on University of Illinois home football game Saturdays and

— Automatically take University Avenue across town when you are going from southwest Champaign to southeast Urbana during March Madness.

— Still refer to the Champaign Plaza as Lewis's.

—Rave about the beauty of prairie sunsets when newcomers hold forth about the advantages of mountains and lakes.

— Know who Frank A. Somers is (it helps if you've pushed a baby carriage or stroller or done some snow-shoveling in Urbana). His name is stamped into many sidewalks.

— Say "The Krannert Center is at it again" when a shingle flies by on a windy day.

— Do not cover your head with your arms and start to howl with fear when you see a small red car obviously being strangled by a luminous green octopus at night but calmly realize that the Flying Tomato Brothers are making a pizza delivery.

— Can discern a subtle change in the topography which is the origin of place names like Yankee Ridge.

— Can remember when the local telephone exchanges were called FLeetwood and EMpire.

— Know that the place to let a 15-year-old budding driver practice for his or her driving exam is the Assembly Hall parking lot.

— Are not consumed with envy when a friend says she is just back from Paris, but inquire further and find out that she has visited the charming town southeast of Tuscola.

— Reel off the names of the states in the order of Illinois, California, Oregon, Nevada instead of Alabama, Alaska, Arizona.

You have lived in Urbana a long time if you taunt your friends with Urbana's superiority over Champaign based on the fact that most Champaign people have the sun in their eyes driving to and from work, while Urbana people don't.

258

And you have lived in Champaign a long time if you revel in a feeling of superiority over Urbana people based on the strength of the Maroon football team as compared to the Urbana Tigers.

August 1977

To Say Goodbye Is to Die a Little

The French have a saying, Dire adieu c'est mourir un peu — to say goodbye is to die a little.

Today we at The Morning Courier all died a little.

After two months and six days of agonizing limbo, of alternating hope and despair for the fate of the paper, we got the word from editor Pete Selkowe that the paper has died.

Now, 20 minutes after the announcement, I am sitting here for the last time in the warm womb of the newsroom with its beloved cacophony of hammering Teletype machines and reporters' typewriters.

And, mixed in with the all-pervading feeling of loss and sadness, I feel a sense of pride in this splendid group of professionals who are doggedly going about their jobs of putting out the last paper, even though tearstains are still visible on many faces.

I have worked for newspapers almost all of my working life but never have I been blessed with such a group of colleagues — tough, gifted, hard-headed, professionally superb workers and yet at the same time the gentlest and most emotionally responsive friends I have ever known.

Where else but among this group would you find people like Phil Greer and Curt Beamer — those incredible combinations of artists, craftsmen and journeymen photographers — who spent all their free time Thursday attempting to hock their homes in a last-ditch effort to save this great paper?

Because this is the time to say it, friends: We did put out a great paper. When the padlock snaps shut on the door early this morning, when each of you leaves with grocery bags stuffed full with the contents of your desks, when the resume-writing begins, say to yourselves and repeat it through the dark months to come: we did put out a great paper.

For years I have ended my talks to women's organizations about my work on The Courier with a little story about my daughter's attempt to put courage into me as I left my house five years ago to apply for a job on The Courier.

"You'll do fine," she said with all the fervor of her 10 years as I quaveringly prepared myself to re-enter the job market. "Just don't let them know that you really think the New York Times is a better paper."

The story always got a laugh but sometimes I felt like a faker using it. Because, considering the size of The Courier and the huge news-producing area it covered, I am not sure I have not come to believe that we, and not the New York Times with its vast resources, are not indeed the better paper.

In the early morning hours tomorrow a light that has shone steadfastly in my own life as a reader for 21 years and as a writer for five will be extinguished. The voices of many good people, whether heard in words or given life through photos, will be stilled. An entity which lived and breathed as surely as if it had a physical heart and lungs will have died.

In the words of Viscount Grey at the outbreak of the First World War, "The lamps are going out all over Europe; we shall not see them lit again in our lifetime."

During these last two terrible months a number of my co-workers have said to me, "I don't know why but somehow I can't seem to cry."

We can cry now, singly or together. But before we start, let us put aside our usual semi-cynical, self-deprecating attitude towards ourselves and our work and say, "We did put out a great paper." Or, even better, let us speak the way we do among ourselves and not in the cleaned-up words of reporting and say, "We did put out one hell of a newspaper."

March 31, 1979

POTPOURRI

Football to a Foreigner

"With all the vast space available in America, it seems strange to see 22 grown men fight for a few yards of territory."

This is the opinion of Boris Korenblum, a Russian visiting the University of Illinois for a few days. He attended the Illinois-Washington State football game Saturday with a Scot and a Dane as instructors in the intricacies of the all-American game.

Korenblum left Russia in December to emigrate to Israel, where he is now a professor at the University of Tel Aviv.

The Scot, Milne Anderson, teaches at University College, London, and is spending his sabbatical at the University of Illinois. Both men are mathematicians.

Anderson had seen one football game at the University of Michigan on a previous visit 10 years ago. Korenblum saw the last half of a game, also at Michigan, two weeks ago.

The guide (this Danish-born reporter) quickly proved inadequate and was supplanted by a University of Illinois alumnus in the next seat, Dan Smith of Richmond, Va. After wincing visibly at the guide's explanations about batters and pitchers and holes-in-one, Smith took over and outlined the plays and penalties to the two foreign visitors.

Their national characteristics showed quickly in their response to the game. Anderson took the reverses of the first half in good humor and was the only person in the section to leap to his feet and applaud when the Washington State placekicker kicked a field goal.

"What a beautiful kick!" he shouted with a typical British sense of fair play.

The Russian showed the emotional mobility of his great nation, when Illinois was behind, 10-0, at the end of the first half.

"Why are they rejoicing?" he muttered when the pompon girls went into a frenzied dance.

"I am disappointed, deeply disappointed," he said. "Of course, when a team loses in Russia, they say the players must have neglected their political education."

When the Illini card-section showed some Illini-boosting displays, he said, "This is like the Russian expression: to give incense to a dead man."

Hearing the Marching Illini perform the Schubert "Marche Militaire" at half-time, he suggested that they should rather play Chopin's Funeral March.

"I feel to rejoice with success, but the success is all Washington's," he lamented as the second half began.

The second half, with its quick reverses of fortune and fantastic instant replay of two passes caught in the end zone for a touchdown, the first having been nullified on a penalty, lifted Korenblum's spirits, and at the end of the game he was enthusiastic about the game of football and the Illini team.

Both men said they attended the game for its pageantry and spectacle. The fact that the game turned out to be so exciting convinced Anderson to attend future games.

They both commented on the good-naturedness of the crowd and admired the calmness and lack of anger of the spectators when the Illini were down.

They were delighted to be told by Smith that time-outs are occasionally called to make time for a TV commercial. A small airplane pulling a sign, "Jim loves sweet Shirley mucho," pleased them both.

After the game the visitors saw an improvised "Spirit of '76" group made up of three fraternity men with a trumpet, a trombone and an upended wastebasket beaten with a pair of scissors. Grinning broadly, the three musicians marched down Fourth Street playing "We are marching to Pretoria" and serenading cars with "You are my sunshine."

"Only in America—so childlike, so happy," Korenblum said.

"Yes," said Anderson, the Scot. "It was worrrth every penny!"

September 1974

For Love of Luciano

Or 5,200 characters in search of a ticket

An opera buffa in five acts
Music by Mozart, Puccini, Donizetti, Rossini and Wagner
Libretto by Nina Rubellini

Dramatis Personae

Luciano Pavarotti, tenor, the world's greatest singer.

Diana Nollen, soprano, keeper of the treasure (the 186 tickets available at the box office at 10 a.m. last Monday plus about 100 tickets reserved for mail orders).

Richard Blocher, tenor, a lover of opera in search of the Holy Grail (two tickets).

R. J. Coleman, baritone, a friend.

Chorus of townspeople of Champaign-Urbana and points east and west of the moon.

Setting: The sepulcher of the Holy Grail and its vestibule (the Krannert Center ticket office and outdoor terrace).

Time: Acts I-II, spring to fall 1980. Acts III-V, Oct. 4-6.

Synopsis

Act I

The heralding of the coming of Luciano Pavarotti to Champaign-Urbana, two towns of the golden Midwest, to give a concert is followed by a record sell-out of the Krannert Center subscription series which includes the concert. By late April all 1,700 subscription tickets are sold. (Chorus by Krannert ushers: "In diesen heil'gen Hallen" (In these hallowed halls.)

Act II

During the three months preceding the sale of the remaining 186 tickets, opera lovers from coast to coast lay siege to the Holy Sepulcher by mail, phone and in person. The inquiries include tearful pleas, veiled threats and attempts to cross the vendors' palms with silver. (Soft lament by quintet of vendors: "Un bel di vedremo" — On a beautiful day we shall see him.) The vendors stalwartly adhere to their sacred pledge not to sell tickets until 10 a.m. Oct. 6.

Higher powers decide to add 250 seats on stage. The pursuit of the Holy Grail now has about 286 possible Lancelots including mail-order knights.

Act III

The pursuit grows intense. Fifty-two hours before the opening of the vault containing the Holy Grail the first supplicant (No. 1 on a list developed by Richard Blocher at his arrival) starts the line, equipped with folding chair, sleeping bag and Thermos. Members of No. 1's family occasionally take over the vigil. They are joined 10 hours later by R. J. Coleman (No. 2) and two of his friends, neophytes at the revered seat of learning, the University of Illinois, (Nos. 3 and 4). The vigil continues through the bitter night as the students intone "O du mein holder Abendstern" (Oh you my lovely evening star).

Act IV

The sun has risen and other pilgrims join the throng. By late afternoon Blocher arrives and heroically decides to number the faithful to avoid sneaking-in by late-arriving infidels, himself becoming No. 27. (Tenor version by Blocher of Leporello's list aria, "Madamina"). By 3 a.m. Monday, although Blocher explains only 120 tickets will be sold in lots of two per supplicant, 30 believers (Nos. 61-90) remain staunch in their quest through the dark and starry night. (Tenor aria: "Che gelida manina" — Your tiny hand is frozen.)

Act V

At cock's crow, as the sun rises above the huddled group of pilgrims, many late-comers (estimated Nos. 91-250) seek to join the numbered throng and are repulsed by Nos. 1-90 who mumble the calumny aria, "La calunnia," under their breath. A rousing chorus of thanksgiving to Blocher sung by Nos. 1-90 precedes the opening of the barriers to the Holy Sepulcher. The time is 10 a.m. The crowd surges forward, still in Blocher's formation. The phones ring off the hook. Mail order fillers scribble furiously.

Twenty minutes later, Diana Nollen, the soprano, and her handmaidens have sold the 120 tickets and filled 66 phone orders. The townspeople who sought in vain depart, singing an eloquent dirge, as No. 61's bass soars above their voices in the lament "Soffriva nel pianto languia nel dolore" (My sufferings and sorrow I've borne without repining). Blocher, the tenor, raises his tickets to his lips and breaks into "Il mio tesoro" (My treasure). The soprano, tenor and baritone sing the haunting trio, "Luciano, o Luciano mio" (Luciano oh my Luciano) as the curtain descends slowly.

With apologies to Mozart, Puccini, Donizetti, Rossini and Wagner. The first-act aria is borrowed from Mozart's "The Magic Flute." The second-act aria is from Puccini's "Madama Butterfly." The song to the evening star in Act III is from Wagner's "Tannhauser." The fourth-act "Madamina" and fifth-act "Il mio tesoro" are from Mozart's "Don Giovanni." The fourth-act "Che gelida manina" is from Puccini's "La Boheme" and the fifth-act "Soffriva" is from Donizetti's "Lucia di Lammermoor." The calumny aria (Act V) is from "The Barber in Seville."

Pavarotti made his original debut in his native Italy as well as his Metropolitan Opera debut in "La Boheme" as Rodolfo who sings "Che gelida manina." He has frequently appeared in "Lucia di Lammermoor" and will perform Don Ottavio's aria, "Dalla sua pace," from "Don Giovanni" on Sunday.

October 1980

Tales of Two Cities

The List

Listed in alphabetical order by the authors' last names, here are 20 novels with settings in Champaign-Urbana or the surrounding area.

Gary Adelman: **Honey out of Stone.** Doubleday and Co., Garden City, N.Y. 1970.

Garreta Busey: **The Windbreak.** Funk and Wagnalls Co., New York and London. 1938.

Gail Godwin: **The Odd Woman.** Alfred A. Knopf, New York. 1974.

William Groninger: **A Proper Price.** The New American Library, New York. 1966.

Robert Henderson: **Whether There Be Knowledge.** J. B. Lippincott Co., Philadelphia and London. 1935.

Thomas Hinde: **High.** Walker and Co., New York. 1968.

Olive Deane Hormel: **Co-Ed.** Charles Scribner's Sons, New York. 1926.

Michael Kenyon: **The Trouble with Series Three.** William Morrow and Co., New York. 1967.

Herbert Kubly: **The Whistling Zone.** Simon and Schuster, New York. 1963.

Meyer Levin: **The Old Bunch.** Simon and Schuster, New York. 1937.

John Manson: **It Is a Dream.** Henry Holt and Co., New York. 1957.

William Maxwell: **The Folded Leaf.** Harper and Brothers, New York. 1945.

Louis L. Miller: **The New Minister.** Pageant Press, New York. 1952.

Lois Seyster Montross: **The Perfect Pair.** Doubleday, New York. 1934.

Lynn Montross and Lois Seyster Montross: **Town and Gown.** George H. Doran Co., New York. 1923.

Lynn Montross and Lois Seyster Montross: **Fraternity Row.** George H. Doran Co., New York. 1926.

Odette Newman: **So You Think Sex Is Dirty.** Olympia Press, Paris. Publication year not established.

Philip J. Simon: **Cleft Roots.** Priam Press, Chicago. 1975.

Richard Unekis: **The Chase.** Walker and Co., New York. 1962.

Yves Velan: **Soft Goulag.** Galland, Switzerland. 1977.

A gigantic boar is hognapped from the Large Animal Clinic, a futuristic couple makes its home at 10015 de la rue de la Prairie in Urbana, and Red Grange completes six triumphant touchdowns in one game.

These are among the scenes found in 20 novels set in Champaign, Urbana and Champaign County.

Romantic encounters in the novels include a seduction in a cemetery in which the book's author later was buried, a tryst inside the whale in Lincoln Square, and a wildly imaginative sexual romp involving a graduate student wife and a fictional Chief Illiniwek in a pornographic novel.

In no fewer than nine of the 20 novels the Champaign-Urbana setting is utilized to detail the main characters' quest for an undergraduate education at the University of Illinois.

Of the 20 novels, the ones strongest in local color are "High," "The Trouble with Series Three," "The Whistling Zone," "Co-Ed" and the three books by Lynn and Lois Seyster Montross.

"High"

Thomas Hinde, the author of "High" (1968), is a pseudonym for Sir Thomas Chitty, an English Third Baronet who has written more than a dozen books.

Chitty was a visiting lecturer at the University of Illinois from 1965 to 1967. He is described on the dustjacket of "High" as "one of England's finest living writers."

The book details the story of a love affair between a visiting English lecturer at a big midwestern university and a student. Employing the novel-within-a-novel technique, Hinde has his narrator, Maurice Peterson, writing a novel about a man named Peter Morrison.

In the novel, the two narrators mention the IGA, McBride's drug store and the K-Mart by name and talk about the Danish Shop and the Swedish Shop located in Jefferson Place (the Scandinavian Shop in Lincoln Square).

The lecturer and the student make love inside "the hollow black belly" of "a child's giant play-porpoise" in Jefferson Place (the whale in Lincoln Square), and the student upgrades her wardrobe by shoplifting in "Carson Pirie's."

Hinde published a novel, "Our Father," in 1976.

"The Trouble with Series Three"

The author of "The Trouble with Series Three" (1967), Michael Kenyon, is an English writer with more than half a dozen novels to his credit. He was a member of the journalism department at the University of Illinois in 1964-65.

The heroes of his humorous suspense novel are an English swine nutritionist and a 400-pound boar, both connected with the Large Animal laboratory at "Illinois State University."

The two get caught up in murder and international intrigue when the Englishman discovers a feed formula with an ingredient of importance for the space race.

The hero's department head tells him to call pigs "hawgs if you can manage it" and expresses the hope that he will like the university saying "There's nothing to do but work and drink." The title of the book's English edition is "The Whole Hog."

To kidnap the hog, the villain gets the hero out of the way by sending him to the main reference library to find a football ticket secreted in the Zoological Record for 1951, Vol. 88. The hero then proceeds to attend the university Homecoming football game — in September!

Kenyon drops many local names including "Meadow Gold Strawberry Butter Pecan Ice Cream" and the Cosmopolitan Club for faculty wives and sends an injured character to "Charles Clinic" — Charles being, of course, the French version of the name Carl, thus Carle.

"The Whistling Zone"

Herbert Kubly's "The Whistling Zone" (1963), portrays the big state university as a vicious environment which brings destruction to many of its inhabitants.

The main character's marriage collapses, two of the minor characters commit suicide, and a female midget dies after being gang-raped in "the low-cost housing barracks for unmarried men, Stadium Stalag."

The faculty types shown are obsessed with petty intrigues and backbiting and spend most of their time at departmental meetings arguing about cookie funds.

Among the identifiable landmarks in the book are "a large square plot of wheat stubble" (the Morrow Plots), "Fertile Acres" housing units (the Stadium Terrace housing for graduate students, now torn down), and a hotel "in chateau style with turrets and balconies" (the pre-Lincoln Square Urbana-Lincoln Hotel).

Kubly was a member of the speech department staff from 1949 to 1954. He has lived in Italy for some years and is the author of many travel books, plays and articles.

"Co-Ed"

Olive Deane Hormel's "Co-Ed" was a smash hit at its appearance in 1926, its first printing selling out within three weeks. Today's booklovers may find a certain wistful nostalgia in learning that the original hardcover edition was priced at $2.

Although the university in the novel is unnamed, the book abounds in descriptions of campus landmarks and activities easily identifiable as belonging to the University of Illinois.

The book outlines the college career of a sorority girl of the 1920s. It is divided into five sections called Enchantment, Disillusion, Readjustment, Romance and Realization.

Part of its appeal to local contemporary readers at its appearance was its roman a clef aspects. Many faculty members of the time appear under thinly disguised names, among them Stuart P. Sherman, head of the English department, who is called Tudor P. Sherman in the book, William R. Oldfather ("Old-man") and H. S. V. Jones ("R. S. V. P. Smith").

Hormel was a 1916 graduate of the University of Illinois and a member of the English department staff from 1917 to 1918.

The Three Montross Books

A husband-and-wife writing team (later divorced), Lynn and Lois Seyster Montross collaborated on two books of short stories loosely strung together into novels, "Town and Gown" (1923) and "Fraternity Row" (1926) about sorority and fraternity life in the 1920s.

Lois also authored a novel on the same theme, "The Perfect Pair" (1934).

The clearly identifiable University of Illinois background for all three books was obtained by Lois, a 1919 University of Illinois graduate.

"Fraternity Row" and "Town and Gown" contain series of lighthearted episodes about a group of gay blades and their flapper girlfriends, all considering the pursuit of pleasure more important than their university studies.

The characters observe the construction of Memorial Stadium — "The mighty steel structure of the new stadium was rearing itself out of the prairie on the edge of town" — and cheer as a Red Grange-like character catches the football on the kick-off and runs it back 78 yards, later making five more touchdowns in the same game.

"Town and Gown" includes a seduction scene set in the cemetery east of the stadium — a cemetery in which Mrs. Montross later was buried, according to Bruce Weirick, Universty of Illinois professor emeritus of English.

Professor Weirick recalls "the indignation (the seduction scene) caused in President Kinley's and Dean Clark's offices and the embarrassment it caused when Lois was called in, on the carpet, so to speak, and her pleasure in being able to pull out of her bag a note from Stuart Sherman, head of the English department, congratulating her on her book."

In addition to "Co-Ed" and the three Montross books, the five novels centering on undergraduate life at the University of Illinois are, in order of their appearance, those of Robert Henderson, Meyer Levin, William Maxwell, John Manson and Philip J. Simon.

"Whether There Be Knowledge"

Robert Henderson's "Whether There Be Knowledge" (1935) describes the disappointments and enlightenment of a college senior in his campus relationships.

The main character, who becomes editor of the University Daily (the Daily Illini), views Champaign-Urbana at his arrival as a freshman thus,

". . . the bright, noonday streets. Boys in white sweaters. Boys in knickers . . . Everybody was young. The boys had a jaunty air and were handsome. The girls, walking in twos and threes along the streets, were graceful and all of them laughing."

Henderson graduated from the University of Illinois in 1928 and was a member of the English department the following six years. He has been an editor of The New Yorker for about 40 years and has had many short stories published in the magazine.

"The Old Bunch"

Parts of Meyer Levin's long (766 pages in paperback) novel, "The Old Bunch" (1937), describes the years spent by some of the main characters as students at the University of Illinois.

According to Champaign novelist Elizabeth Klein, the book is seen by "many members of Sinai Temple Sisterhood now in their sixties as the definitive novel about growing up in Chicago and coming to Champaign to attend the university."

One of the protagonists views Champaign thus: "This was just an Illinois town, with houses set back from the streets, each on its lawn. And he suddenly had a complete idea of how he wanted his life to be, to live in some such house as one of these, with gables and cupolas, and a crazy little glass observatory on the roof, to have a garage fixed over into a studio with a big skylight, to walk back into the garage and work at sculpture all day, to walk up to the house and wash, and Sylvia would be waiting, dinner ready, maybe a kid with a snotty nose."

The author of many novels and plays, Levin is best known for his novel, "Compulsion."

"The Folded Leaf"

William Maxwell, the American novelist and short story writer, worked for 40 years as an editor of The New Yorker until his recent retirement.

A 1930 graduate of the University of Illinois, he taught freshman composition at the university from 1931 to 1933.

The first half of his novel, "The Folded Leaf" (1945), is set in Chicago, the second half at an unnamed university similar to the University of Illinois.

The plot deals with the troubled college years of a sensitive young man and his relationship with his friends.

Recognizable settings include the Men's Old Gym (now renamed Kenney Gym), the long-gone streetcars, the university orchards and barns, and the Boneyard.

"It Is a Dream"

Most of the first 73 pages of John Manson's "It Is a Dream" (1957) deal with student life at the University of Illinois in the period shortly preceding the United States' entrance into the second World War.

The main character is an undergraduate at the university.

The book contains many local references, among them to Lincoln Avenue, California Street, Bidwell's, singing the Loyalty Song, football coach Zuppke's last year of coaching, the university farms, and Bunny's, "a dumpy little tavern in an alley on the other side of town."

Manson was a student at the University of Illinois in 1940-41 and left to serve in the Armed Forces in World War II.

"Cleft Roots"

Parts of Philip J. Simon's "Cleft Roots" (1975) take place in Champaign-Urbana (identified by name) while the book's protagonist attends the University of Illinois.

The period spanned by the novel is 1918-23. The hero starts his studies bankrolled with $2,738.16. This munificent sum supports him, aided by some part-time jobs, until the end of the fourth year.

The book contains many identifiable local place names.

One description reads, "The coming of spring arrayed the campus in vernal glory. Soft winds murmured through the trees and swept over the velvety carpet of green in a touch of caressing tenderness. The ivy-covered buildings . . . weekly band concerts in front of the Auditorium were held at twilight . . . the serenades rang beneath the windows of sorority houses."

The following six novels are listed in the order of their appearance.

"The Windbreak"

Garreta Busey's "The Windbreak" (1938) features Hugh Brundage as its protagonist. The novel starts in 1863 when Brundage is 13 and takes him through his experiences as an itinerant peddler, a farmer in Champaign County and, later, the owner of a tile factory in Corinth (Urbana).

" 'By Jingo, Grace! We're going to feed the world, some day!' ", says Brundage, dreaming of the day he will be able to drain his marshy farmland.

The book includes this description of Corinth-Urbana around 1870: "Fine wooden pavements had been put in everywhere, even in the residence districts, and a good many folks had built sidewalks in front of their houses. The courthouse square was building up all around with new brick buildings."

Miss Busey was a member of one of the oldest families in Urbana. Born in 1893 in her grandparents' house, which stood where Carle Foundation Hospital now is located, she died in 1976. She was a member of the University of Illinois English department from 1930 to 1961.

"The New Minister"

Louis L. Miller's "The New Minister" (1952) incorporates the 1939 fatal shooting of a University of Illinois student outside a Champaign house of prostitution as a major part of its plot.

The shooting created a sensation throughout the state when it occurred.

The novel deals with the attempts of a minister to try to effect social reform in a college town.

At the time of the novel's publication Miller was a minister in Normal.

"The Chase"

Richard Unekis' "The Chase" (1962) is set in Champaign County, according to clippings in the Urbana Free Library's newspaper file. No information is available on the author.

The novel is a mystery in which a state police superintendent employs the theory of games to capture criminals fleeing in a car through a maze of cornfields.

The tautly written novel gives little information about the town of "Bucola" where some of the action takes place and concentrates mainly on the landscape of "the black, flat farming country" with "eight-foot corn standing in marching rows in late July."

"A Proper Price"

William Groninger's "A Proper Price" (1966) tells the story of an aging sheriff and his attempts to keep a nationwide crime syndicate out of his county.

The book contains many descriptions of Champaign County farm landscapes. The city landmarks described include the courthouse and its clock tower and city hall.

One passage reads: "The courthouse was in the old section of Landing where the houses stood on quiet, narrow, brickpaved streets unlike the sprawling too-bright city, which had grown up impatient and unplanned to the west and north of the original settlement, beyond the band of crumbling old mansions of the city's original families that ringed the courthouse."

Groninger worked as a reporter and columnist for more than 25 years for the Champaign-Urbana Courier until its demise in 1979. He now is editor of The Champaign-Urbana Weekly.

His first novel, "The Run from the Mountain," was published in 1959.

"Honey Out of Stone"

Gary Adelman, who has taught English at the University of Illinois since 1963, drew on his own life for the novel, "Honey Out of Stone" (1970). Adelman became blind at the age of 30 from the effects of a childhood injury.

After the novel's protagonist, Ben Storch, becomes blind, his wife leaves him. His life receives new meaning when his childhood sweetheart leaves her own unhappy marriage to come to him.

A blend of poetry and prose, the book contains many direct references to local places and people, among them Smith Music Hall, the Vocational

Rehabilitation Center, and Champaign streets like Willis, Green and White.

Adelman also is the author of "Political Poems", published in 1968.

"The Odd Woman"

Gail Godwin's third novel, "The Odd Woman" (1974), was written after she had been a visitor to the University of Illinois on a postdoctoral fellowship at the Center for Advanced Study.

The novel describes a woman's search for identity as she measures herself against other women and their lifestyles.

Most of the book is set in North Carolina, New York and Chicago, but the parts in Urbana contain many local references.

The town is described "as a disturbing dream. Set in the midst of dead-flat prairie, its plain streets and houses huddled together as if trying to cheer one another up" and as having 1930s street lamps and bicycling lanes.

The book contains several portraits of current University of Illinois faculty members and also makes repeated references to the Enema Bandit and his attacks on women.

The Enema Bandit was an elusive criminal who was finally caught in 1975. He pleaded guilty to the charge of armed robbery at his trial.

Among her published works since "The Odd Woman" are a collection of short stories, "Dream Children," (1976) and a novel, "Violet Clay."

"Soft Goulag"

The only one of the 20 novels to be written in French, "Soft Goulag" was published in 1977 by the Swiss publishing firm, Galland.

The winner of the International Prize of Science Fiction for French-Speaking Writers, the book was the third published novel by Yves Velan, professor of French at the University of Illinois at the time of the book's publication.

The futuristic novel is set throughout in Champaign-Urbana.

The main characters, Ad and Eve, live at 10015 de la rue de la Prairie in Urbana and spend at least one Sunday a month at Allerton Park.

Ad commutes to his job at "l'Illinois Accounting Division" in Kankakee on a bus operated by a company called Illinois Transportation Included.

"So You Think Sex Is Dirty"

Champaign and Urbana even have the dubious distinction of serving as a setting for a pornographic novel, "So You Think Sex Is Dirty."

The book's author is Odette Newman (probably a pseudonym). It was published by the Olympia Press in Paris, according to several people who have read the book.

Unfortunately the book has proved to be unobtainable. It was, however, reviewed in the Oct. 1, 1969 issue of the Laputa Gazette & Faculty News which was published from 1968 to 1970.

According to the unsigned review, the early parts of the novel are set at the University of Illinois and in Champaign-Urbana.

The book begins with this lament, "O Lord, Urbana, Illinois is a dull place. We deserve a better place, my lover and me. They all swear that it used to be a pretty town, all the streets lined with ancient elms. But all the trees are gone. The streets exposed with a merciless barrenness that accentuates the flatness of the town . . . Only the starlings love Urbana, Illinois."

The main characters are two graduate students, in the architecture and English departments at the University of Illinois, and their wives.

The reviewer reveals that the book contains several thinly disguised portraits of University of Illinois faculty members.

Among the key scenes, according to the reviewer, is a sexual encounter between one of the graduate student wives and a fictional Chief Illiniwek in which the chief's war bonnet is put to a decidedly unconventional use.

When the couple "finish with the war bonnet, the university will have to tap an alumnus for 300 new egret feathers," the reviewer writes.

Novel Use of Two Towns

"The city of Flatville, a giant cow turd on the landscape, all breadth, no height, a concrete turd with psychedelic fringes of neon-lit gas stations, bowling alleys, drive-in hamburger joints . . ."

This is how a character in Thomas Hinde's novel, "High," describes the city known to the rest of us as the fair town of Urbana.

If this quote elicits snickers from the town west of Wright Street, here is the outcry of a bride whose husband has brought her to live in Champaign in Herbert Kubly's novel, "The Whistling Zone:"

" 'Take me away!' she cried, beating the pillows with her hands. 'Take me away from these hicks and yokels!' "

The cities get a better press in Philip J. Simon's "Cleft Roots."

A character in the novel writes in a letter to a friend, "Champaign is right next to Urbana, in fact they're like one town with only a street between them. Murray, you can't begin to imagine what a wonderful place it is. The campus is something to rave about and the college spirit just can't be beat."

A relatively unloaded view of Champaign-Urbana is depicted in Michael Kenyon's novel of intrigue, "The Trouble with Series Three."

Memorial Stadium is described thus: "The stadium stood like a fortress on the southern edge of the campus. The besiegers were a thousand parked cars, paintwork glinting in the sunlight."

The novel includes a characterization of the menu of the Pancake Pantry (a disguised version of Uncle John's Pancake House) as "a lunatic encyclopedia of numbered and documented pancakes," followed by an approximately 175-word detailing of the menu.

In most of the 20 novels Champaign and Urbana appear thinly disguised under fictional names. In some of the novels, though, such as "Soft Goulag" by Yves Velan and "So You Think Sex Is Dirty" by Odette Newman, Urbana is called by its rightful name. Champaign receives the same distinction in several of the books, among them "Cleft Roots" and "The Old Bunch" by Meyer Levin.

The 20 novels were identified after much digging in library archives and questioning of knowledgeable local people.

The earliest of the novels was published in 1923, the last in 1977.

Three of the novelists on the roster are not American. Hinde ("High") and Kenyon ("The Trouble with Series Three") are from England while Velan is Swiss and wrote and published "Soft Goulag" — the winner of a major science fiction award — in French.

The identity of the author of "So You Think Sex Is Dirty," a pornographic novel published by Olympia Press in Paris, was the subject of much speculation when a copy of the book was passed from hand to hand locally in the late 1960s. The name attached to the novel, Odette Newman, is widely believed to be a pseudonym.

The range of genres in the 20 novels is breathtaking, spanning from science fiction (Velan) to pornography (Newman), women's movement (Gail Godwin's "The Odd Woman") to faculty expose ("High" and "The Whistling Zone"), international intrigue thriller ("The Trouble with Series Three") and social reform (Louis L. Miller's "The New Minister").

A huge sub-category of nine novels is in the undergraduate novel genre, dealing in the Champaign-Urbana setting part of the novels with the main characters' undergraduate college years at the University of Illinois.

In fact, the main reason the two cities have been used so frequently as novelistic settings is the presence of the University of Illinois.

In no fewer than 16 of the novels the main characters are in Champaign-Urbana because of their studies or teaching at the University of Illinois. The four novels not in this category are Garreta Busey's "The Windbreak," William Groninger's "A Proper Price," Richard Unekis' "The Chase" and "Soft Goulag."

Most of the authors either have taught at the University of Illinois, attended the university or, in some cases, first attended the university and later taught there. Even Garreta Busey and Yves Velan, whose novels' setting in Champaign-Urbana is not connected with the university's presence, were at some point members of the University of Illinois faculty.

Gary Adelman ("Honey Out of Stone") is the only one of the writers who still teaches at the university.

Many of the novels treat Urbana and Champaign as one town. The identifiable references to specific places are far more numerous for Urbana than for Champaign in most of the books.

This fictional single town is given a name in some of the books and left unnamed in others. Among the fictional names are Landing in "A Proper Place," Flatville in "High," Avon Bluff in "The Whistling Zone" and Grigg's Corner and later Corinth ("Some folks wanted to change its name to something more high-toned") in "The Windbreak."

Some of the fictional names for the University of Illinois are the State University (the Montross novels), the University (John Manson's "It Is a Dream"), Illinois State College ("The Trouble with Series Three") and Alakomo University ("The Whistling Zone").

Among the pithy observations about university life are the derisive comments of a college senior to a friend who plans to attend classes on the first day of the semester, found in "Whether There Be Knowledge":

" 'Don't act like a freshman. You haven't been to a first class for two years. Nothing happens. The instructor tells you what a swell text he's written and what a break it is for you to buy the thing, and then he stalls for fifty minutes!' "

A character in "Cleft Roots" describes the south campus as "the place where a fellow takes his best girl walking when they want to be alone."

Some aspects of local nature are mentioned in many of the books. The beauty of prairie sunsets is a recurrent theme, as is the smell of burning leaves in the fall.

The most salient feature of the Champaign County landscape, the towering rows of corn in midsummer, functions as an important plot device in three of the books—"The Chase," "The Trouble with Series Three" and "A Proper Price," which all end with manhunts or violent one-on-one confrontations amid the not-so-alien corn.

The Orpheum Theater is mentioned by name in several of the books. Memorial Stadium figures in many of the books, and the Boneyard appears as the Styx in "The Folded Leaf" and receives a reference of "by the banks of the bonny Boneyard" in "Co-Ed."

Disguised under assorted names, the Illini Union is featured in many of the books, among them "The Odd Woman," "The Whistling Zone" and "The Trouble with Series Three." The latter book even gives the contemporary prices for fried and boiled eggs (10 cents each) and scrambled eggs (23 cents).

Other indications of the loss of purchasing power of the dollar is the $1,200 academic-year salary of a rhetoric instructor in "Fraternity Row", the $2,738.16 which, with some help from part-time jobs, provided four years of college tuition and living expenses for a character in "Cleft Roots" and the purchase of a set of walnut furniture including a drop-leaf table, six chairs and a sideboard for $106 in "The Windbreak."

Two local advertising slogans feature in English in the French-language "Soft Goulag." They are "You are a go getter" and "We help people become neighbors" and have their genesis in Ozark Air Lines' slogan of the mid-1970s and in the Bank of Illinois of Champaign's "We help newcomers become new neighbors."

March 1981